Engineering Analysis of

FIRES and EXPLOSIONS

Engineering Analysis of
FIRES and
EXPLOSIONS

Randall Noon

CRC Press
Boca Raton   London   Tokyo

Library of Congress Cataloging-in-Publication Data

Noon, Randall.
  Engineering analysis of fires and explosions / by Randall Noon
      p.   cm.
  Includes bibliographical references and index.
  ISBN 0-8493-8107-X
  1. Fire investigation.   2. Explosions.   3. Forensic Engineering.
I. Title.
Th9180.N66   1995
    363.2'5964—dc20

                                                                        95-3187
                                                                            CIP

© 1995 by CRC Press, Inc.

No claim to original U.S. Government works
International Standard Book Number 0-8493-8107-X
Library of Congress Card Number 95-3187
Printed in the United States of America 1 2 3 4 5 6 7 8 9 0
Printed on acid-free paper

Get the facts, or the facts will get you.
And when you get 'em, get 'em right,
or they will get you wrong.

Thomas Fuller

Preface

Forensic engineering is defined as the application of engineering principles and methodology to answer questions of fact that may have legal ramifications. Forensic engineers apply engineering knowledge and skills to analyze car accidents, building collapses, fires, explosions, industrial accidents and other types of catastrophic events. Typically, forensic engineers have the task of answering the question: how did this happen?

This text is about forensic engineering as it applies to fires and explosions. It assumes that the reader has studied science or engineering and is familiar with chemistry, thermodynamics, heat transfer, materials, general engineering science and college-level mathematics. Assuming this, it is likely then that no new fundamental scientific concepts or principles will be presented to the reader. That is not the book's purpose; its purpose is to show the reader how professionals use these familiar concepts and principles to analyze fires and explosions.

In the academic world, subjects tend to be compartmentalized into neat, well defined disciplines like chemistry, physics, and engineering. With respect to demonstration and practice problems, typically, there is only one "right" answer. If there is any doubt about what the "right" answer is, it is listed at the back of the text or the professor provides it. If the class is chemistry, the practice problem will generally involve the application of only chemistry principles; if the class is physics, the problem will involve the application of only physics principles, and so on. Rarely in academia will the practice problems in one discipline call for the application of another discipline to reach an answer.

This tendency towards compartmentalization at the undergraduate level often also extends into the graduate schools, and in some ways is magnified there. Interdisciplinary graduate-level projects are often discouraged; they are viewed as "cheap" ways of obtaining an advanced degree in either department. In the main, as students move up from undergraduate to graduate school, their educational focus becomes narrower, not broader. The old saw about education is often true: as a person becomes more educated, he or she learns more and more about less and less.

Unfortunately, or perhaps fortunately depending upon your point of view, academia is not real life. The application of science and engineering to real-life problems can be messy. It is full of all kinds of complications which do not respect the artificial boundaries of academic disciplines. Real-life problem solving is interdisciplinary.

In a fire or explosion, all kinds of effects may have occurred at the same time, in quick succession, or both. A fire may cause walls to cave in, barrels of fuel to explode, metal structural components to melt, electrical systems to short, sprinkler systems to activate, and all kinds of bedlam, mayhem, and general confusion to take place. A real-life fire or explosion reminds me of the abstract Picasso painting *Guernica:* everything seems to be chaotically going on at the same time.

Determining the cause of a fire or explosion typically requires the simultaneous or sequential application of several disciplines. Information gleaned from the application of one discipline may provide the basis for another to be applied, which in turn may provide the basis for still another. The logical relationships among these many pieces of information then form the basis for the solution of what caused the fire or explosion.

For example, suppose there is a fire in a warehouse. Assume that the floors of the warehouse are supported by large horizontal I-beams. The actual load on the floors at the time of the fire can be reasonably estimated from inventory lists and building plans. If some of the beams are found permanently "sagged" after the fire, then the strength versus temperature properties of the steel beams can be used to determine at which temperature the beams would have begun to sag. The specific time when various beams began to sag may have been observed by a passer-by. Fire spread through the building later on may have then been observed by other witnesses.

Putting all this information into a logical time and place sequence can be used to re-create the fire spread through the building. Re-creation of the fire spread may even be done using sophisticated computer tools. A finite element "net" image of the building can be drawn, and the known positions of the fire can be plotted in stepped time increments. From this information, heat transfer and flame velocity information specific for the warehouse can be determined. When the known divergence or spread pattern of the fire has been quantified, the time line can then be reversed, using finite-element analysis techniques and the known fire spread velocities, until it converges back to the origin.

To accomplish the above sophisticated analysis requires the application of metallurgy, strength of materials, architectural design, computer skills, thermochemistry, finite element modeling, inventory auditing, and interviewing skills.

In the design process, design engineers typically start out with a clean sheet of paper. Everything that ends up on that sheet of paper they have either designed or deliberately selected to be incorporated in the design. Then they build the item and sell it to the client. If everything goes well, the item gives good service for a reasonable time, and the client is satisfied.

Forensic engineering, however, is a kind of "reverse" design process. The forensic engineer investigating a fire or explosion does not start with a clean piece of paper; he or she starts out with the physical reality of scattered heaps of dirty fire debris; to most people, fire debris is just a polite name for garbage.

In a typical assignment, there is a damaged building or facility in disarray. Some portions of the fire scene may be obscured by piles of debris. Other portions may be structurally unstable and dangerous to enter. Fire fighting and rescue activities may have moved some items from their "during the fire" positions to new locations.

The scene itself sometimes resembles a circus. Investigative teams representing separate or competing interests may be simultaneously "working" the fire scene and examining evidence. The owners may be trying to recover salvageable items. There may be several anecdotal accounts of what happened, volunteered by witnesses and excited neighborhood "experts." Some of the supposed "eyewitness" accounts may not factually agree with the others, or even with the obvious physical evidence.

Representatives of local newspapers and television stations may be trying to get that prize-winning interview or story. They sometimes end up interviewing the neighborhood "experts" and usually have the solution to the fire or explosion in time to make the evening edition or newscast. This is fortunate for the newspeople, as it may take much longer for the investigating engineer to figure out what occurred.

In addition, the fire or explosion scene is usually dirty, smelly, and hazardous. Often there are projecting nails, jagged pieces of sheet metal and glass shards. Sometimes there is decaying food and organic materials. In walking around, there is always the danger of stepping into hidden smolders, or falling through weakened flooring.

With any luck, the engineer will have to visit the scene when it is raining, snowing, $+110°F$ or $-20°F$. Since water is generally used to put out fires, when it is very cold the engineer will be standing on ice for many hours. And, importantly, there usually are no working toilets or hot coffee in a burned out building.

From out of this chaos the forensic engineer has to find order. The skill of his or her work is knowing how to relate seemingly disparate facts and observations into a cohesive account to answer the question: how did this happen? Far from being a specialist, a skilled forensic engineer is a consummate generalist. In this regard, it has been my intention to prepare an instructional text that shows how various engineering and scientific disciplines are applied to analyze fires and explosions. I have tried to incorporate practices and lessons learned from first-hand experience, both my own and my professional colleagues'. I have also included some related items that are just interesting to know about.

However, please be warned: this text is certainly not exhaustive. There are other disciplines and sciences which can be useful in the diagnosis of fires and explosions that I have not even touched upon. The reader should consider this text to be just a starting point.

Because it is not intended to be a strictly academic text, I have used footnotes sparingly. The traditional practice of inserting copious footnotes in the text to demonstrate the author's erudition is generally distracting to the reader, and makes the task of absorbing new material even more difficult.

No work such as this is done in a vacuum, and I would be remiss if I did not acknowledge the body of work upon which I have drawn. For this reason, there is a bibliographic chapter at the end of the book containing an ample list of references. The reader can use the books and papers listed there to verify and augment the principles, concepts, and information introduced in the text.

For those readers who may choose forensic engineering as a profession, I wish you good luck. The work never ceases to provide interesting puzzles and problems to test your abilities and skills. Sometimes an assignment is a little like watching a theatrical drama unfold. There is intrigue, suspense, plot twists, tragedy, triumph, heroes and heroines, villains and rogues, and at the end, hopefully, a resolution. In this drama, however, no one knows the ending until the final curtain falls. And because of the Byzantine workings of our legal system, that can sometimes take years.

Last, and not least, I want to thank the reader for his or her interest in the subject.

The Grizzley Bear is huge and wild;
He has devoured the infant child.
The infant child is not aware
It has been eaten by a bear.

A. E. Housman

Acknowledgments

It is customary after the preface to thank those persons who have helped the author in preparing the text. This is a very practical tradition, since it provides the author with additional scape goats to share the blame if the reader finds the text wholly unpalatable and useless.

So, thank you, Chuck Jacobs, for sharing cups of coffee with me while talking over fire evidence. Thank you, Don Dressler, Mike Hanson, Mara Wills, Frank Young, Paul Cabell, and all the rest of the Dressler Consulting Engineers gang for helping me dig through the mud and crud for evidence. Thank you, Dr. Don Miller for providing first class forensic chemistry support, and for giving a few lessons on the side.

Thank you, Prof. John Love for introducing me properly to combustion engineering at the University of Missouri-Columbia. Thank you Mr. Horina at Pattonville H.S. and Mr. Ivester at Poplar Bluff H.S. Everyone should be as lucky as I was in having you two for chemistry teachers. Thank you Mr. Wizard, alias Dr. Don Herbert, for so many awe-inspiring Saturday mornings which began after the test pattern stopped. Thank you George Novotny, for your kind editorial encouragement. And thank you Leslie, for faith and forbearance.

The reader will find a small piece of everyone listed above between the lines of every chapter. I thank them all very much.

R.K.N.
August 11, 1994

Faith is a fine invention
For Gentlemen who see;
But microscopes are prudent
In an emergency!

Emily Dickinson

About the Author

Randall Noon is Director of Engineering Services at the firm of Dressler Consulting Engineers, Incorporated, in Overland Park, Kansas. In this capacity, Randy directs the engineering activities of the firm related to investigative engineering, which includes fire and explosion reconstruction work.

Randy holds a B.S.M.E. from the University of Missouri-Columbia, an M.S.M.E. from the University of Missouri-Rolla, and a Ph.D. from Pacific Western University. Randy is professionally licensed in both the U.S. and Canada, and is also the author of two other texts about forensic engineering: *Introduction to Forensic Engineering*, and *Engineering Analysis of Vehicular Accidents*. Both are published by CRC Press, Inc. and are available through many bookstores, or directly from the publisher.

TABLE OF CONTENTS

Chapter 5: Electrical Shorting   **135**

The difference between primary and secondary shorting is explained. A simple thermodynamic model of a resistive circuit is derived. Some of the basic theoretical underpinnings of parallel and series shorting are discussed. The causes of beading are explained. Overcurrent protection devices are explained and their relationship to shorting is discussed. Common points where shorting occurs are listed and discussed.

Chapter 6: Explosions   **173**

The differences between deflagrations, detonations, and high pressure gas expansion explosions are discussed. The minimum ignition energies for deflagrations in air and oxygen are compared. Common sources of ignition energy for explosions are listed. The explosive limits for various gases are explained and listed. Overpressure fronts are briefly discussed, and the abuse of the term "explosive yield" is detailed.

Chapter 7: Determining the Point of Origin of an Explosion   **187**

The use of the flammability limits in diagnosing explosions is demonstrated. Fick's Law is explained. Explosion vectors are discussed. The determination of the explosion epicenter is discussed. Energy considerations with respect to diagnosing an explosion are demonstrated with a hypothetical example.

Chapter 8: Arson   **195**

The definition of arson and incendiary fires is given and explained. The profile of the typical arsonist is given, and the seven motives for arson are listed. Arson characteristics are exemplified in discussing the problems that confront an arsonist. The "Prisoner's Dilemma" problem is briefly discussed. Typical characteristics of an arson or incendiary fire are listed. Some arson precursors are noted. The arson immunity laws are explained. Pour patterns, spall patterns, and items relating to the detection of accelerants are discussed.

Chapter 9: Automotive Fires   **217**

Fuel related fires, electrical related fires, automotive arson, fires due to smoking materials, and other miscellaneous causes for fires in automobiles are discussed. Fires caused by catalytic converters are also included.

Chapter 10: Fire and Explosion Case Study   229

The fire and resulting two explosions which occurred November 29, 1988, in Kansas City, Missouri, in which six firemen were killed, is analyzed. The amount of explosive materials consumed by fire prior to the explosions is determined, and the amount of overpressure and ground vibration levels resulting from the largest blast are determined.

Chapter 11: Study Problems   243

A number of study problems for each chapter are posed. Answers are not given, and in some cases the information needed to solve the problems is not to be found in the text; this may require the reader to do some library work or small-scale laboratory experimentation to reach a solution. This is done purposely to give the reader a taste of what professional forensic engineers do all the time to solve cases.

Bibliography   259

A number of books and papers are listed which are pertinent to the topics of fire and explosion analysis. Many of the items are considered "standards" in fire and explosion analysis, and could, in themselves, constitute a set of "core" readings and information for professionals in the field. Other items are listed because they contain basic information which either augments or supplements topics discussed in this text.

Index   267

This is dedicated to my family:
the Noons,
the Jiles,
my Cousins,
the Fosters,
and all the other shady characters
that claim me as kin.

Ashes denote that fire was;
Respect the grayest pile
For the departed creature's sake
That hovered there awhile.

Fire exists the first in light,
And then consolidates, —
Only the chemist can disclose
Into what carbonates.

Emily Dickinson from *Poems*, published 1890

Chapter 1: Introduction

A. General

This book is about forensic engineering as it applies to the analysis of fires and explosions.

The term *forensic engineering* is generally understood to mean the application of engineering principles and methodology to answer questions of fact. Often, the questions of fact have legal ramifications.

Regarding fires and explosions, the most frequently posed questions of fact are: where did the fire or explosion start; and what caused it? The terms of art for these questions are, respectively, the determination of the point of origin, and the determination of the cause. Sometimes the two inquiries are jointly referred to as the determination of the cause and origin, commonly abbreviated as "C/O" or "C&O."

To establish a sound basis for analysis, a forensic engineer relies mostly upon the actual physical evidence found at the scene and verifiable facts related to the matter. The forensic engineer then applies accepted scientific methodologies and principles to interpret the physical evidence and facts. Often, the analysis of the physical evidence and facts requires the simultaneous application of more than just one scientific discipline: in this respect, the practice of forensic engineering is highly inter-disciplinary.

The disciplines primarily applied in the analysis of fires and explosions include inorganic and organic chemistry, materials and metallurgy, thermodynamics, physics, heat transfer, machine design, structural engineering, building systems design, electrical engineering, and ergonomics. A familiarity with codes and standards is also required. This includes building codes, mechanical equipment codes, fire safety codes, electrical codes, material storage specifications, product codes and specifications, installation methodologies, and various safety rules and regulations.

Because many of these subjects are normally a part of traditional mechanical and civil engineering curricula, graduates of these two engineering disciplines tend to dominate the forensic engineering field involved in the analysis of fires and explosions. However, there are also a small number of electrical, industrial, and safety engineering practitioners.

In essence what a forensic engineer does is this:

- he or she assesses what was there before the event and the condition it was in.
- he or she assesses what is present after the event, and the condition it is in.
- he or she hypothesizes plausible ways in which the pre-event conditions can have led to the post-event conditions.
- he or she searches for evidence which either denies or supports the hypotheses.
- he or she applies engineering knowledge and skill to relate the various facts and evidence into a cohesive scenario of how the event may have occurred.

Implicit in the above list of what a forensic engineer does is the application of *logic:* logic provides order and coherence to all the interdisciplinary facts, principles and methodologies which appear to bear on a particular case.

In the beginning of a case, the available facts and information are like pieces of a puzzle found scattered about the floor: a piece here, a piece there, and one perhaps which has mysteriously slid under the refrigerator. At first, the pieces are simply collected, gathered up, and placed in a heap on the table. Then, each piece is fitted to all the other pieces until a few pieces match up with one another. When several pieces match up, a part of the picture begins to emerge. Eventually, when the all the pieces have been fitted together, the puzzle is solved and the picture is plain to see.

It is for this reason that the scientific investigation and analysis of a fire or explosion should be structured like a pyramid. There should be a large foundation of facts and evidence at the bottom, which support a few conclusions at the top. Conclusions should be based directly upon facts, not upon other conclusions or hypotheses. If the facts are arranged logically and systematically, the conclusions should be almost self-evident. Conclusions based on other conclusions or hypotheses, which in turn are only based upon a few facts or upon very generalized principles, are a house of cards. When one point is proven wrong, they all fall down.

For example, consider the following case. It is true that propane gas systems are involved in some explosions and fires. A particular house that was equipped with a propane system sustained an explosion and subsequent fire. The epicenter of the explosion, the point of greatest explosive pressure, was located in a basement room which contained the propane furnace. From this information, the investigator concludes that the explosion and fire was caused by the propane system and in particular, the furnace.

However, the investigator's conclusion is based on faulty logic. There is not sufficient information to firmly conclude that the propane system was the cause of the explosion, despite the fact that the basic facts and the generalized principle upon which the conclusion is based are all true.

Consider again the given facts and principles in the example.

Principle: Some propane systems cause explosions and fires.
Fact: This house had a propane system.
Fact: This house sustained a fire and explosion.
Fact: The explosion originated in the same room as a piece of equipment that used propane, the furnace.
Conclusion: The explosion and fire was caused by the propane system.

The principle upon which the whole conclusion depends asserts only that *some* propane systems cause explosions, not *all* of them. In point of fact, the majority of propane systems are reliable and work fine without causing an explosion or fire for the lifetime of the house. Arguing from a statistical standpoint, it is more likely that a given propane system will *not* cause an explosion and fire.

In our example, the investigator has not yet actually checked to see if this propane system was one of the *some* that work fine or one of the *some* that cause explosions and fires. Thus, a direct connection between the general premise and the specific case at hand has not been made; it has only been assumed. A verification step in the logic has been deleted.

Of course, not all explosions and fires are caused by propane systems; propane systems do not have a corner on the market in this category. There is a distinct possibility that the explosion may have been caused by something not related to the propane system which is unknown to the investigator at this point. The fact that the explosion originated in the same room as the furnace may be only a coincidence.

Using the same general principle and available facts then, it can equally be deduced (albeit also incorrectly) that the propane system did not cause the explosion. Why? Because it is equally true that some propane systems never cause explosions and fires. Since this house has a propane system, then it could be concluded that this propane system could not have been the cause of the explosion and fire.

As is plain, our impasse in the example is due to the application of a general principle for which there is insufficient information to provide a unique, logical conclusion. The conclusion that the propane system caused the explosion and fire is based implicitly on the conclusion that the location of the explosion epicenter and propane furnace is no coincidence. It is further based upon another conclusion that the propane system is one of the "some" that cause explosions and fires, and not one of the "some" that never cause explosions and fires. In short, in our example we have a conclusion, based upon a conclusion, based upon another conclusion.

Figure 1.1: Remains of farm house after fire.
Fire originated at propane water heater line.

The remedy to this dilemma is simple: additional information must be gathered to either uniquely confirm it was the propane system, or uniquely eliminate it as the cause of the explosion and fire.

Going back to our example, compressed air tests at the scene find that the propane piping found after the fire and explosion does not leak, despite all that it has been through. Since propane piping which leaks before an explosion will not heal itself so that it does not leak after the explosion, this test eliminates the piping as a potential cause.

Testing of the furnace and other appliances finds that they all are in good order. This now puts the propane equipment in the category of the "some" that do not cause explosions and fires. We have now confirmed that the conclusion which assumed a cause and effect relationship between the location of the epicenter and the location of the propane furnace was wrong. It was a coincidence that the explosion occurred in the same room as the furnace.

Further checks by the investigator even show that no propane was missing from the tank, as one would expect to be the case if the propane had been leaking. Thus, now there is an accumulation of facts showing that the propane system was not involved in the explosion and fire.

Finally, a thorough check of the debris in the epicenter area finds that within the furnace room there were several open one-gallon tins of paint thinner which the owner had assumed to be empty when he finished doing some painting. Closer inspection of the tins finds that some of them are expanded as if they had withstood an internal explosion of their vapors.

Upon further questioning, the owner recalls that the tins were placed only a few feet from a high-wattage light bulb, which was turned on just before the time of the explosion. A review of the safety labels finds that the tins contained solvents that would form explosive vapors at room temperature even when the tin was to all appearances empty. A back-of-the-envelope calculation finds that the amount of residual solvent in the tins taken together would be more than enough to provide a cloud of vapor in the room at a concentration exceeding the lower threshold of the solvent's explosion limits.

The above example demonstrates the value of the "pyramid" method of investigation. When a large base of facts and information is gathered, the conclusion almost suggests itself. When only a few facts were gathered to back up a very generalized premise, the investigator can "steer" the conclusion to nearly anything he wants. Unfortunately, there are some fire investigators who do the latter very adroitly. This point is discussed again in Section I which is titled, "A Priori Biases."

B. Eyewitness Information

Eyewitness accounts are important sources of information, but they must be carefully scrutinized and evaluated. Sometimes eyewitnesses form their own opinions and conclusions about what took place; they may then intertwine these conclusions and opinions into their account of what they say they observed. Skillful questioning of the eyewitness can sometimes separate the factual observations from the personal assumptions.

Consider the following example. An eyewitness initially reports seeing "Bill" leave the building just before the fire broke out. However, careful questioning reveals that the eyewitness did not actually see "Bill" leave the building at all; the witness simply saw someone drive away from the building in a car similar to Bill's, and assumed it must have been Bill. Of course, the person driving the car could have been Bill, but it also could have been someone with a car like Bill's, or someone who had borrowed Bill's car.

Of course, some eyewitnesses are not impartial. They may be relatives, friends, or enemies of persons involved in the event. They may have a personal stake in the outcome of the investigation. For example, it is not unusual for the arsonist who set the fire to be interviewed as an eyewitness. Let us also not forget the eyewitnesses who are scalawags, psychotics, and blowhards. They may swear to anything to pursue their own agendas, or just to get attention.

What an honest and otherwise impartial eyewitness reports observing may also be a function of his location with respect to the event. His perceptions of the event may be colored by his education and training, his life experiences, his physical condition such as eyesight or hearing, and social or cultural biases. For example, the sound of a gas explosion might variously be reported as a sonic boom, cannon fire, blasting work, or an exploding sky rocket. Because of this, eyewitnesses to the same event will sometimes disagree on the most fundamental facts.

Further, the suggestibility of the eyewitness in response to questions is also an important factor. Consider the following two exchanges during *"statementizing."* This is a term of art which refers to interviewing a witness to find out what the witness knows about the incident. The interview is often recorded on tape and later transcribed to a written statement. Usually it is not done under oath, but it is often done in the presence of witnesses. It is important to "freeze" a witness' account of the incident as soon as possible after the event. Time and subsequent conversations with others will often cause the witness' account of the incident to change.

Exchange I

> *Interviewer: Did you hear a gas explosion last night at about 3 a.m?*
> *Witness: Yeah, that's what I heard. I heard a gas explosion. It did happen at 3 a.m.*

Exchange II

> *Interviewer: What happened last night?*
> *Witness: Something loud woke me up.*
> *Interviewer: What was it?*
> *Witness: I don't know. I was asleep at the time.*
> *Interviewer: What time did you hear it?*
> *Witness: I don't know exactly. It was sometime in the middle of the night. I went right back to sleep afterwards.*

In the first exchange, the interviewer suggested the answers to his question. Since the implied answers seem logical, and since the witness may assume that the interviewer knows more about the event than himself, the witness agrees to the suggested answers. In the second exchange, the interviewer provided no clues to what he was looking for; he allowed the witness to draw upon his own memories and did not suggest any.

C. Magnitude of Fire and Explosion Problem

The following fire loss statistics have been gathered from a number of sources, including the National Fire Protection Association, located in Quincy, Massachusetts; *Accident Facts* published yearly by the National Safety Council; the *Information Please Almanac* published yearly by the Houghton Mifflin Company, and the *World Almanac* published yearly by Pharos Books. They are presented to show the scope and breadth of fire and explosion losses in the U.S.

In 1990, about 7.8 billion dollars in property damage and 3,300 deaths were caused by fires in the U.S. Of this total, fires that damaged structures totaled about 6.7 billion dollars, or about 86% of the total. The loss to residential property was about 4.2 billion dollars. On a per capita basis, monetary losses from fire damages in 1990 were a little over 30 dollars.

Staying with the same reporting year, 1990, fire departments across the U.S. responded to over 2 million calls. By individual count, there were 624,000 fires in structures, and 467,000 fires in residential properties. Interestingly, there were almost as many automobile fires, 436,000, as there were fires in residential properties.

There were about 28,600 injuries directly associated with fire losses in 1990 in the U.S.; of this total, about 20,000 injuries were associated with residential fires. This figure excludes injuries to fire department personnel.

On an average annual basis, about 100,000 fires are deliberately set. In 1990, about 16% of all U.S. structure fires were considered deliberately set or were suspected of being deliberately set. Suspicious fires in structures alone were associated with 715 deaths in 1990. Similarly, about 12% of automotive fires were considered deliberately set or were suspected of being deliberately set.

The U.S. has the highest rate of arson in the world. Of course, this may be a function of the fact that the U.S. is also one of the most insured countries in the world. In some U.S. cities, the high arson rate has been a major factor in the abandonment of whole neighborhoods. Besides the high number of annual arson-related deaths, arson costs the U.S. over 1.5 billion dollars a year in property losses.

In addition to the annual aggregate death and destruction problem, fires and explosions are also the root cause for some of the worst single-event disasters. The following is just a small sampling from a very long list. (For brevity, many whole categories of fire and explosion disasters have been omitted, e.g., grain bins, airplanes, ships at sea, oil platforms, forests, grasslands, etc.).

- On September 3, 1991, 25 people died in a fire in Hamlet, North Carolina, at a chicken processing plant. Many of the deaths were related to the fact that emergency fire exits were blocked unusable. The poor management of the state's fire safety inspection program in North Carolina was also blamed for the event. The U.S. federal government stepped in to partially administer the state's inadequate fire inspection program.

- On December 31, 1986, 96 people died in a fire at the Dupont Plaza Hotel in Puerto Rico. Investigation found that the fire had been deliberately set by a disgruntled employee. Many of the deaths were related to the occupants' inability or reluctance to promptly leave the building. Some did not wish to leave their winnings behind in the casino.

- On April 16, 1947, 561 people died and 3,000 people were injured in an explosion at the Texas City, Texas, pier. The explosion originated on a French freighter, the *SS Grandchamp,* which was carrying ammonium nitrate. It has been called the worst accidental explosion in U.S. history. Resulting property damages exceeded $59,000,000 (in 1947 dollars), and workmen's compensation losses were about $8,000,000. The next day, the ammonium nitrate cargo in the *SS High Flyer* also detonated, killing one more person and injuring about 100 more.

- On April 22, 1992, 190 people were killed in Guadalajara, Mexico, when an explosion ripped through the city sewers. Investigation found that flammable liquids from a nearby refinery had gotten into the sewer system. The ensuing political scandal caused several high ranking officials to resign; some were indicted criminally.

- Perhaps the worst explosion in North America took place on December 6, 1917 in Halifax Harbor, Canada. The French ammunition ship, the *Mont Blanc,* collided with a Belgium steamer. 1,654 people were killed by the explosion.

- The New York City Social Club fire of March 25, 1990 caused 87 deaths. The building was noted to have many fire code deficiencies, and many deaths were related to a lack of fire exits. New York was publicly criticized for lax building code enforcement.

- The crew of Apollo I, Grissom, White and Chaffee, were killed on January 27, 1967, in a fire which broke out in the Apollo capsule while undergoing ground tests. Investigation of the fire resulted in the designers incorporating more nonflammable materials into the design of the Apollo capsule.

- On May 22, 1975, about $100,000,000 worth of damage occurred to the nuclear plant at Brown's Ferry, Decatur, Alabama. A technician, checking for air leaks with a lighted candle, inadvertently set fire to some wiring. The initial small fire could not be put out, and spread. The resulting fire burned up the plant's electrical controls which lowered the cooling-water level in the reactor to dangerous levels. Subsequent investigation by the Nuclear Regulatory Commission resulted in many design changes in U.S. nuclear plants.

- One of the more infamous fires occurred on November 28, 1942, at the Cocoanut Grove nightclub in Boston, Massachusetts; 492 people were killed. The lack of adequate fire exits was determined to have contributed greatly to the loss of life. The event was widely publicized in U.S. newspapers and became a *cause célèbre* for rigorous enforcement of building codes.

- Shortly after takeoff on January 28, 1986, the space shuttle *Challenger* exploded in flight and killed all its crew; the event was witnessed live on television by millions of viewers worldwide. As a result the U.S. space program was delayed by several years. Investigation traced the problem to a lapse in the application of established safety procedures, and to an o-ring design deficiency. The o-ring seal design of the main booster rocket casing was revamped, and safety launch procedures were made more independent of political and business concerns.

  An interesting facet of the televised proceedings of the investigation involved Dr. Richard Feynman, the Nobel Laureate physicist. While listening to NASA officials argue that the 28°F temperature that occurred on the morning of the launch could not have affected the pliancy of the o-ring, he placed a sample o-ring in his ice water and tightened a C-clamp on it. While it was still cold, he loosened the C-clamp and observed how the o-ring retained its flattened shape instead of returning to a round cross section as claimed. To engineers and persons knowledgeable about materials, this simple demonstration, done without a word while the world watched and the NASA officials continued presenting their case, was simply stunning.

- In April 1986, the fire in the Chernobyl nuclear plant near Kiev, Ukraine, spread radioactive materials over several European countries and contaminated the immediate 60-mile radius area making it unlivable. The deaths and sickness resulting from this have not yet been fully counted but number in many thousands. The heroism of the firefighters who put out this fire was remarkable; many fought the fire knowing full well they would shortly die due to radiation exposure, and some died even before they could be removed from the scene.

- In reviewing the U.S. mine statistics between 1900 and 1968, I counted 47 mine disasters in each of which 60 or more miners were killed; most of these disasters involved fires and explosions. From 1968 to 1992, I estimate about 300 or more miners have similarly been killed in mine fires and explosions.

- In Chasnala, India, 431 miners were killed in a single fire/explosion event on December 27, 1975.

- A single explosion at a gas pipeline in the former U.S.S.R. on June 3, 1989 killed more than 650 people.

- A tanker truck exploded in a traffic tunnel in Oakland, California, on April 7, 1982. The explosion and fire resulted in 7 deaths.

- In Kansas City, Missouri, on November 29, 1988, six firemen died when about 25 tons of ANFO explosive was set on fire by vandals and subsequently exploded. The firemen had responded to a report of vandalism fires at a construction site and were extinguishing the fires when the explosives detonated. This particular incident is the subject of Chapter 10.

With only a little effort, the above list of infamous fire and explosion catastrophes could be expanded many times over. However, no further elaboration is really needed; this list is more than sufficient to make the point of why it is necessary to spend the time and effort to investigate fires and explosions. The next question is then, have any of the lessons learned to date been put to good use?

According to the National Safety Council's *Accident Facts*, 1991 edition, U.S. deaths in the home resulting from fires have significantly decreased: in 1960, such deaths numbered 6,350, and in 1990, they numbered 3,300. This gross decline occurred despite the general increase in the total U.S. population from 179,000,000 in 1960 to 249,000,000 in 1990. If the 1960 home fire death rate is applied to the 1990 population figures, deaths in the home from fires would have been 8,833 instead of 3,300.

Of course, it could be argued that the lower death rate in 1990 is the result of better medical treatment rather than "real" improvements in fire safety. It is true, for example, that the treatment of severe burns was better in 1990 than in 1960. Hence, it could be hypothesized that the lower death rate in 1990 may be simply because fewer people die from fires, not that there are fewer fires.

However, it is also true that medical treatment for all types of injuries and problems was better in 1990 than in 1960. Thus, one way to ferret out the "real" progress in fire safety, as opposed to improvements in medical treatment of fire injuries, is to compare the ratio of fire related deaths to all accidental deaths in general. The premise of this comparison is that since the medical treatment for both categories has improved about the same, then any change in the ratio of one category to another must indicate "real" increases or decreases of that category.

In checking the total accidental deaths in the home for all reasons, we find that this category has also decreased in the same period of 1960 to 1990. This then apparently substantiates the argument that better medical care in general has caused the death rate to decline. However, a closer look at the statistics finds that deaths resulting from fires have decreased more than the general rate of decline for all accidental deaths in the home. Specifically, fire related deaths in 1960 constituted 23% of all home accident deaths, which totaled about 28,000. However, fire related deaths in 1990 constituted 15% of all home accident deaths, which numbered 21,500.

In other words, while the gross number of deaths between 1960 and 1990 due to all types of accidents in the home decreased by 23%, the gross number of deaths in the home related to fires decreased by 48%. All the while, the population of the U.S. increased by 39%. These statistics show that some of the lessons learned are, indeed, being put to good use.

As an aside, it is too bad that such a remarkable "good news" story has not been noticed by the major newspapers or news services. But for that matter, when smallpox, the all-time disease scourge of the ages, was finally wiped off the face of the earth, the event was hardly noticed by the news services.

The decline of accidental fire deaths in the home is credited to the adoption and enforcement of many fire-related safety codes and standards. These codes and standards apply to the home itself, and to the appliances and furnishings put into it. Even children's pajamas have become safer with respect to fire; they are no longer made of easily flammable materials.

Unfortunately, many of the regulations and standards promulgated for fire and explosion safety are the result of a particular tragedy, or perhaps a number of related tragedies. In truth, it is often the case that a number of people have to die, or at the very least lose a lot of property, before a particular fire code regulation is adopted. Whenever contractors and builders carp about the inconvenience of having to comply with this or that fire code provision, I hope that they may also reflect upon how inconvenient death and destruction is.

However, lest we become too proud of our achievements in reducing fire deaths, it is worth noting the following: Chicago has three times the number of fire caused deaths as Hong Kong, a city with twice the population. Amsterdam and Baltimore have approximately the same population, but Baltimore has 13 times more deaths by fire than Amsterdam.

D. Who Investigates Fires and Explosions?

In the investigation of a fire or explosion, several types of professional investigators can be involved. The following is a short list and description of the *dramatis personae:*

1. **Forensic Engineer:** Usually a state licensed professional engineer, the forensic engineer assesses the technical aspects of a fire or explosion. Forensic engineers are typically employed by private consulting firms, and their services are engaged by insurers, attorneys, private individuals, companies, and sometimes governmental agencies. Some large governmental investigating agencies, like the Bureau of Alcohol, Tobacco, and Firearms (BATF); the Federal Bureau of Investigation (FBI), and various state level "FBI's" may also employ forensic engineers as members of their investigation team.

2. **Fire Department Fire Investigator:** This is most often a former fireman with specialized training and experience in cause and origin work. Usually the fire department fire investigator works alongside the regular firemen, especially during overhaul[1], to determine the point of origin of the fire, and if possible, the cause. In small fire departments, the fire investigator may be the Fire Chief, the Fire Captain, or a Lieutenant in the regular fire fighting unit. In large fire departments, the fire investigator may hold a special but parallel position outside the regular fire fighting unit.

3. **Fire Marshal:** This is a fire investigator for the state, usually involved at the request of a city or county fire department. Such requests are made when it appears that more investigative resources are needed than the local fire fighting unit can provide.

---

[1] After a fire has been largely put out, *overhaul* is when firemen carefully go through a building looking for small fires and smolders hidden in walls, ceilings, attics, or floor cavities which could rekindle into a second fire.

This might occur if the fire or explosion is very large and complex, if a crime like arson or sabotage is suspected, if criminal negligence is suspected, if hazardous materials are involved, or if the public interest is involved. The latter category might include fires and explosions at utilities, pipelines, fuel storage dumps, or where there has been substantial loss of property and injuries.

Some large cities have a position of *city fire marshal*, which is similar in scope to the state fire marshal position. Fire marshals are often former firemen or former fire investigators. However, in some states they may be former policemen or law enforcement investigators.

4. **Fire Investigator (Private):** This is often a former fire department fire investigator, fireman, fire marshal, or other law enforcement professional employed by a private company. Sometimes called cause and origin specialist, the services of a private fire investigator are often engaged by insurers, private individuals, companies, attorneys, or governmental agencies.

5. **Private Investigator:** A private investigator is differentiated from a private fire investigator in that the former handles all types of cases, while the latter deals mostly with fires and explosions. However, it is not uncommon for a private fire investigator to also be a licensed private investigator. The requirements for private investigator vary widely from state to state. Some states require formal law enforcement training and a passing grade on a test; others only require that a person fill out a form, undergo a criminal warrant check and pay a fee. Private investigators are engaged by insurers, private individuals, companies, and attorneys.

6. **Fire/Explosion Reconstructionist:** This is a term used by some attorneys and insurers that may be applied to most of the professionals in this list. It simply refers to a person who determines how and why a fire occurred, that is, a person who "reconstructs" how the fire occurred.

7. **BATF Investigator:** The Bureau of Alcohol, Tobacco, and Firearms has jurisdiction in fires and explosions that may involve explosives, firearms, or certain types of criminal activity.

8. **Police, State Police, and FBI Investigator:** In fires and explosions that involve criminal activity, local, state, and even federal law enforcement investigators may be involved in the investigation. This is especially true in cases involving arson, insurance

fraud, fires or explosions that are set to hide other crimes, or deliberately set fires or explosions that result in loss of life.

9. **Forensic Chemist:** In some respects a forensic chemist is similar to a forensic engineer: both typically hold college-level degrees in a scientific discipline. However, a forensic chemist's role in fire or explosion investigation is generally limited to the detection and identification of substances related to the fire or explosion. Some forensic chemists work for private companies, and some are employed in governmental laboratories providing support for their particular investigation agency.

10. **Insurance Adjuster:** To determine whether a particular fire or explosion is covered under the terms of the insurance policy, an insurance adjuster investigates what occurred. Some adjusters have training in cause and origin work and will conduct a preliminary investigation on their own. More often, however, an adjuster will engage the services of a forensic engineer, private fire investigator, private investigator, or forensic chemist to investigate the fire or explosion on his behalf.

11. **National Transportation Safety Board Investigator:** In cases where the fire or explosion involves an airplane, train, truck, or other interstate type transportation vehicle, the NTSB may conduct investigations on behalf of federal interests.

12. **Miscellaneous Government Investigators:** Other government agencies that may be involved from time to time in investigating fires and explosions include the following:
a. *Occupational Safety and Health Administration (OSHA):* When a fire or explosion occurs at a work place, construction site, or other area covered by O.S.H.A. regulations.
b. *National Bureau of Standards (NBS):* When there are public issues involved related to material standards, codes, etc.
c. *Mine Safety and Health Administration:* When explosions occur in mines due to dust, gas accumulations, or safety problems.
d. *Maritime Administration:* When ships catch fire or explode.
e. *National Parks Service:* When protected wilderness areas are burned.
f. *Local codes administrators:* When significant building code violations are related to the cause or severity of the fire or explosion.

E. Role in the Legal System

From time to time, a person who does this type of engineering analysis is called upon to testify in deposition or in court about the specifics of his or her findings. Normally the testimony consists of answers to questions posed by an attorney for an involved party. The attorney will often be interested in the following:

- the engineer's qualifications to do fire or explosion analysis,
- the basic facts and assumptions relied upon by the engineer,
- the reasonableness of the engineer's conclusions, and
- plausible alternative explanations for the fire or explosion not considered by the engineer, which often will be his client's version of the event.

By virtue of the appropriate education and experience, a person may be qualified as an "expert witness" by the court. In some states, such an expert witness is the only person allowed to render an opinion to the court during proceedings. Because the U.S. legal system is adversarial, each attorney will attempt to elicit from the expert witness testimony to either benefit his client, or disparage his adversary's client.

In such a role, despite the fact that one of the attorneys may be paying the expert's fee, the expert witness has an obligation to the court to be as objective as possible, and to refrain from being an advocate. The best rule to follow is to be honest and professional both in preparing the original analysis, and in testifying. Prior to giving testimony, however, the expert witness has an obligation to fully discuss with his or her client both the favorable and unfavorable aspects of the analysis.

Sometimes the forensic engineer involved in preparing a fire or explosion analysis is requested to review the report of analysis of the same event by the expert witness for the "other side." This should also be done honestly and professionally. Petty "one-upmanship" concerning academic qualifications, personal attacks and unfounded criticisms is unproductive and can prove embarrassing to the person who engages in them. When preparing a criticism of someone else's work, consider what it would sound like when read to a jury in open court.

Honest disagreements between two qualified experts can and do occur. When such disagreements occur, the focus of the criticism should be the theoretical or factual basis for the differences.

F. The Scientific Method

Roger Bacon, a 13th century English Franciscan monk, is often credited with defining the modern scientific method. He believed that scientific knowledge should be obtained by close observation and experimentation. He experimented with gunpowder, lodestones, and optics to mention a few items, and was dubbed "Doctor Admirabilis" because of his extensive knowledge.

For his efforts to put knowledge on a verifiable basis, the curious friar was accused of necromancy, heresy, and black magic by the chiefs of his order. He was confined to a monastery in Paris for ten years so that he could be watched. He attempted to persuade Pope Clement IV to allow experimental science to be taught at the university, but his efforts failed. After Pope Clement IV died, Bacon was imprisoned for another ten years by the next pope, Nicholas III; this Pope specifically forbade the reading of Bacon's papers and books. This was somewhat moot, however, since his work had generally been banned from publication anyway. Some scholars believe that Roger Bacon was the original inspiration for the Doctor Faustus legend.

Why all the fuss over a friar who wants to play in the laboratory? It is because he threatened the "correctness" of theories promulgated by the Church. At the time of Bacon, the doctrine of *apriorism* was the accepted basis for inquiry. Apriorism is the belief that the underlying causes for observed effects are already known, or at least can be deduced from some first principles. Under apriorism, if a person's observations conflict with the accepted theory, then the person's observations must be imperfect. They may even be the product of the Devil tempting a foolish mortal.

For example, in Bacon's time it was assumed *a priori* that the sun revolved about the earth and that all celestial motions followed perfect circles. Thus, all other theories concerning the universe and the planets had to encompass these *a priori* assumptions. This led, of course, to many inaccuracies and difficulties in accounting for the motions of the planets. Why then were these things assumed to be correct in the first place? It was because they were deemed "reasonable" and compatible with accepted religious dogma. In fact, various Bible verses were cited to "prove" these assumptions.

Because Holy Scripture had been invoked to prove that the earth was the center of the universe, it was then reasoned that to cast doubt on the assumption that the earth is at the center of the universe was to cast doubt, by inference, on the Church itself. Because the Holy Scriptures and the Church were deemed above reproach, the problem was considered to lie within the person who put forward such heretical ideas.

Fortunately, we no longer burn people at the stake for suggesting that the sun is the center of our solar system, or that planets have elliptical orbits. Modern scientific method does not accept the *a priori* method of inquiry. The modern scientific method works as follows: first, careful and detailed observations are made. Then, based upon the observations, a working hypothesis is formulated to explain the observations. Experiments or additional observations are then made to test the predictive ability of the working hypothesis.

As more observations are collected and studied, it may be necessary to modify, amplify or even discard the original hypothesis in favor of a new one which can account for all the observations and data. Unless the data or observations are proven to be inaccurate, a hypothesis is not considered valid if it cannot account for all the relevant observations.

G. Applying the Scientific Method to the Engineering Analysis of Fires and Explosions

In a laboratory setting, it is usual to design experiments where the variable being studied is not obscured or complicated by other effects acting simultaneously. The variable is singled out to be free from other influences. Experiments are then conducted to determine what occurs when the variable is changed. Numerous tests of the effects of changing the variable provide a statistical basis for concluding how the variable behaves, and predicting what will occur under other circumstances.

In this way, theoretically, any fire or explosion event could be experimentally duplicated or reconstructed. The variables would simply be changed and combined until the "right" combination is found that reconstructs the event. When the actual event is experimentally duplicated, it might be said that the reconstruction of the fire or explosion has been solved.

There are problems with this approach, however. Foremost is the fact that a fire or explosion is a singular event. From considerations of cost and safety, the event will not be repeated over and over in different ways just so some engineer can play with the variables and make measurements.

It can be argued, however, that if there is a large body of observational evidence and facts about a fire or explosion, this is a suitable substitute for direct experimental data. Only the "correct" reconstruction hypothesis will account for all of the observations, and also be consistent with accepted scientific laws and knowledge.

An analogous example is the determination of an algebraic equation from a plot of points on a Cartesian plane. The more data points there are on the graph, the better the curve fit will be. Inductively, a large number of data points with excellent correspondence to a certain curve or equation would be proof that the fitted curve was equal to the original function that generated the data.

Thus, the scientific method, as it applies to the reconstruction of fires and explosions, is as follows.

- a general working hypothesis is proposed based upon "first cut" verified information.

- as more information is gathered, the original working hypothesis is modified to encompass the growing body of observations.
- after a certain time, the working hypothesis could be tested by using it to predict the presence of evidence that may have not been obvious or was overlooked during the initial information gathering effort.

A hypothesis is considered a complete reconstruction when the following are satisfied:

- the hypothesis accounts for all the verified observations.
- when possible, the hypothesis accurately predicts the existence of additional evidence not previously known.
- the hypothesis is consistent with accepted scientific principles, knowledge, and methodologies.

The scientific method as applied to the reconstruction of fires and explosions is not without some shortcomings. The reality of fires and explosions is that the event itself may destroy evidence about itself. The match that started a fire will likely be wholly consumed and never be found. Important evidence can be lost or obscured in the debris. Fire fighting may inadvertently destroy important evidence. In short, there can be observational gaps.

Using the previous graph analogy, this is like having areas of the graph with no data points, or few data points. Of course, if the data points are too few, perhaps several different curves might be fitted to the available data.

Thus, it is possible that the available observations can be explained by several hypotheses. Gaps or paucity in the observational data may not allow a unique solution. In effect, two qualified and otherwise forthright experts could proffer two conflicting reconstruction hypotheses, both equally consistent with the available data.

H. The Scientific Method and the Legal System

Having several plausible explanations for a fire or explosion may not necessarily be adverse in our legal system. It can sometimes happen that an investigator does not have to know exactly what happened, but rather what did not happen.

In our adversarial legal system, one person or party is the accuser, prosecutor or plaintiff, and the other is the accused, or defendant. The plaintiff or prosecutor is required to prove that the defendant has done some wrong to him or the state. However, the defendant has merely to prove that he, himself, did not do the wrong; he does not have to prove who else or what else did the wrong.

For example, suppose that a gas range company is being sued for a design defect that allegedly caused a house to burn down. As far as the gas range company is concerned, as long as it can be proved that the range did not cause the fire, the gas range company has no further concern as to what did cause the fire. Likewise, if the plaintiffs cannot prove the gas range caused the fire, they also may quickly lose interest; this is because there may be no one else for the plaintiffs to sue.

Thus, even if the observational data are not sufficient to provide a unique fire or explosion reconstruction, they may be sufficient to deny a particular one.

I. A Priori Biases

One of the thornier problems in the reconstruction of fires and explosions is the insidious application of *a priori* methodology. This occurs when legal counsel hires a forensic engineer to find out only information beneficial to his client's position. The counsellor will not specifically state what findings are to be made, but may suggest that since the "other side" will be giving information detrimental to his client, there is no pressing need to repeat that work.

While the argument may seem innocent enough, it serves to bias the original data. This is because only beneficial data will be considered, and detrimental data will be ignored. If enough bad data is ignored, the remaining observations will eventually force a beneficial fire or explosion reconstruction. Like the previous graph analogy, if enough data points are erased or ignored, almost any curve can be fitted to the remaining data.

A second version of this *a priori* problem occurs when a client does not provide all the observational data base to the forensic engineer for evaluation. Important facts are held back. This similarly reduces the observational data base, and enlarges the number of plausible hypotheses which might explain the facts.

A third variant of *a priori* reasoning takes place when the forensic engineer becomes an advocate for his client. In such cases, the forensic engineer assumes that his client's legal posture is true even before he has evaluated the data. This occurs because of friendship, sympathy, or a desire to please his client in hope of future assignments.

To guard against this, most states require that licensed professional engineers accept payment only on a time and materials basis; unlike attorneys, they may not work on a contingency basis. This at least removes the temptation of a reward or a share of the winnings.

Further, it is common for both the adversarial parties to question and carefully examine technical experts. During court examination by the attorneys for each party, the judge or jury can decide for themselves whether the expert is biased. During such court examinations, the terms of hire of the expert are questioned, his or her qualifications are examined, any unusual relationships with the client are discussed, all observations and facts he considered in reaching his conclusions are questioned, etc.

While an expert is considered a special type of witness due to his training and experience, he is not held exempt from adversarial challenges. While not perfect, this system does provide a way to check such biases and *a priori* assumptions.

J. A Little Fire History

Mankind's use of fire can be traced back to great antiquity, even prior to the advent of *homo sapiens* as a distinct species. Fire remains in proto-human dwelling areas have been found in Ethiopia and Kenya which date to 1.5 million years before the present. It is not specifically known if people were able to make fire then, but it is inferred from the association of ashes and charred animal bones alongside human artifacts that fire was being used by mankind.

It is hypothesized by some anthropologists that paleolithic mankind may have discovered fire through spontaneous combustion. People were not particularly sanitary in those times. Old food, animal parts, excrement, and other organic wastes usually were not segregated from the living areas. Thus, a person's bed could get egregiously rank. Periodically, a new layer of grass or leaves would be needed to cover up the nastiness before a person could lie down in it.

Such an arrangement of layered decaying organic matter overlaid by insulating grass and leaves are the basic components necessary for spontaneous fire generation. Thus, it is possible that the first person to discover fire may have simply been unsanitary rather than particularly intelligent. Even today, a small number of fires in livestock barns still occur where hay is stored in bulk and the hay is soiled or somewhat "green" in the middle of the pile.

A disgusting bed of decaying organic material may have even been desirable from a paleolithic person's point of view. If such a bed of organic materials is kept covered in the right way, it will generate an even warmth for a long period of time. Such a warm bed might have been very welcome on a cold, prehistoric night no matter how bad the stench. (Without deodorants and baths, who could tell the difference anyway?) Further, the distinctive stench may have been useful in warding off wild animals which prefer to avoid contact with humans.

Besides the spontaneous combustion theory of first fire, more conventional anthropologists suggest that mankind first discovered fire through forest fires started by lightning, lava flows or other natural causes. These theories, however, are not nearly as amusing to imagine as a bewildered caveman hot-footing it out of his bed in the middle of the night.

There is substantial evidence that proto-humans were regularly making and using fire by about 500,000 years before the present era. Drill-type tools and flints that can be used to start fires in the Boy Scout fashion have been found in association with hearth ash layers and human habitation debris.

In the famous Lascaux Cave in Montignac, France, the walls are decorated with prehistoric friezes of animal scenes. These scenes were painted by neolithic artists about 15,000 to 17,000 years ago. Mankind, or course, had evolved by that time into *homo sapiens.* On the ceiling of that cave have been found smoke residues resulting from the use of fat-burning lamps and torches by the artists for illumination in the otherwise lightless caves. This indicates a certain sophistication in the use of fire.

Some anthropologists note the parallel development of mankind's ability to utilize and generate fire with the advancement of mankind itself as a species. First, to make fire using the friction method requires manual dexterity and the ability to make tools. Keeping fires continuously burning requires communication and cooperation within a group. With fire, humans could migrate into colder climates and expand their range. Food that would otherwise be indigestible could be cooked and eaten. Fire could make wood stronger for better spears and turn clay into pottery. Fire kept away wild animals and extended the working day.

Of course, fire was not always mankind's idyllic friend; there was always the threat of forest fires and range fires. Dwellings and villages frequently caught fire and burned down due to errant hearth fires. The first arson must have occurred during the paleolithic period. Some thoughtful warrior likely saw the havoc created by an out-of-control fire in a village, and conjured up the notion of deliberately setting fire to the villages of his enemies. Setting fire to an enemy's buildings and property is still a time-honored facet of warfare; General Sherman became famous for his "scorched earth" policy of warfare during the U.S. Civil War. A similar "scorched earth" policy was recently used by the retreating Iraqi army in the Kuwaiti oil fields. Some traditions apparently do not change much over time.

To early mankind, fire was also a kind of magic. Fire dances and darts about almost in an animate way, but there is no apparent substance to it. A blazing fire casts ephemeral shadows and the flames create flickering luminous images. As with Rorschach ink blots, a person's imagination can find significance in such shadows and images. Like the sun, fire provides heat and warmth. Thus, having a fire is like having a small piece of the sun; it is a link to the power of the sun.

Magically, a solid object can be burned by fire and turned into smoke. The smoke can then float away with the wind like a cloud or spirit. To some, the ethereal qualities of smoke provide a medium between the tangible world of substances and the intangible world of spirits. In this way, sacrifices can be burned by mankind on earth, and sent directly to God in heaven (e.g. Genesis 22:1–13).

This co-equal imagery of fire and spirit is still present in many religions where incense is burned, e.g. Catholicism, Jainism and Buddhism. In the Christian religion, the Holy Spirit is often portrayed as a tongue of fire (see Acts 2:3). Angels and other spirits are also associated with fire (see Exodus 3:2 and Leviticus 10:1–2).

Some American aboriginal tribes revered ancestral fire spirits. The Aztecs worshipped the fire-god Xiuheuctli. Early Semitic tribes worshiped the fire-god Moloch, often sacrificing their first-born sons to him. The Greeks had the fire cult of Hestia, and the Romans had a corresponding fire cult centered around Vesta, the goddess of the hearth, and Vulcan, the god of fire and smithing. The ancient Celts and Slavs also worshipped various fire deities.

In Zoroastrianism, the dominant religion of ancient Persia which preceded Islam, fire worship was an important component. Each temple kept a holy flame burning, and it was symbolically important to keep it burning continuously. And in fact, the name for a Zoroastrian priest, *athravan*, means "belonging to the fire." Zoroastrianism is still practiced today by some 140,000 adherents in both Iran and India. Despite its Persian origins, however, the main contingent of adherents is in India due to aggressive persecution of followers in its native Iran.

Even earlier than Zoroastrianism, there was an organized fire cult which worshipped the god Mithra. Mithra was not only the god of fire, light, and the sun, but was also the god of wisdom and knowledge. The belief in Mithra was later adopted by and then integrated into the Zoroastrian religion.

Interestingly, the cult of Mithraism was at one time commonly practiced throughout most of Western Europe. It was a favorite religion of Roman soldiers, who established fire temples and shrines dedicated to Mithra throughout the Roman Empire. It was introduced into Western Europe during the 1st century A.D., and by the 4th century A.D. it had become the preeminent religion. Notably, the birthday of Mithra was celebrated on December 25. Ancient fire temples dedicated to Mithra are still standing in London, Rome, France, Turkey and Iran.

Systematic persecution of Mithraism by the Catholic Church after the conversion of the Roman Emperor Constantine, however, eventually stamped out the practice of the religion in Western Europe. Today, despite its historical significance to Western civilization, few Occidentals have even heard of it, and almost no secondary-level history books even mention the Mithra fire cult.

In several religions, it is believed that fire came to mankind as either a gift from the gods, or by theft from the gods. In the Greek myths, the Titan Prometheus stole fire from Mount Olympus and gave it to mankind. For this transgression, Prometheus was punished by Zeus, who chained him to a rock and allowed an eagle to eat out his liver. In the Polynesian myths of the Cook Islands, the epic hero Maui goes to the underworld where he is taught fire making by the gods.

One of the first instances of regulations about the responsible control of fire is found in the Old Testament, Exodus 22:6. The King James Version is quoted in full as follows:

If a fire break out, and catch in thorns so that the stacks of corn or the standing corn, or the field be consumed therewith; he that kindled the fire shall surely make restitution.

Before modern times, if a fire broke out, bucket-brigade type efforts would be used to put it out. Such volunteer firefighting units are known to have been organized in ancient Egypt and later in Rome.

In Europe during and after the Middle ages, some large towns had fire watchmen. These people would roam the city or stand post on towers looking for fires; when a fire was spotted, they would sound alarms and convene bucket brigade volunteers to the scene. This is essentially the same function performed by modern forest fire spotters. Similarly, the U.S. military still posts fire watchmen or fire guards when soldiers are housed in the older, wooden type military barracks.

While some mention of a type of fire engine in the first century A.D. was made by the Roman historian Pliny, the earliest fire engine for which a complete description exists was in Nürenberg, Germany in 1657. It was drawn by two horses, and needed 28 men to power and operate the pumps. It reportedly could shoot a one-inch diameter jet of water 80 feet high.

The application of a little algebra and Bernoulli's equation for incompressible flow to the above finds that the nozzle velocity must have been about 71 ft/sec, and the head pressure at the nozzle must have been about 136 psig. This is impressive when we consider the state of seal technology in 1657 and the fact that the pressure was pumped up manually.

Fire insurance was invented shortly after the Great Fire of London in 1666; in that fire, some 13,000 buildings burned down. Mr. Nicholas Barbon, a London businessman, devised a system where small payments or premiums would be collected periodically from a pool of people to establish a fund. The fund would then be used to compensate persons in the pool who sustained accidental property loss by fire.

Another result of the Great Fire of London was the enactment of the first fire code regulations to reduce fire risks. These regulations specified the use of more fireworthy building materials and construction methods. Shortly after these regulations were adopted in England, some American colonies adopted similar regulations. Unfortunately, the regulations were not particularly effective because they were generally not enforced.

Some fire insurance companies founded after the Great Fire of London organized fire brigades to protect their insured members. Some of these brigades were equipped with pumps mounted on handcarts. These various insurance fire brigades were taken over by the City of London in 1865, and were reorganized into the London Metropolitan Fire Brigade; this formed the basis for the current fire protection system in London.

The first permanent fire company in the U.S. was organized in Philadelphia in 1736 by none other than Benjamin Franklin; the second permanent fire company was organized in New York City one year later. The first fire insurance company in the U.S. was the Philadelphia Contributorship for the Insurance of Houses from Loss by Fire, which began operation in 1752. Perhaps not surprisingly, one of the first directors of the company was also Benjamin Franklin.

During the 1800's, numerous large conflagrations destroyed whole sections of large cities in the U.S., killing thousands of people. Most notable, perhaps, is the Great Chicago Fire of 1871, which by legend was started when Mrs. O'Leary's cow knocked over a coal oil lantern in the barn.

These urban fires easily spread through the congested tenement sections of cities, because building construction methods and materials exacerbated fire spread. Fire fighting was also hampered by insufficient water resources and uncoordinated fire fighting efforts. Many people died in such fires because they had no warning, and because often there were no safe exits once a fire had begun.

By the turn of the 20th century, fire fighting had advanced greatly. Large cities had salaried, professional fire fighting units. Fire fighting units were now integrated into the city government instead of competing with one another for business and territory. Steam-driven fire pumps, which could deliver large volumes of water at high pressure, were employed instead of low pressure, manually operated pumps. This allowed water to reach the upper stories of the newer, taller buildings.

Systems of underground water pipes and hydrants were installed in the cities. Instead of taking the water to the fire or relying on nearby horse troughs and ponds, a city-wide fire hydrant system made ample water available at regular points close to the fire. Telegraph fire alarm systems were installed, and public fire call boxes were installed. The first modern fire engine, where one motor provided power to both operate the pump and drive the vehicle, was built in 1903.

After the Great Chicago Fire of 1871, cities adopted a number of regulations with respect to the use of fire-retardant materials and fireproof construction. Around 1900, tenement house laws were enacted in New York City which set standards for public apartment houses. The laws were quickly adopted by other cities with large concentrations of tenement buildings.

At the same time as the adoption of tenement house laws, insurance companies developed their own fire codes. While these codes had no legal standing like a city or state law, compliance was achieved by charging higher insurance premiums for buildings which did not meet the codes. These insurance fire codes formed the foundation for most modern building and fire safety codes.

For example, the *National Electric Code*, which has been adopted by nearly every city and principality in the U.S., is an outgrowth of the first electrical code published in 1897 by a consortium of insurance, electrical, and architectural companies. Concomitant with the above developments of codes and standards since about 1900, the scientific investigation of fires and explosions has emerged as a specific field of study and research. A subdivision of mechanical engineering, fire protection engineering has also emerged which specializes in the design of fire protection systems for large buildings, factories, and facilities.

K. Some Brief Notes About Fire Insurance Policies

The modern fire insurance policy in most U.S. states is derived from the standard policy adopted by the State of New York in 1943. In that prototype policy, two types of premium rates were established: class rates and schedule rates.

Class rates are based on homogeneous groupings of building types according to occupancy, construction, and available fire protection in the area. The same premium rate is applied to all buildings which fall into the same category. Residences and apartments are usually insured according to class rates.

Because commercial and industrial facilities comprise a wide range of risk types, they are usually *schedule rated.* This means that specific risk factors are assessed and weighed for each particular facility. These factors might include the statistical loss history of similar industries, internal protection measures including safety training of employees and safety equipment, the available fire protection in the area of the facility, and any special hazards within the facility.

Most fire insurance policies cover losses caused by fire or lightning, and any resulting smoke and water damages. Damages to the structure proper are often distinguished from damages to the building's contents. This is because the owner of the building may not be the same as the owner of the contents, as in a leased building or apartment. Many policies have special provisions which make allowances for economic disruption, and for out-of-pocket expenses caused by the unavailability of the facility or its contents.

The two most common bases for compensation are *actual cash value,* and *replacement cost.* Actual cash value, or ACV, is the market value of the item at the time it was damaged. For example, a car which originally cost $10,000 may have only been worth $750 at the time of the loss due to its age and high mileage. Since the car is old, repairs would cost many times more than the ACV of the vehicle. Thus, under ACV compensation, the fire loss would be valued at $750, and not the amount needed to restore the car to its pre-fire condition.

Replacement cost is the amount of money it would take to replace the damaged item in like condition as before the fire. Using the same car fire as before, it might be that while the car was only worth $750, it might cost $1,200 to find a similar car to replace it. This might be because an car identical in age, condition, and mileage cannot be found. Thus, to functionally replace the car with like quality and features, $1,200 would be needed.

One term often used in fire and explosion losses is *betterment*, which is best explained by the following example: assume that a building originally built in 1950 burns down; it was insured for replacement costs. Changes in the local building code since 1950 require that buildings like the one which burned down have additional safety equipment and features in order to obtain an occupation permit.

In such a case, the insurance company would likely have an obligation to repair or replace the building as needed, and in like quality and quantity as existed prior to the fire. However, the insurance company would likely have no obligation to pay for any additional safety equipment and features which are now required but which were not required in 1950. This is true even if the building cannot be issued an occupancy permit without the new equipment and features. The difference between the building's equipment and features which existed prior to the fire, and the equipment and features now required by the current local building code is called the betterment; many insurance fire policies do not pay for betterment.

Science is simply common sense at its best-
that is, rigidly accurate in observation,
and merciless to fallacy in logic.

Thomas Huxley

Chapter 2:
Some Combustion Chemistry

A. General

Fire or combustion is basically a chemical reaction; more specifically it is a rapid, self-sustaining oxidation process. In order to diagnose fires and explosions, a person must understand the basic chemical and thermodynamic principles involved in the fire process. If these basic principles are well understood, much of the mystery of how and why fires occur and propagate becomes plain. The understanding and application of these principles is what separates the *science* of diagnosing fires and explosions from the *art* of diagnosing fires and explosions.

In most fires, the fuel or fire load reacts with the oxygen in the air, heat and light are given off, and products of combustion are generated. A simple example involving methane and pure oxygen is given below:

reactants   products
(i) $CH_4 + 2O_2 \rightarrow CO_2 + 2H_2O +$ heat of combustion
    gas   gas   gas   gas

In this combustion reaction, the single methane molecule is completely oxidized by the two oxygen molecules and heat is given off. The resulting products of combustion are one molecule of carbon dioxide and two molecules of water vapor.

In equation (i), the number and kind of atoms on the left side are algebraically equal to the number and kind of atoms on the right side, so that both quantities are conserved in the reaction. This is, of course, because in any chemical reaction the total mass of the materials before the reaction must equal the total mass of the materials after the reaction. Also, the total count of any particular type of atom before the reaction must be equal to the total count of the same type of atom after the reaction. Atoms of hydrogen, for example, do not turn into atoms of antimony during a fire.

In short, although the reactants involved in combustion may recombine into new compounds, change form, and appear very different

27

after combustion has taken place, all the atoms that were present before combustion are still present after combustion.

If the atomic weight of each component involved in the reaction is summed and noted under equation (i), then a *mass balance* of the reaction can be calculated. This is shown below.

$$
\begin{array}{ccccccc}
\text{(ii)} & CH_4 & + & 2O_2 & \rightarrow & CO_2 + 2H_2O & + \ \text{Heat of Combustion} \\
& (12 + 4 \times 1) & + & 2(2 \times 16) & = & (12 + 2 \times 16) & + \ 2(2 \times 1 + 16) \\
& 16 & + & 64 & = & 44 & + \quad 36 \\
& & 80 & & = & & 80
\end{array}
$$

For convenience, the mass units initially used to set up equation (ii) are the given atomic weight units for the particular elements found in the periodic table. However, the units used in equation (ii) are arbitrary, and can be modified to suit the situation. They could just as easily represent grams, kilograms, pounds mass, slugs, or carats. And, as long as all the items in the equation are multiplied by the same factor, they can be doubled, halved, increased by a degree of magnitude, or decreased by a degree of magnitude.

For example, equation (ii) indicates that 16 grams of methane will burn with 64 grams of oxygen to produce 44 grams of carbon dioxide and 36 grams of water vapor. Alternatively, it also indicates that 8 pounds of methane will burn with 32 pounds of oxygen to produce 22 pounds of carbon dioxide and 18 pounds of water vapor.

Reaction calculations like the preceding, which describe the numerical relationships between reactants and resulting products, constitute a branch of chemistry called *stoichiometry.* More properly, stoichiometry is defined as the study of the quantitative relationships between the reactants and the products of a reaction.

As has been done in the methane and oxygen combustion example, the usual method in setting up a combustion chemical equation is as follows: first, a complete list of the reactants and products involved in the reaction, and their relative proportions, is written down in chemical equation form. Then the relationships between the reactants and products are worked out. The total mass of reactants is set equal to the total mass of the products, and the total count of each type of reactant atoms is set equal to the total count of each type of product atoms. Usually, the relationship between reactants and products is worked out using the lowest possible whole number ratios.

The principle of using the lowest ratio of whole numbers to represent reaction relationships is often called the *Law of Combining Weights,* or *Dalton's Law of Multiple Proportions.* The latter name is in honor of John Dalton (1766–1844) who was one of the first to recognize that chemical reactions involving the same substances will combine in the same proportions, no matter what amounts are involved. In other words, all elements and compounds combine or decompose in specific, simple weight ratios, and these weight ratios are exactly proportional to the sum of the atomic mass units of the substances.

Incidentally, Dalton was the first significant scientist since Democritus to propose that substances are composed of fundamental particles which retain the same chemical properties as the substance in larger bulk. The fundamental particle of an element is an *atom,* and the fundamental particle of a compound is a *molecule.* Molecules are made up of two or more atoms which have reacted with one another and combined to make a compound.

When the reaction involves mainly gases, Dalton's Law of Multiple Proportions is sometimes referred to as *Gay-Lussac's Law of Combining Volumes,* which can be stated as follows: the volumes of gases involved in a chemical reaction can be represented by ratios of small whole numbers when the gases are at the same temperature and pressure. Both laws, Gay-Lussac's Law of Combining Volumes and Dalton's Law of Multiple Proportions, are based on the same fundamental principle.

A practical extension of Gay-Lussac's Law is *Avogadro's Law,* which states that equal volumes of gas at the same conditions of pressure and temperature contain equal numbers of atoms or molecules. Thus, the same chemical equation for the methane and oxygen combustion reaction can be used to determine the volumes of gases involved in the reaction. This is shown in the following chemical equation.

(iii) CH_4 + $2O_2$ → CO_2 + $2H_2O$ + Heat of Combustion
    gas   gas   gas   gas
1 mole vol. 2 mole vols.   1 mole vol.   2 mole vols.

As before in the mass balance equation, the mole volume units are arbitrary. They can be liters, cubic feet, or barrels. However, the mass units that are selected to set up the mass balance equation lock in the volume units in the volume balance equation, and vice versa.

For example, in the metric system one gram molecular weight, or one mole, of a gaseous substance has a volume of 22.4 liters at standard conditions of pressure and temperature. Standard conditions are 1,013.3 millibars of pressure, which is one atmosphere, and 0°C. Thus, if 16 grams or one mole of methane were used in the reaction at standard conditions, the methane would have a volume of 22.4 liters.

An item worth noting in the methane and oxygen reaction is the water vapor. The water produced in the combustion reaction is initially in gas form. However, upon cooling, the water vapor will condense into liquid water.

Dalton's Law of Partial Pressures states that the total pressure of a mixture of gases is the sum of the pressures of the individual gases as if each one were present by itself in the same volume.

Thus, if a mole of methane and two moles of oxygen were placed in a sealed vessel of 67.2 liters at standard conditions of 1,013.3 millibars and 0°C, then the methane would exert a partial pressure of 337.8 millibars and the oxygen would exert a partial pressure of 675.5 millibars.

After combustion occurs between the methane and oxygen in our example, the resulting products of combustion would consist of three mole-volumes of a mixture of carbon dioxide and water vapor. Thus, there would be the same number of gas molecules after combustion as there were before combustion. However, due to the heat given off during the reaction, the pressure in the sealed vessel after combustion would be higher.

If the combustion takes place slowly enough for heat to be transferred away from the vessel during the combustion process, then the pressure in the vessel after combustion is complete can be calculated by using the Ideal Gas Law. If the temperature of the resulting gases sometime after the reaction is completed is T_2, then the pressure at that time can be calculated by combining the Ideal Gas Law and Dalton's Law of Partial Pressures as follows:

Dalton's Law of Partial Pressures

(iv) $P_{1total} = P_{1methane} + P_{1oxygen}$ pressure inside vessel before combustion

$P_{2total} = P_{2carbon\,dioxide} + P_{2steam}$ pressure inside vessel after combustion

Ideal Gas Law

(v) $PV = nRT$ $P = [nR / V] T$

where P = pressure,
      T = temperature on the absolute scale,
      n = number of moles of particular gas, and
      R = gas constant, 83.14 (millibar-liters) / (g-moles)(°K) or 8.314 joules/(g-moles)(°K).

Thus,

(vi) P_{1total} $= [n_{meth.}RT_1 + n_{oxygen}RT_1]/V_1$ before combustion

      P_{2total} $= [n_{car.diox.}RT_2 + n_{steam}RT_2]/V_2$ after combustion

Since the reaction takes place in the same vessel, then $V_1 = V_2$. Thus, the before and after pressures can be related to each other as follows:

(vii)
$$\frac{P_{1total}}{P_{2total}} = \frac{[n_{methane} + n_{oxygen}]}{[n_{car.diox.} + n_{steam}]} \times \frac{[T_1]}{[T_2]}$$

$$\frac{P_{1total}}{P_{2total}} = \frac{[1 + 2][T_1]}{[1 + 2][T_2]} = \frac{[T_1]}{[T_2]}$$

Equation (vii) shows that in the methane and oxygen combustion reaction, as long as the water is in a vapor form, the after combustion pressure within the vessel is just a ratio of the before and after combustion temperatures, i.e.

$$P_{2total} = [P_{1total}][T_2/T_1]$$

As the gaseous mixture of combustion products cools to standard temperature, 0°C or 273°K, the water vapor condenses out as liquid water. Thus, instead of 3 mole volumes of gaseous products, there is only one, carbon dioxide. Equation (vii) becomes:

(viii)
$$\frac{P_{1total}}{P_{2total}} = \frac{[n_{meth.} + n_{oxygen}R]}{[n_{car.diox.}R} \times \frac{[T_1]}{[T_2]}$$

$$P_{1total} = [3/1][P_{2total}][T_1/T_2]$$

When the sealed vessel finally cools to 0°C or 273°K, the resulting pressure will be 337.8 millibars, or about 1/3 atmosphere.

Up to this point, it has been assumed that the reaction has proceeded slowly and the heat generated has been allowed to transfer freely out of the vessel and into the environment more or less as it is released by the reaction. When this assumption is made, the Ideal Gas Law is applicable. These types of reactions are often described as being *isothermal*. However, strictly speaking, an isothermal reaction is one that occurs at a constant temperature.

However, there are instances where this assumption is not valid. In cases where the reaction proceeds rapidly enough where there has not been enough time for significant energy to be transferred to the environment, or where there is enough insulation to prevent significant transfer of energy to the environment, the reaction is *adiabatic*. In adiabatic reactions, there is no heat transfer; all the energy produced by the reaction is kept within the system. Adiabatic reactions are discussed later in Section K of this chapter.

To further add to the sometimes confusing list of chemical laws that have been presented, there is a corollary to Dalton's Law of Partial Pressures that is sometimes handy to know. It is called *Amagat's Law;* it states that the total volume of a mixture of individual gases which all have the same temperature and pressure is the sum of the volumes of the individual gases at that same temperature and pressure. Whereas in Dalton's Law of Partial Pressures the individual pressures are summed, in Amagat's Law, the individual volumes are summed.

If a person wants to be more precise with respect to the post-- combustion pressure in the vessel in our methane and oxygen reaction example, then the volume of the liquid water has to be accounted for. The mass of 2 metric moles of liquid water is 36 grams and occupies a volume of about 36 milliliters or 0.036 liters. Thus, the 44.8 liters of water vapor produced in the reaction would, upon cooling, condense to 0.036 liters of liquid water. Because of this, the remaining gaseous carbon dioxide would not expand into a vessel of 67.2 liters, but into one containing 67.164 liters. The liquid water would occupy the rest.

This slight change in available volume into which the gaseous carbon dioxide would expand changes slightly the calculated pressure of the carbon dioxide to 337.9 millibars. If even more precision is needed, the vapor pressure over the liquid water also has to be accounted for. At 0°C, liquid water has a vapor pressure of 3.4 millibars. Thus, the total pressure in the vessel after it has cooled to standard temperature is 341.3 millibars.

For most purposes, the volumes of the non-gases can be neglected in volume calculations. In this example, the liquid water is only 1/1,866th the volume that the water vapor occupied in the vessel.

B. Limitations of the Ideal Gas Law

One advantage of the Ideal Gas Law is that it is a relatively simple algebraic expression. It is easy to solve, easy to work with in equations, and for most common applications, it provides accurate results.

However, the Ideal Gas Law has some limitations that the reader should be aware of. It assumes that the attraction or repulsion between individual gas molecules is negligible. Thus, when pressures and temperatures are in the ranges where such intermolecular forces are low, the Ideal Gas Law is accurate.

If, however, the pressures and temperatures are in ranges where the intermolecular forces are not negligible, such as when the gas is very dense and hot, a better model for the behavior of the gas is *van der Waal's Law*. The expression for van der Waal's Law is given in the following equation.

(ix) $[P + n^2a / V^2][V - nb] = nRT$ van der Waal's Law where a and b are constants, and n = number of moles.

Some typical values for the "a" and "b" constants used in the van der Waal's Law are given below. The values are given in metric units using liters and millibars. (One atmosphere is equal to 1,013.3 millibars.) Note that if "a" and "b" were both zero, van der Waal's Law would reduce to the Ideal Gas Law.

Table 1. Some van der Waal's Constants

gas	"a"	"b"
O_2	1378 $(l^2)(millibars)/(g\text{-}mole)^2$	0.0318 (l)/g-mole
N_2	1408$(l^2)(millibars)/(g\text{-}mole)^2$	0.0391 (l)/g-mole
CO_2	3638$(l^2)(millibars)/(g\text{-}mole)^2$	0.0427 (l)/g-mole
CO	1510$(l^2)(millibars)/(g\text{-}mole)^2$	0.0399 (l)/g-mole
CH_4	2283$(l^2)(millibars)/(g\text{-}mole)^2$	0.0428 (l)/g-mole
C_3H_8	8780$(l^2)(millibars)/(g\text{-}mole)^2$	0.0845 (l)/g-mole
H_2O	5537$(l^2)(millibars)/(g\text{-}mole)^2$	0.0305 (l)/g-mole
H_2	247.7$(l^2)(millibars)/(g\text{-}mole)^2$	0.0266 (l)/g-mole

The "a" value in van der Waal's equation is a measure of the attraction between molecules of the gas. The "b" term is related to the volume of the molecules themselves, and their relative incompressibility with each other. Gases with high "a" values will generally liquify at a higher temperatures than ones with lower "a" values due to the greater intermolecular attractions.

Similarly, molecules with low "b" values tend to liquefy at lower temperatures, due to the smaller size of the molecule which prevents the attractive forces from coming into play sooner due to intermolecular distance.

Because of the mathematical advantages of the Ideal Gas Law over van der Waal's Law, another way of dealing with the deviation of real gas behavior from the Ideal Gas Law has been developed, involving the use of a correction factor, often called the compressibility factor, which is substituted into the Ideal Gas Law in the following way:

(x) $PV = ZnRT$

where Z = compressibility factor.

In more concrete terms, the compressibility factor Z is the ratio of the volume of the real gas to the volume of the ideal gas, as predicted by the Ideal Gas Law, at the particular conditions of pressure and temperature. Thermodynamic reference texts have tables, graphs, or formulas from which Z factors can be selected for each type of gas at various conditions of pressure and temperature.

A related concept, called *fugacity*, is also used to correct for deviations of a real gas from the Ideal Gas Law. In this method, a corrected pressure, or *fugacity pressure* is substituted for the pressure "P" in the Ideal Gas Law expression. Substitution of the fugacity pressure makes the Ideal Gas Law more exactly model the behavior of the real gas. Thermodynamics references provide tables, graphs or formulas that allow the conversion of the actual pressure "P" to the corresponding fugacity pressure.

Despite the shortcomings of the Ideal Gas Law, in most situations involving open air-fires its application is satisfactory.

C. Combustion in Air

In Section A, the simple combustion of methane and pure oxygen was discussed. However, in most fire situations, oxygen is not available as a pure substance. In open-air fires, oxygen is supplied to the fire as a component of the air.

Table 2 lists the typical component gases found in dry air at sea level. Pollutant gases and particles and water vapor are omitted from the list, although in some localized areas pollutant gases and particles may be significant components.

Table 2. Typical Composition of Dry Air at Sea Level

component	at. wt.	volume percent	ppm
N_2	28	78.08	780,800
O_2	32	20.95	209,500
Ar	39.9	0.93	9,340
CO_2	44	0.033	330
Ne	20.2	0.0018	18
He	4	0.0005	5
CH_4	16	0.0002	2
Kr	83.8	0.0001	1
H_2	2	0.00005	0.5
NO	30	0.00005	0.5
Xe	131.3	0.000009	0.09

Inspection of Table 2 finds that the components of air can be divided into two subgroups: major components and minor components. Diatomic nitrogen and oxygen are the major components; they comprise 99.03% of the air by volume. All the other components combined comprise only 0.97% of air by volume. From Table 2, a little application of algebra finds that the weighted average atomic weight of air is 28.94.

If the composition of air is arbitrarily set to be 78% nitrogen, 21% oxygen, and 1% argon and the other components are simply ignored, the weighted average atomic weight of air would be 28.96.

This simplifying assumption introduces only a 0.07% error with respect to the average atomic weight of air. Considering the day-to-day variations in average atomic weight due to humidity and local conditions, the loss of accuracy introduced by this simplifying assumption is statistically hidden by other variations anyway.

But a further simplification can be made if air is considered to be composed of just 79% nitrogen and 21% oxygen. With this assumption, the weighted average atomic weight of air is 28.84. This varies from the "actual" calculated average weighted atomic weight from Table 2 by only 0.35%.

Thus, for most instances, it is practical to consider air as being composed of 21% oxygen and 79% nitrogen, and this greatly simplifies the combustion chemical equations without introducing significant error. If greater accuracy is required, air can be considered to be 78% nitrogen, 21% oxygen, and 1% argon. It is doubtful that any calculations involving open-air fires would require a level of accuracy which would necessitate the use of the whole list of components in Table 2.

Applying Gay-Lussac's Law to the simplified version of air, it is found that for every molecule of diatomic oxygen there are about 3.762 molecules of diatomic nitrogen. Thus, whenever a mole of oxygen is used in a chemical reaction, 3.762 moles of diatomic nitrogen are also introduced into the reaction. If an arbitrary mole of air is hypothesized that corresponds one-to-one with a mole of oxygen, then such a mole of air could be represented by the following:

(xi)   Air $= O_2 + (3.762)N_2$

Recall that in Section A, the chemical equation for the combustion of methane with pure oxygen was given as:

(i) $CH_4 + 2O_2 \rightarrow CO_2 + 2H_2O +$ heat of combustion

Using equation (xi), we can now modify equation (i) to show the chemical equation for the combustion of methane in air. The following equation shows this:

(xii) $CH_4 + 2O_2 + 7.524\ N_2 \rightarrow CO_2 + 2\ H_2O + 7.524\ N_2$
$+$ heat of combustion

A useful parameter often cited in combustion reactions is the *air-to-fuel ratio*. The air to fuel ratio may be expressed in mass-to-mass units, or volume-to-volume units when the fuel is gaseous. The air-to-fuel ratio indicates the theoretic amount of air that will exactly burn one unit of fuel.

For example, in equation (xii) the atomic weight of the fuel is 16, and the atomic weight of the air is 274.7. Thus, on a mass-to-mass ratio, the air-to-fuel ratio of methane is (274.7)/(16) or 17.17 to 1. On a volume-to-volume basis, the air to fuel ratio is 9.524 to 1.

For purposes of this analysis, the nitrogen in the combustion equation is considered to be inert. It does not react with any of the reactants or products and does not break down or reconfigure itself into a different compound. Basically, it goes in one side of the reaction, and comes out the other more or less chemically unchanged. However, its inclusion in the reactant and product mix does cause some interesting physical and thermodynamic changes in the combustion reaction.

For example, it often significantly changes the reactant-to-product volume relationships. Compare the combustion of methane in pure oxygen, as shown in equation (i), to the following combustion equation of methane in air.

(xiii) $CH_4 + 2\ O_2 + 7.524\ N_2 \rightarrow CO_2 + 2\ H_2O + 7.524\ N_2$
$$+ \text{heat of combustion}$$

1 vol   2 vols   7.724 vols $\rightarrow$ 1 vol   2 vols   7.524 vols

10.524 vols $\rightarrow$ 10.524 vols

If the reaction takes place in a closed vessel at standard conditions as before, then the methane exerts a partial pressure of 96.3 millibars, the oxygen exerts a partial pressure of 192.6 millibars, and the nitrogen exerts a partial pressure of 724.4 millibars.

After the reaction has been completed, the water vapor has condensed out as a liquid and the gaseous products have returned to standard temperature, the pressure of the products would be about 843 millibars or about 0.83 atmosphere. Thus, the condensation of water from the products of a methane and air combustion would not result in as much of a pressure drop in the vessel as when only methane and pure oxygen are combusted.

In addition to changing the volume relationships, the presence of the inert diatomic nitrogen in the product mix tends to lower the temperature of the products. The amount of heat given off by the combustion of the fuel is constant on a per mole of fuel basis; one molecule of methane produces only so much heat when oxidized. When considering the methane and pure oxygen reaction, there is only carbon dioxide and water vapor to soak up the heat afterwards. The heat of combustion released by the reaction is only used to raise the temperature of those two products.

However, when air is used instead of pure oxygen, the products of combustion are mixed with a large amount of inert nitrogen which heats up along with the rest of the combustion products. In fact, there is more nitrogen by weight in the mixture than any other component. In the reaction noted in equation (xiii), the total atomic weight of the products is 290.7. The atomic weight of the nitrogen alone is 210.7 or 72% of the total mass. Because the same amount of heat must now be distributed to 3.63 times more mass, the temperature reached by the products just after combustion will be significantly less.

This is the reason why, when extremely high temperatures are desired, fuels are burned in pure oxygen instead of air. However, air is free and pure oxygen is expensive. Besides, operating at significantly higher combustion temperatures requires the use of high-temperature resistant materials, which is also expensive. Since pure oxygen is itself a fire risk, certain precautions and safety regulations must be followed when it is used. This, of course, introduces an added level of design complexity to the combustion equipment. Since only a few processes can justify the additional expense associated with using pure oxygen, most industrial, commercial and domestic combustion is done with plain air.

In industrial conflagrations, however, the principle about combustion occurring with a pure oxidizing material should be well considered. If there is a source of pure oxidizing material within a warehouse or factory, the resulting fire when that material burns may be significantly hotter and more dangerous. Such fires may burn so fiercely that the heat from radiation alone may be too intense for unshielded firemen to get close enough to fight the fire. This is why large concentrations of oxidizing agents stored in warehouses require special protection to prevent combustion, and call for special procedures when fire fighting operations are underway.

D. Imperfect Combustion

In all the combustion equations examined so far, the combustion reaction was assumed to be perfect. In this sense, "perfect" is used to mean that all the fuel is burned, all the reactant oxygen is consumed, all the products are fully oxidized and cannot react further, and there are no left-over reactants except possibly for some atmospheric nitrogen which is along for the ride. Such a perfect combustion situation is often called a *stoichiometric* reaction.

While controlled combustion in a high-efficiency boiler, gas turbine, or furnace may get very close to stoichiometric conditions, uncontrolled fire usually does not. In an uncontrolled fire where air is supplied by natural convective effects there is usually not enough air to fully combust the available fuel load. In such cases, the combustion reaction proceeds with only partial oxidation of the fuel.

For example, suppose that a stable combustion reaction could be sustained using only half the amount of air needed for the stoichiometric combustion of methane. The combustion equation then might look something like the following:

(xiv) $CH_4 + O_2 + 3.762 \, N_2 \rightarrow$

$$wCO_2 + xCO + yH_2O + zH_2 + 3.762 \, N_2 + Heat$$

where w, x, y, and z are unknown coefficients.

From the conservation of mass in the above equation, it is known that

$$w + x = 1; \quad y + z = 2 \, ; \quad and \quad w + (x/2) + (y/2) = 1.$$

A little algebraic manipulation finds the following additional relationships:

$$x = y; \; w + y = 1; \; w = z; \; and \; z + x = 1.$$

From the equations just above, it is seen that there is no unique algebraic solution to the formation of products of combustion. The only way to tell for sure what is going on in the combustion reaction is to note the conditions of combustion, sample the combustion products, chemically analyze the samples, and then determine the quantitative relationships between the various products.

However, as the above equations show, if the single unknown coefficient x were determined from chemical analysis, the other coefficients can be immediately solved. Thus, a single test to determine the ratio of carbon dioxide to carbon monoxide would be sufficient to define all the other components in equation (xiv).

The sampling of stack gases or flue gases is routinely done in order to check the efficiency of combustion of commercial boilers, furnaces and combustion equipment. It is done with a variety of test equipment. The most complete analysis of flue gas is done with an *Orsat Apparatus*; this device physically samples the flue gas and passes it through a series of reagents. Each reagent selectively absorbs and thereby detects the amount of a particular component within the flue gas sample. Specialized devices are also available which check either singly or in combination for oxygen content, carbon dioxide content, carbon monoxide content, unburned fuel content, oxides of nitrogen, and oxides of sulfur.

E. Smoke and Fire Coloration

Usually the clouds of smoke seen billowing from an uncontrolled fire are colored primarily by particles of unburned or partially burned fuel. Sometimes the color of the smoke can provide a clue as to what is burning.

For example, the smoke from burning gasoline, rubber tires, asphalt and motor oil often appears opaque black or gray. Some types of hydraulic fluid may have a gray or white colored smoke. Burning chlorine may emit a green or yellowish green smoke. Nitric acid may appear yellowish brown, bromine may appear brown, iodine may appear purple, and so on.

Table 3 lists some substances that may color smoke when burned or partially burned.

Table 3. Some Compounds or Elements Which May Color Smoke

compound/element	color of fumes or smoke
aluminum	whitish, perhaps with sparkles
nitrates and nitrites	brown
iodine	violet
nitric acid	yellow or brown
NO_2 from nitrates	brown
Ca^{++} cations	brick red
Sr^{++} cations	crimson
Ba^+ cations	green
K^+ cations	violet
Na^{++} cations	yellow
Cu^{++} cationsborates	green
borates	green
cesium compounds	same as potassium compounds, violet
$CuCl_2$	azure
$CuBr_2$	azure blue/green
lead, arsenic	light blue
compounds of thallium	green
lithium compounds	green
Fe	brown or yellow (green in a reducing flame)
Bi	brown or yellow (gray in a reducing flame)
white phosphorus	whitish, with sparkles

Before the advent of modern analytical methodologies such as gas chromatography, mass spectroscopy, and infrared spectroscopy, a common laboratory technique for substance identification was the *flame test.* In this procedure, samples of substances to be identified are placed in the flame of a Bunsen burner, usually in the oxidizing portion of the flame, and the resulting color is noted.

One commonly used type of flame test is called the *Borax Bead Test.* In this procedure, a loop of wire is heated until red hot, and then is plunged into some borax. The borax-covered loop is then placed back into the flame until it melts and forms a clear, glass-like bead within the wire loop. Small sample amounts of the items to be tested are set aside, and are then picked up by being touched with the hot borax bead. The material is then put into the oxidizing zone of the Bunsen burner until the sample materials blend into the bead. The resulting coloration of the bead is an indicator of what substances the unknown material might be composed.

Tables of colorations associated with the application of the Borax Bead Test are still listed in some chemistry reference texts, most notably the *Handbook of Chemistry and Physics,* published by CRC Press. While largely supplanted in the laboratory by more sophisticated identification techniques, the Borax Bead Test is still a useful field identification method for inorganic compounds, especially when it is inconvenient to lug around a gas chromatograph, a motor-generator set to run it, and the supporting laboratory hardware. The materials needed for the Borax Bead Test are cheap, simple and easy to get, and the test is relatively easy to do even for persons with little laboratory experience.

However, getting back to the topic at hand, in reviewing the correspondence of the various colors in Table 3 to their associated substances, it is apparent there is a significant problem with using smoke or fire coloration as an identifier. First and foremost is the fact that several compounds and elements can produce the same coloration, or nearly so. Brown, for example, is a common color produced by a large number of compounds, cations, and elements. In short, many different substances can produce the same coloration.

Second is the fact that most of the fires that require investigation are uncontrolled. In a laboratory setting, only one item at a time is flame tested. Thus, the resulting coloration corresponds to just one substance. A burning warehouse, however, may be composed of steel, concrete, glass, aluminum, wood, linoleum, gypsum board, and various textiles. Additionally, there may hundreds of different items stored in inventory; all of these items may burn or oxidize, and the colors of their individual flames and smoke will blend in unknown proportions with one another.

For example, a yellow-colored smoke produced by the combustion of a sodium compound may mix with a green-colored smoke formed from the combustion of chlorides to produce a brown-colored smoke. This brown-colored smoke could be mistakenly interpreted to indicate any of the following: that nitrates were being burned; that bismuth compounds were being burned; or that iron shavings were being burned.

In short, while flame or smoke coloration can provide clues to the nature of the fire load, by itself it cannot be considered a reliable and unique indicator.

F. Heat of Formation

When a compound freely forms from the reaction of two or possibly more substances, heat is given off during the formation of the new compound. This heat is called the *heat of formation* of the substance; sometimes it is also called the *enthalpy of formation*. A reaction that gives off heat is called an *exothermic reaction*. Since the energy given off during the formation of a substance can vary with pressure and temperature, the measurement of the heat of formation has to be standardized to be meaningful. Thus, the heat of formation is more properly defined as the heat given off when one mole of a substance is formed from its constituent elements in their standard states at 25°C and 1013.3 millibars of pressure.

For obvious reasons, all combustion reactions where the combustion is self-sustaining are exothermic; otherwise, the fire would go out by itself. Reactions that require the constant addition of heat to make them go are called *endothermic* reactions. The distinction between naturally occurring endothermic and exothermic reactions can be very important in arson cases. When the primary material which burned cannot itself sustain fire without external fuel or heat being applied to it, it may indicate it was "helped" to burn.

If amorphous pure carbon reacts with pure oxygen, the product of the reaction is carbon dioxide, as shown in equation (xv) below. As the carbon dioxide is formed from the amorphous carbon and oxygen, heat is evolved or given off. From numerous experiments it has been found that every time carbon dioxide is formed in this way, the same amount of heat is evolved per mole of amorphous carbon.

(xv) $C + O_2 \rightarrow CO_2 + 408{,}970$ joules

Once started, the reaction of amorphous carbon with pure oxygen to form carbon dioxide will proceed on its own until the reactants are used up. The heat given off during the combustion process keeps the reaction going. Also, as heat is released and the temperature of the reactants increases, the reaction rate itself will quicken.

This is because the rate at which reactions proceed increases as the temperature of the reactants increases. Thus, once started, a fire often appears to feed upon itself and increase in intensity as long as the fire load and air supply holds out.

If it is desired to cause carbon dioxide to decompose back into carbon and oxygen, that is, to reverse the reaction shown in equation (xv), it is necessary to add at least 408,970 joules of energy to one mole of carbon dioxide. This "reverse combustion" reaction is endothermic, because it cannot proceed by itself unless at least a minimum specific amount of heat energy is added. The endothermic reaction equation for the decomposition of carbon dioxide is shown below.

(xvi) CO_2 + 408,970 joules → C + O_2

Equations (xv) and (xvi) demonstrate *Lavoisier's Law*, which was originally proposed in 1780. Lavoisier's Law states that the amount of heat evolved in the formation of a compound is equal to the amount of heat necessary to decompose the compound back into its initial constituents.

G. Joules

Since the unit of heat energy used in the chemical equations in this chapter is the joule, a word of explanation about joules should be given at this point: a joule is the current international metric unit of energy, defined as the work done when a force of one newton is applied through a distance of one meter. For those who may have forgotten, a newton is a unit of force: one newton is the force needed to accelerate one kilogram of mass at a rate of one meter per second.

Unfortunately, the joule as formally defined is not a unit which most people can easily get a feel for. The more traditional units for heat are the metric calorie and the British Thermal Unit, or BTU. A calorie is the amount of heat needed to raise the temperature of one gram of water at 15°C by one degree Celsius. Similarly, the BTU is the amount of heat needed to raise the temperature of one pound of water at 60°F by one degree Fahrenheit.

If the joule is defined in the same way as the calorie or BTU, then it takes 4.186 joules to raise the temperature of one gram of water at 15°C to 16°C, and 1054.8 joules to raise the temperature of one pound of water from 60°F to 61°F. For convenience, the conversion of joules to other units is given below.

Table 4. Conversion of Joules

1 joule =	10^7 ergs	energy
	0.2389 calories	
	0.000948 BTU	
	0.7376 foot-pounds	
1 joule/sec	1 watt	power

H. Heat of Combustion and Hess's Law

The term *heat of combustion* is very similar in meaning to the term *heat of formation*. However, the difference is that the heat of combustion is the heat evolved when a substance is oxidized or burned; the heat of combustion is always exothermic. The heat of formation may describe the heat either given off or absorbed in any reaction, not just combustion reactions.

One of the fundamental rules for working with heats of combustion and heats of formation was established experimentally in 1840 by G. H. Hess. Strangely enough, it is called *Hess's Law*, or the Law of Constant Heat Summation. It states that in a chemical reaction, the change in energy or heat content between reactants and products is constant. It does not matter whether the reaction takes place in one step or several steps.

The ramifications of Hess's Law are very important. It means that the heat of formation equations and the heat of combustion equations can be manipulated together algebraically to accurately calculate the heats of formation or combustion of substances whose values have not been previously determined experimentally.

To show how this works, consider again the combustion of methane in pure oxygen.

(i) $\qquad CH_4 + 2O_2 \rightarrow CO_2 + 2H_2O + 887{,}000$ joules,

where the heat of combustion of methane is 887,000 joules per mole methane.

Let us now consider the heat of formation equations associated with the products of the above combustion reaction.

When two moles of diatomic hydrogen are mixed with one mole of pure oxygen in the presence of a spark or small flame, the hydrogen will burn in the oxygen.[1] Water is produced and heat is evolved. Since the

---

[1] Be aware that this is an understatement. Usually the hydrogen will explode with a loud bang and scare you into having kittens. It can also be hazardous if you are using glass containers.

heat of formation of one mole of water is 285,970 joules, then the chemical equation for the formation of water is given below.

(xvii) $2H_2 + O_2 \rightarrow 2H_2O + 571,940$ joules,

where the water has cooled to a liquid form at 25°C.

As previously discussed, the reaction of one mole of amorphous carbon with one mole of oxygen produces carbon dioxide and heat in the following way:

(xv) $C + O_2 \rightarrow CO_2 + 408,970$ joules

Now, applying Hess's Law, if equation (xv) is subtracted from equation (i), then the following is obtained:

$$CH_4 + 2O_2 \quad \rightarrow \quad CO_2 + 2H_2O + 887,000 \text{ joules}$$
$$C + O_2 \quad \rightarrow \quad CO_2 + 408,970 \text{ joules}$$

(xviii) $CH_4 - C + O_2 \quad \rightarrow \quad 2H_2O + 478,030$ joules

If equation (xviii) is now subtracted from equation (xvii), the following is obtained:

$$2H_2 + O_2 \quad \rightarrow \quad 2H_2O + 571,940 \text{ joules}$$
$$CH_4 - C + O_2 \quad \rightarrow \quad 2H_2O + 478,030 \text{ joules}$$

$$2H_2 - CH_4 + C \rightarrow \quad 93,910 \text{ joules}$$

Rearranging terms, the above becomes:

(xix) $2H_2 + C \quad \rightarrow \quad CH_4 + 93,910$ joules.

The above equation, derived from equations (i), (xv) and (xvii), indicates that the heat of formation of methane made from one mole of amorphous carbon and 2 moles of diatomic hydrogen is 93,910 joules per mole of methane. A check with experimentally determined information in reference texts confirms that the heat of formation for methane from amorphous carbon is indeed 93,910 joules.

When Hess's Law is applied to simply determine the heat of formation for a particular substance, it can be simplified to the following: the heat of formation of a substance is equal to the heat of combustion of the substance less the sum of the heats of formation of the products of the combustion of that substance. Algebraically, this is expressed by the following:

(xx) $Q_f = Q_c - \Sigma(P_f)$

where Q_f = heat of formation of the substance,
        Q_c = heat of combustion of the same substance, and
        P_f = heat of formation of the individual products of combustion of the substance.

I. Combustion of Wood

By crude analysis, wood has the following elemental composition:

hydrogen 8%
carbon   38%
oxygen   54%.

It is also known that kiln-dried wood typically has a water content of 12% by weight.

In basic elemental content, the above crude analysis and moisture content for wood closely matches the empirical formula for cellulose mixed with 12% water by weight, which is $C_6H_{10}O_5 + (1.22)H_2O$. As an aside, the empirical formula for cellulose is also the same as that for plant starch and sugars, two other important components of trees and plants.

Based upon the above, a stoichiometric formula for the combustion of wood can then be modeled:

         solid   liquid   gas   gas
xi) $C_6H_{10}O_5 + 1.22H_2O + 6O_2 + 22.572N_2 \rightarrow$
                        $6CO_2 + 6.22H_2O + 22.572N_2 + Q_c$
                        gas   liquid   gas

where Q_c = the heat of combustion.

Since our chemical model for wood is the first two terms on the left side of equation (xxi), then the molecular weight of one mole of bone dry wood is 162. For wood with a moisture content of 12%, the molecular weight is 184. From equation (xxi), it is seen that about 4.48 kilograms or 3,479 liters of air are needed to combust each kilogram of 12% moisture wood.

Inspection of equation (xxi) also finds that if the water vapor contained in the products is allowed to condense, the gaseous volume of the products is the same as the gaseous volume of the reactants.

Fig. 2.1: Classic alligatoring of burned wood.

Various reference texts show that the heat of combustion for seasoned wood with a moisture content of 12% by weight is about 4.28 kcal/g. This figure includes recapturing the heat used in turning liquid water into steam and burning the wood as completely as possible. This converts to 17,916 j/g. If bone dry wood is considered to have a molecular weight of 162, then the heat of combustion is about 2,902,400 joules per g-mole of bone dry wood.

The heats of formation for the products of wood combustion are as follows:

$$H_2 + (\tfrac{1}{2})O_2 \rightarrow H_2O + 285,970 \text{ j/g-mole (liquid)},$$
$$C + O_2 \rightarrow CO_2 + 393,710 \text{ j/g-mole (from graphite)}.$$

From the above, an energy balance can be done to determine the heat of formation of the wood itself.

(xxi) $C_6H_{10}O_5 + 1.22H_2O + 6O_2 + 22.572N_2 \rightarrow$
$$6CO_2 + 6.22H_2O + 22.572N_2 + Q_c$$

where
$$6.22H_2O - 1.22H_2O = 5(285,970 \text{ j})$$
$$6CO_2 = 6(393,710 \text{ j})$$
$$22.572N_2 - 22.572N_2 = 0$$
$$6O_2 = 0$$
$$Q_c = 2,902,400 \text{ j/g-mole cellulose, and}$$
$$C_6H_{10}O_5 = Q_f.$$

In equation (xxi), the $(1.22)H_2O$ on the left side cancels out the same amount of water on the right side. The diatomic nitrogen, which is assumed to be inert, also balances itself out of the equation. However, the heats of formation for diatomic hydrogen, oxygen, and nitrogen are zero anyway, because they are their own constituent parts at 1 atmosphere and 25°C. In other words, at 1 atmosphere and 25°C, diatomic oxygen, hydrogen and nitrogen are at their lowest naturally occurring chemical energy states.

Applying Hess's Law in the form of equation (xx) to the energy figures listed under equation (xxi) above and substituting the appropriate heats of formation and combustion, the following is obtained for the heat of formation of wood:

(xxii) $Q_f = 2,902,400j - [6(393,710j) + 5(285,970j)]$

$Q_f = -889,700j/g\text{-mole} = -212,600\ cal/g\text{-mole} = -1,312\ cal/g = -5,492\ j/g$

on a bone-dry basis for the wood.

The results of equation (xxii) indicate that the formation of wood is *endothermic*; energy has to be supplied to form wood out of the basic building blocks of carbon, hydrogen, and oxygen. When one gram of wood is formed, about 5,492 joules of heat are supplied in the process. In other words, wood does not form naturally by itself just because the raw materials are at hand.

Of course, this is true for every biologically formed material I can think of. If it were otherwise, apples, pears and chocolate sundaes would spontaneously sprout up all over the surface of the earth. As noted previously, the distinction between reactions that proceed naturally due to their exothermic nature, and reactions that can only proceed when energy is supplied due to their endothermic nature, is very important in analyzing fire scenes.

Since the polymer unit formula for cellulose is also the same polymer unit formula for starch, the heat of combustion for starch can form a sort of theoretical check of our cellulose model of wood.

As noted in chemical reference texts, the heat of combustion of starch is 4,179 kcal/kg. Converting units and again assuming a bone-dry molecular weight of 162, this gives a heat of combustion for starch of about 2,834,000 j/g-mole. Since the heat of combustion for bone dry wood used in our example was 2,902,400 j/g-mole, then the heat of combustion of plant starch varies only 2.4% from the heat of combustion of wood used in our simple model. It appears then that using cellulose or plant starch as a model for wood combustion equations is very reasonable.

The preceding wood combustion analysis is very important in understanding common fires. It applies to most types of wood products such as plywood, roof shakes, construction lumber, and wooden furniture. It also applies to a host of wood-derived products such as paper, cardboard, and even some types of plastic.

Further, since the primary constituents of wood combustion are cellulose, plant starch, and plant sugars, which have the same or very similar elemental composition, the wood combustion analysis also applies equally well to cotton textiles, flax derived textiles, sisal derived textiles, grains, feeds, certain plastics, and other similar products derived from plant fiber and starch, like disposable diapers.

Additionally, since plant starch is identical in its empirical formula to animal starch, glycogen, it also applies to products and items that contain significant amounts of glycogen and glycogen-like components.

While it has little direct bearing upon the diagnosis of fires, it is interesting to note the similarities between plant chemistry and animal chemistry. The interested reader may wish to check out the similarities of the structure of heme (as in hemoglobin) and chlorophyll.

J. Changing Phase

When water is heated at atmospheric pressure from say 15°C until it forms steam, for every 4.186 joules of heat added to one gram of water, the water temperature will rise about 1°C. Because the temperature of the water rises in proportion to the heat added, this is sometimes referred to as the *sensible heat region* of the water.

This is true until the boiling point, 100°C, is reached. From then on, the addition of more heat does not cause the temperature to rise further; instead, the temperature stays the same until all the water has vaporized, but the additional heat is consumed by the process of turning liquid water into steam.

Because the addition of heat at this point does not cause a corresponding increase in temperature, this is sometimes referred to as the *latent heat region* of water. It is called latent because the heat put into the water is "hidden," that is, it does not manifest itself by a temperature increase.

The amount of heat needed to accomplish the change of phase from liquid to vapor is called the *latent heat of vaporization,* or more simply the heat of vaporization. The heat of vaporization of water at the boiling point and one atmosphere pressure is 2,259 joules per gram, or about 40,654 joules per g-mole.

When all the liquid water has been turned into steam, then the temperature of the steam will again increase in proportion to the added heat. This is the sensible heat region of the water vapor.

A similar effect occurs when water solidifies or freezes. As water is cooled from 15°C, for every degree Celsius of temperature drop about 4.186 joules of heat must be extracted from each gram of water. This is true until 0°C is reached; at that temperature, the extraction of more heat from the water does not cause the temperature to drop any more; instead, the temperature stays the same, and continues the same until all the water is frozen. When all the water is frozen, then the extraction of more heat will cause the temperature of the ice to again drop in proportion to the extracted heat.

Figure 2.2 below is an idealized graph for a single-component substance showing these phase change effects. The vertical axis is temperature, and the horizontal axis is heat. Note that in the sensible regions, the temperature increases linearly as heat is added or vice versa. In the latent heat regions, the temperature stays flat as heat is added, and does so until the phase change is complete.

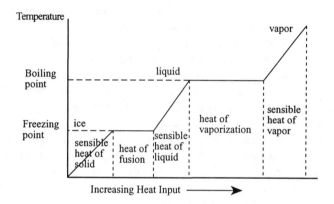

Figure 2.2. Phase change diagram for single substance

Phase changes in a substance occur not only between obviously different forms of matter, such as solid to liquid, or liquid to gas, but can also occur between different types of solids of the same substance. What occurs in such solid solution phase changes is that the molecular structure of the solid changes from one crystalline form to another.

Ice, for example, has nine separate molecular arrangements or phases in the solid state; most of them are indistinguishable from one another with the unaided eye. However, it is typical for the different solid phases of a substance to have different ratios of heat input to temperature rise, and also to have measurably different physical properties.

Pure iron undergoes three phase changes when its temperature is raised above room temperature. At room temperature and up to about 910°C, iron is in the phase called *alpha-iron*. Its molecules are arranged in what is called a body-centered cubic system. Briefly, a body-centered cubic crystal resembles a box with a molecule at each corner of the box plus a molecule in the center of the box.

From 910°C to 1,391°C, iron is in the *gamma-iron* phase, which is a face-centered cubic crystalline arrangement. Face-centered cubic is a box with a molecule at each corner, and also a molecule centered in each face of the box. From 1,391°C to 1,539°C, iron is in the *delta-iron* phase, where it reverts to a body-centered cubic crystalline arrangement. Above 1,539°C, pure iron melts, which is the beginning of the *liquid phase.*

As before, when a phase change occurs in a solid substance, it is accompanied by a region of latent heat absorption, where an input of heat does not cause a corresponding change in the temperature of the substance. When the change in phase is from one solid crystalline structure to another, the latent heat needed to do accomplish the change is called the *latent heat of transition,* or more simply, the heat of transition.

Besides ice and pure iron, which are single-component substances, phase changes in solids also occur in metals and alloys which may be composed of several components. The presence of more than one component in a substance significantly complicates the formation of phases. Generally, the number of possible phases in a solid solution increases significantly as the number of components in the substance is increased.

When high-strength alloy steels and heat-treated steels are heated to elevated temperatures such as might occur during a fire, they may undergo molecular realignment or phase changes if the temperatures exceed certain temperatures. The realignment of their crystalline structure often causes corresponding changes in strength, durability, and other mechanical properties.

For example, a high-strength, heat-treated steel may have a strength of 185,000 pounds per square inch at room temperature, and up to about 600°F its strength may not significantly drop. In fact, for various arcane reasons, the strength may actually increase slightly. However, at 800°F or above, while the steel does not melt, it undergoes "tempering" and loses significant strength and stiffness. Tempering is a type of phase change where the internal crystalline structure is realigned.

Tempering is not detectable by simple visual inspection, but can be detected in the field by the use of metal hardness testers, and in the laboratory by a number of techniques, including examination of specially prepared samples under a microscope. Hardness testers actually check the hardness of the metal by poking at it with a tiny diamond-tipped stylus. The depth of penetration per applied force of the stylus provides an indication of the hardness and strength of the steel.

High-strength alloy steel that has been fully tempered due to exposure to an intense fire is soft and relatively weak as compared to its original, fully heat-treated condition. Further, removing the temperature source does not reverse the tempering. Once tempered, the metal stays tempered; the process is not readily reversible.

Thus, steel that will hold up a floor at 500°F during a fire for hours on end, may not be able to hold up the same floor at 800°F for even an hour or less. This is why building fire codes often require structurally important steel support columns and beams to be wrapped in gypsum board or other fire-impeding materials; this slows down the fire in getting to the supports and keeps them cool for a longer time and gives people more time to get out of a burning building before it collapses.

Sometimes the amount of tempering that has occurred to a high-strength alloy steel makes it possible to deduce the temperature which occurred in that area. This is because the amount of tempering is a function of both temperature and time.

Figure 2.3 shows the strength versus tempering temperature of a heat treatable, AISI 410 stainless steel. Note the sharp decline in both the breaking strength and the yielding strength beginning at about 800°F.

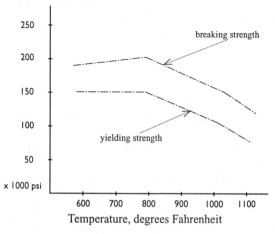

Figure 2.3 Strength versus temperature of heat treated 410 stainless steel

K. Heat Capacity, Enthalpy, and Internal Energy

Besides the heat associated with reactions and combustion processes, a material also contains a certain amount of heat by virtue of its mass and its temperature. For example, a brick at room temperature has obviously less heat in it than a brick that has been baked in an oven at 400°F for an hour or two. Also, anyone who has boiled water knows from experience that it takes more heat to boil two gallons of water in a large pot than to boil a cup of water in a saucepan.

The amount of heat a substance can hold by virtue of its mass and temperature is called its *heat capacity.* In general, if we know how much mass of a substance there is, and at what temperature it is, then the amount of heat it contains can be calculated from a simple algebraic expression or read from a table. Typically, the algebraic expression to calculate the amount of heat the substance contains is applied in the sensible heat regions of the substance, where the addition or extraction of heat causes a regular, proportional change in the temperature of the substance.

The measurement of the exact amount of heat a substance contains can be somewhat arbitrary or relative. In our example using the bricks, if a person tries to hold the baked brick without protective heat pads it is obvious the baked brick contains more heat than the one at room temperature. The difference is simply the heat added to the brick by the oven to make it hotter than the one at room temperature.

If a similar brick had been placed in a refrigerator, it would also be obvious that the one which had been in the refrigerator has less heat energy than either the one at room temperature, or the one which had been baked in the oven. In fact, it might be suggested that the brick in the refrigerator has negative heat, since it will begin to absorb heat from the environment as it warms up to room temperature.

For these reasons, heat energy is usually measured from some convenient reference temperature, usually $0°C$, $15°C$ or $25°C$. In using such a reference temperature, what is actually being measured is the difference in heat content of the substance at its current temperature as compared to itself were it at the reference temperature.

However, if a person wished, the heat contained in a substance at any temperature could be measured against the amount it would contain at absolute zero, $-273.15°C$ or $0°K$.

By definition, the amount of energy a substance contains at absolute zero is either zero, or its least theoretical amount. Thus, using absolute zero as the reference temperature would tell a person the absolute amount of heat energy a substance contains rather than a relative amount. People who work in cryogenics, the study of really cold stuff, regularly use absolute zero as their reference point for heat capacity measurements.

Since water and air are common materials, the heat capacity of a substance is often compared to water or air at standard conditions. The ratio of the heat capacity of a substance to water or air is called its *specific heat*. In general, the specific heats of solids and liquids are measured against water. The specific heats of gases are also usually measured against water, but occasionally they are measured against air at standard conditions of pressure and temperature. When using specific heat values for gases from a reference text table, be sure to check whether the gases are being compared to water or air.

For example the heat capacity of water as a liquid at room temperature is generally 4.186 joules per $°C$ per gram of water, or

$$C_{water} = (4.186j)/(°Cg).$$

The heat capacity of copper at room temperature is:

$C_{copper} = (0.386j)/(°Cg)$.

Thus, the specific heat of copper with respect to water is:

Sp. ht. Cu = 0.386/4.186 = 0.0921

The advantage of listing specific heats instead of heat capacities is that the number is a dimensionless ratio, valid for any set of consistent units. For example, since the specific heat of copper from the above example is 0.0921, and it is known that water in the English system of units has a heat capacity of 1 BTU per pound of water per degree Fahrenheit, then the heat capacity of copper in English units is:

C_{copper} = (Sp. ht. Cu)(C_{water}) = (0.0921)(1 BTU/lb°F) = 0.0921 BTU/lb°F

However, to slightly complicate matters, there are two kinds of heat capacity: the first is the heat capacity of a substance measured at constant volume conditions; this is usually symbolized by C_v. The second is the heat capacity of a substance measured at constant pressure conditions, usually atmospheric pressure; this is symbolized by C_p.

The reason for these two types of heat capacity measurements will be apparent to the reader if the situation with respect to gases is considered. When energy is added to a gas at constant pressure, not only will the mass of the gas heat up due to temperature increase, but the gas will also expand and do work (see Ideal Gas Law, in Section A). To maintain a constant pressure as the temperature of the gas increases, the volume must get larger. Recall that the definition of work is the application of force through a distance. In this case, the pressure against the sides of the container supplies the force, and the expansion of the container to maintain constant pressure supplies the distance.

When gas is heated at constant volume, the pressure increases inside the volume, but no work is done. This is because without an increase in container size or volume, the force has not been applied through a distance. The distance term is zero. Thus, since there is no change in volume, there is no "P–V" work done when heat is added at constant volume.

For this reason, the values for C_p are larger than the values for C_v. It takes more heat to raise the temperature of a gas at constant pressure conditions than constant volume conditions, because in addition to heating up the mass of the gas, work must be done in expanding its volume.

Usually, when only the energy associated with mass is being considered, this parameter is called the *internal energy*. The internal energy of an amount of material depends only on its temperature. When the energy of the mass, and the energy associated with work done in causing expansion or contraction of the material are considered, this parameter is called *enthalpy.* The enthalpy of a material is the sum of its internal energy and the work done by expansion of the material at constant pressure.

The change in heat capacity of a substance at constant pressure from a reference temperature is given by the relation:

(xxiii) $\delta H = (m)(C_p)(T - T_o)$

where H   =   the heat contained in the substance at constant pressure
                which includes a work term (i.e., the enthalpy),
      m   =   mass of the substance,
      C_p =   heat capacity coefficient at constant pressure,
      T   =   temperature, and
      T^o =   reference temperature.

The change in heat capacity of a substance at constant volume from a reference temperature is then given by the relation:

(xxiv) $\delta U = (m)(C_v)(T - T_o)$

where U = the heat contained in the substance at constant volume (i.e., the internal energy).

Because the C_p term includes both the internal energy of the substance and the work done by the substance in expanding at a constant pressure, the heat capacity at constant pressure is related to the heat capacity at constant volume by the following:

(xxv) $\delta H = \delta U + \delta(PV).$

Substituting the relations in (xxiii) and (xxiv) into (xxv) gives the following:

(xxvi) $(m)(C_p)(T - T_o) = (m)(C_v)(T - T_o) + P(V - V_o)$

$(C_p)(T - T_o) = (C_v)(T - T_o) + (P)(V - V_o) / m$

$C_p = C_v + (P)(V - V_o) / (m)(T - T_o)$

If the Ideal Gas Law, equation (v), is appropriately substituted into the last term on the right in equation (xxii), and the equation is put on a gram-mole basis instead of a gram mass basis, then the following relation is noted:

(xxvii) $C_p = C_v + R$

where R =   the Ideal Gas Constant, 8.314 joules/(g-mole)(°K), and C_p
            and C_v are both on a gram-mole basis in units of joules/
            (g-mole)(°K).

The above relation is very useful, since it means that if either C_p or
C_v are known, the other can be easily derived. Of course, equation (xxiii)
can also be put on a gram mass basis. However, in that case, the gas
constant R would have to adjusted for the atomic weight of the particular
gas.

For example, the C_p value for diatomic oxygen on a gram mass basis
is 0.913 joules/(g)(°K). A gram-mole of diatomic oxygen is 32 grams. The
gas constant or R for oxygen on a gram mass basis instead of a gram-mole basis is then about 0.260 joules/(g)(°K). Thus, the calculated value for
C_v as derived from the value for C_p using the Ideal Gas Constant R on a
gram mass basis is about 0.653 joules/(g)(°K). This calculated value is
within three-place accuracy of experimentally determined values of C_v for
diatomic oxygen.

More formally, the heat capacity relations can be expressed by the
following differentials:

(xxviii) $C_v = [\delta U / \delta T]v$ and

(xxix) $C_p = [\delta H / \delta T]_p$ or $C_p = [\delta U / \delta T]_v + [\delta(PV) / \delta T]_p$.

where $\delta H = \delta U + \delta(PV)$, and $[\delta U / \delta T]_p = [\delta U / \delta T]_v$ because U is not a
function of either V or P.

Most fires and explosions take place in unconfined spaces where the
pressure is constant at about one atmosphere or 1013.3 millibars. Theoretically, explosions in fully confined areas will initially proceed at
constant-volume conditions until the walls or whatever blow out. After
that, the reaction will proceed at constant pressure conditions.

Since in most buildings the first materials to blow out are the
windows which break when pressure difference exceeds about 0.5 to 1.0
psig, or 3.45 to 6.89 kilopascals, the entire event is considered to have
occurred at constant pressure. However, if the explosion occurs in a
closed vault or similar fully confined space where the building materials
significantly hold up against the explosion and contain it for a time, the
constant volume portion of the reaction may have to be considered in a
step-wise fashion.

Because fires occur at slower rates than explosions, there is usually
enough time for air to infiltrate through the building to maintain atmospheric pressure. Significant constant volume conditions for a fire are
infrequent. Not only would the space have to be confined, but it would

also have to be airtight. Thus, fires are usually considered to be constant-pressure processes even when they occur in seemingly confined spaces.

With respect to "P–V" work, solids and liquids do not appreciably expand or contract when their temperatures rise or fall, assuming there is no phase change. The C_p and C_v values for solids and liquids are essentially the same usually to a precision of three significant figures. Thus, for solids and liquids often only a single value for heat capacity is given in reference tables. When this is done, it is assumed that the value given is for C_p. This is because, unless otherwise stated, most experimentally determined values for heat capacity in the laboratory are done under constant pressure conditions.

Table 5 lists some values for C_p for some common gases involved in combustion reactions.

Table 5. "C_p" Values for Some Common Gases at Room Temperature

gas	"C_p"
CO_2	0.833 j/g°K
H_2	14.27
CO	1.037
N_2	1.042
O_2	0.917
Air	1.005
Steam @ 100–200°C	1.980
CH_4	2.214
C_3H_8	1.667

An interesting approximation concerning heat capacity was discovered in 1819 by Messrs. Dulong and Petit. For elements with atomic weights of more than 35 which are solid at room temperature, the heat capacity can be reasonably estimated from the following relationship:

(xxx)   (26j) / (°K)(g-mole) = (C_p)(AW).

In essence, equation (xxx) is simply the conversion of heat capacity from a per-gram basis, to a per gram-mole basis. Dulong and Petit discovered that for solid elements heavier than an atomic weight of 35, the heat capacity on a per gram-mole basis is approximately constant.

As was mentioned in Section A of this chapter, when a combustion reaction proceeds such that as it releases energy, the energy is able to escape to the environment, the reaction is called *isothermic*. However, when the energy is wholly contained in the system, it is called *adiabatic*. In an adiabatic reaction, it is assumed that no energy, or at least no significant amount of energy, escapes to the environment.

The *First Law of Thermodynamics*, the conservation of energy law, is commonly expressed by the following equation:

(xxxi) $\qquad \delta U = \delta Q - \delta W$

where U = the internal energy,
Q = the heat supplied or produced, and
W = work done by the system on the environment surrounding the system.

Now by definition, an adiabatic reaction has no exchange of heat with the environment. In equation (xxxi), this means that dQ is zero. Thus, an adiabatic reaction is simply:

(xxxii) $\qquad \delta U + \delta W = 0$

Appropriate substitution into equation (xxxii) of equations relating to internal energy, as previously noted in this section, leads to the following expression:

(xxxiii) $\qquad nC_v(\delta T) + P(\delta V) = 0$

where C_v and C_p are on a gram-mole basis instead of a mass basis.

If the Ideal Gas Law is differentiated, the following is obtained:

(xxxiv) $\qquad PdV + VdP = nR(dT)$

Rearranging, this becomes:

(xxxv) $\qquad P(dV / R) + V(dP / R) = n(dT).$

If it is assumed that in equation (xxxiii) the limit of δV and δT is dV and dT as both δT and δV approach zero, then equation (xxxv) can be substituted into equation (xxxiii) to eliminate n(dT). This produces the following expression:

(xxxvi) $C_v[P(dV) + V(dP)] + R[P(dV)] = 0$

By equation (xxvii) it is known that:

$$R = C_p - C_v$$

Substituting this into equation (xxxvi) leads to the following:

(xxxvii) $C_v[P(dV) + V(dP)] + [C_p - C_v][P(dV)] = 0$

$$V(dP) + [C_p / C_v][P(dV)] = 0$$

Letting $k = [C_p / C_v]$, equation (xxxvii) becomes:

(xxxviii) $V(dP) + k[P(dV)] = 0.$

The variables in equation (xxxviii) can be separated and integrated to produce the following:

(xxxix) $PV_k = C$ where C = a constant.

The above equation then is used to describe the pressure-volume relationship in an adiabatic reaction where no heat escapes the system. This equation can be used to determine the pressure-volume relationships from one set of conditions to another by the following:

(xl) $P_1V_1{}^k = P_2V_2{}^k = C.$

Manipulation of equation (xli) gives:

(xli) $P_2V_2 / P_1V_1 = (V_1 / V_2)^{k-1} = [P_2 / P_1]^{(k-1)/k}$

Since PV is proportional to temperature T, then

(xlii) $T_2 / T_1 = (V_1 / V_2)^{k-1}$ and

(xliii) $T_2 / T_1 = [P_2 / P_1]^{(k-1)/k}$

For air, the k value is 1.403. For other gases, the k values can be obtained from Table 5 and the application of equation (xxvii).

In recalling the methane and oxygen combustion reaction discussed in Section A, the reaction occurred in a closed vessel. If either the vessel were well insulated so that no heat could escape, or the reaction were to occur explosively so that there is no time for heat to escape the system, then equation (xliii) could be used to determine the internal pressure of the vessel if the temperature of the gases just after combustion occurred were known.

Conversely, if the vessel were equipped with a pressure gauge to read the maximum pressure produced during the explosion of methane and oxygen, the maximum pressure reading could be substituted into equation (xliii) to calculate the corresponding maximum temperature that occurred during the reaction. This can be a handy thing to do since pressure gauges are often more responsive to rapid changes than tempe-rature probes.

Equation (xl) and the others that follow from it explain why the pressure rise in an explosion is so much greater than if the same amount of heat energy were released in a slow fire. In an explosion, the combus-tion process is so rapid that the reaction is adiabatic. Because of this, the relationship between temperature and pressure is nonlinear. However, in a slow fire, the reaction is slow enough to allow full transfer of heat to the environment. The reaction is isothermal and the relationship of tempera-ture and pressure is linear according to the Ideal Gas Law.

Equation (xliii) explains why the bottom of a bicycle pump gets unusually hot when the pump is used rapidly. When the pump is used rapidly, the process is adiabatic. In that case, a reduction in internal vol-ume causes an exponential rise in temperature according to equation (xliii). On the other hand, if the pump is used slowly, the process is isothermal, the Ideal Gas Law equation applies, and the temperature rise is linear in proportion to the change in internal volume of the pump.

This principle is the basis for the Diesel engine. Rapid compression of fuel-laden air in the engine cylinder causes the temperature of the air to increase nonlinearly to high levels. If the temperature rise is sufficient, it causes the atomized fuel in the air to auto-ignite and explode.

In the 19th century, this principle was used to make walking sticks that could light cigarettes without matches. The walking stick was equip-ped with a bicycle pump-like piston and plunger. The cigarette would be inserted into the walking stick, the plunger would be pulled out, and then the walking stick would be rapidly jammed down into the pavement to quickly depress the plunger. The resulting adiabatic reduction in volume caused an exponential temperature rise which lighted the cigarette. I have also heard reports that certain Indonesian aboriginal peoples used a similar technique to start fires using compression cylinder tubes made of bamboo.

Equation (xxxi), the equation for the conservation of energy, can be also be applied to show why the Ideal Gas Law applies to the case of isothermal processes. In an isothermal process, by definition the internal energy stays the same. Thus, equation (xxxi) becomes:

$$\text{(xliv)} \qquad 0 = \delta Q - \delta W \quad \text{or} \quad \delta Q + \delta W = 0.$$

Since $\delta W = P(\delta V)$ and since $PV = nRT$, then

$$\text{(xlv)} \qquad \delta W = P(\delta V) = (nRT / V)(\delta V) = P[-nRT\,(\delta P)/\,(P^2)].$$

Integration of the above equation gives the following:

$$\text{(xlvi)} \qquad W = nRT\,[\ln\,(V_2\,/\,V_1)] = nRT\,[\ln\,(P_1\,/\,P_2)] = -Q.$$

Thus,

(xlvii) $V_2 / V_1 = P_1 / P_2$ or $P_1V_1 = P_2V_2$

which is a version of the Ideal Gas Law.

L. More About the Heat of Combustion

In most reference texts, the heat of combustion of a fuel is given as either a *higher heating value, HHV,* or a *lower heating value, LHV.* The HHV assumes that the products of combustion have cooled back down to the initial temperature and that the water produced in combustion has condensed to a liquid. Thus, the HHV is a measure of the total amount of heat given off by the combustion reaction when the products of combustion are cooled down to the initial temperature of the reactants. HHV is the maximum amount of heat that can be obtained from the particular fuel by normal combustion.

The LHV assumes that the water in the combustion products is gaseous and disperses or floats away after combustion occurs. In other words, the LHV assumes that the latent heat of vaporization of the water in the reaction products is irretrievable.

When fuel is burned in a combustion chamber and the flue gases are simply vented to the outside, this is exactly what occurs. In that case, the LHV is the maximum amount of heat that will be obtained from the fuel by combustion. However, in newer natural gas home furnaces the latent heat of vaporization of the water vapor is captured and reused. In this case, the HHV is the maximum amount of energy that can be obtained from the fuel by combustion.

In general, the HHV and the LHV are related to each other in the following way:

(xlviii) $LHV = HHV - m(h_{l,s})$

where m = mass of water produced by the reaction, and
        $h_{l,s}$ = latent and sensible heat of the water per unit mass as mea-
                 sured from room temperature to the temperature at which
                 it floated away as a vapor.

The heats of combustion for some common fuels are listed in Table 6.

Table 6. Heats of Combustion for Some Common Fuels

fuel	HHV (j/g)	HHV (j/g-mole)	LHV (j/g)	LHV (j/g-mole)
C	32,700	392,400	no water produced	
CO	10,085	282,400	no water produced	
H_2	141,700	283,400	119,770	239,540
CH_4	55,390	886,240	49,870	797,920
C_3H_{10}	50,270	2,312,000	46,250	2,128,000
octane	48,133	5,487,000	44,670	5,092,000
wood	17,907	2,901,000	16,220	2,627,000

M. Activation Energy

Most people know from direct experience that wood does not readily burst into flames when simply exposed to air. Likewise, natural gas does not catch fire just because it is mixed with some air. In both cases, some type of initial energy input is needed to get the reaction going. Once initiated, the reaction then produces enough excess energy to become self-sustaining. The energy necessary to "get things going" is called the *activation energy.*

The activation energy for a particular combustion reaction can be supplied in several forms. Simple heating is one way. Other ways include electrical spark, friction sparks, radiation, pyrophoric and hypergolic chemical reactions, and adiabatic compression. Thus, there are several ways in which activation energy can be quantified.

In the case of simple heating, the activation energy is usually defined by the *ignition temperature;* this is the temperature at which the fuel material will burst into flames. Since the whole material is being heated up, or at least the whole material in a certain area of the fuel, this activation energy in measured in temperature units instead of strictly energy units. However, it is understood that this is the amount of activation energy necessary to raise the temperature of the fuel to a certain temperature.

For example, the ignition temperature of commercial grade of wood is about 500°F or 260°C, and the ignition temperature of natural gas or methane is 1,004°F or 540°C. In both cases, an amount of heat is added to the fuel to increase its temperature, according to its particular heat capacity, until its ignition temperature is reached.

The term *auto-ignition* or *minimum autoignition temperature* is a more specific laboratory measurement of the general ignition temperature. A small sample of the fuel is placed in a heated vessel, and all the combustion parameters are optimized to determine the lowest possible temperature at which combustion can be initiated without a flame or spark being present. Auto-ignition temperature measurements include the effects of the volume and internal surface area of the test chamber. Usually the minimum auto-ignition temperature will be somewhat less than the ignition temperature.

The *minimum ignition energy* of a fuel material, sometimes referred to as the MIE, is the amount of electrical energy, supplied as a spark, which causes combustible vapors to ignite. Usually the spark is supplied to the fuel from a capacitor across an air gap. The optimum air gap distance which can cause ignition is referred to as the *minimum ignition quenching distance.*

In general, the minimum ignition energy of a fuel varies with pressure, ambient temperature and the air-to-fuel mixture ratio. Depending on these factors, the amount of spark energy necessary to initiate combustion can be as low as tenths of a millijoule, or as large as infinity when either the maximum or minimum air-to-fuel ratio limits of flammability are approached.

Since the topic has already been inferred, this is a good time to discuss the definition of *flash point* of a substance. This is the temperature at which flammable vapors will form in sufficient quantity to ignite and at least temporarily burn at the surface of the substance, usually a liquid. At temperatures below the flash point some vapors may form, but not enough to ignite, even briefly. When flammable liquids are shipped by truck or railroad car, the flash point listed for the liquid was likely measured using the *Tagliabue Open Cup test*, as specified in ASTM D1310-63. This is usually abbreviated TOC after the given flash point temperature.

In this test, some of the liquid is placed in a certain sized metal cup, and the liquid is gently heated to an even temperature. At a particular temperature, a spark is generated near the surface of the liquid to see if there is any "poof" of the vapors. If there is not, the temperature is raised again slightly and the spark is tried again until there is a "poof" which indicates the presence of flammable vapors.

There are other ways to measure flash point: these include the Abel Closed Cup, the Tag Closed Cup, and the Cleveland Open Cup (which sounds like a tennis tournament). In closed cup tests, the liquid is held in a closed container. As a general rule, open cup tests more closely approximate the kind of conditions encountered in fire diagnosis work.

The National Fire Protection Association defines a flammable liquid as having a closed-cup flash point of less than 100°F and a vapor pressure of not over 40 psia at 100°F. For shipping purposes, the definition of a flammable liquid is 80°F (or less) by the open cup method and 73°F by the closed cup method.

A little-appreciated source of activation energy for fires and explosions is static electricity, or the generation of electric charge by triboelectrification. This is the buildup of static electricity caused by friction between two electrically dissimilar materials, which can be solid, liquid or gaseous. In general, the material that is the poorest conductor is the one which will accumulate the static electric charge.

The triboelectric effect occurs often when liquids are pumped from one container to another, when liquids stored in one container are poured into another (especially when one container is a plastic bucket), when concentrations of solid particulants are pneumatically transferred, or when plastic materials are involved in material processes. The latter is because certain plastics have the ability to store electric charge like a capacitor due to their excellent dielectric properties.

It is even possible for people to accumulate enough static charge on their bodies to supply the activation energy to initiate a gas explosion. A person with a capacitance of about 200 to 400 picofarads can accumulate a static charge voltage of as much as 10,000 volts, and this is enough to supply the MIE necessary to ignite natural gas or propane which has collected to explosive levels in a room.

N. Adiabatic Flame Temperature

Using the information already presented, it is possible to estimate the temperature a particular combustion reaction will reach. In order to do this it is first necessary to specify the chemical equation, which includes all the reactants and products and their relative ratios to one another, and the conditions of combustion such as initial temperature, and either constant pressure or constant volume conditions.

When it is assumed that all the combustion energy given off during combustion is retained in the products, the resulting temperature is called the *adiabatic flame temperature.* This temperature is calculated by taking all the energy contained in the reactants before combustion, adding it to all the combustion energy released, and then distributing the total amount of energy among the products so that they reach the same equilibrium temperature.

Often, the adiabatic flame temperature is used to refer to the maximum temperature that a particular combustion reaction will reach. This usually occurs when the reaction is at or near stoichiometric conditions.

For example, consider again the simple combustion of methane and pure oxygen at stoichiometric conditions.

(xlix) $CH_4 + 2O_2 \rightarrow CO_2 + 2H_2O + 797,920$ joules.
　　　16 g　64 g　　44 g　　36 g

In this situation, the lower heating value (LHV) for methane has been used, as it is assumed that the water in the products is already in vapor form. This will save the bother of having to calculate the heat of vaporization of the water later.

If the combustion process has taken place at constant pressure conditions, then the energy of the reactants prior to combustion is simply their enthalpy at room temperature. Assuming a room temperature of 300°K and a reference temperature of 273°K, then the energy input to this reaction is as follows:

(l)	*Reactant*	C_p	*amount*	$mC_p(T{-}T_r)$ *enthalpy energy*
	CH_4	2.21j/g°K	16 g	954.7 joules
	$2O_2$	0.917j/g°K	64 g	1,584.6 joules
		total energy of reactants		2,539 joules

Now, after combustion has occurred, there is a "pool" of energy available to heat up the products. This "pool" consists of the total initial energy of the reactants as estimated in tableau (li) above, and the heat of combustion which has been released during the reaction. Thus, the total energy available to be distributed among the reactants is

(li) E_{total} = energy of reactants + combustion energy

E_{total} = 2,539 joules + 797,920 joules = 800,459 joules

The total energy noted above is now distributed among the products. An algebraic expression for the energy of the products is constructed with the upper temperature left as the unknown. The equation is then set equal to the total energy as noted in equation (liii) below.

(lii) E_{total} = $mC_p(T - T_r)$ + $mC_p(T - 373°K)$
               carbon dioxide   water vapor

800,459 joules =
(44g)(1.427j/g°K)(T − 273°K) + (36 g)(3.107j/g°K)(T − 373°K)

In the above equation, since the lower heating value for the heat of combustion was used, the reference point for the water vapor was the boiling point at atmospheric conditions, or 373°K. Solving equation (liii) for T, the adiabatic flame temperature, gives

(liii)   T = 4,920°K = 4,647°C

The careful reader will note that the C_p values used for carbon dioxide, water vapor, and diatomic nitrogen gas do not match those given in Table 5 of this chapter. Values consistent with a temperature of 3,000°K were used in equation (liii) above.

In equation (liii), an initial guess was made as to the temperature to use for the C_p values for the various products of combustion. The guess was 3,000°K, and the calculated value turned out to be 4,920°K. Since the initial guess is somewhat different from the calculated temperature, a new guess should be made and the equations should be solved again until the two temperatures, the "guessed" one and the calculated one, sufficiently converge. Thus, a second solution is done using a "guessed" temperature of 4,200°K, as follows:

(liv) E_{total} = $mC_p(T - T_r)$ + $mC_p(T - 373°K)$
                    carbon dioxide   water vapor

800,459 joules =
          $(44g)(1.46j/g°K)(T - 273°)+(36g)(3.16j/g°K)(T - 373°K)$

Solving equation (liv) gives:

(lv)   T = 4,833°K or 4,560°C

This is a really high temperature as far as combustion is concerned. However, as noted before, when a fuel is burned in pure oxygen, the fire is much hotter than when air is used. This is, of course, why pure oxygen is often used in special alloy foundries, welding processes, and similar applications involving materials with very high melting temperatures.

A point to note in this case with respect to the solution of the adiabatic flame temperature equation is that this combustion temperature is not actually achieved in practice, because of dissociation effects which start to become significant at about 2,500°C. At temperatures such as these and higher, some of the carbon dioxide and nitrogen will break apart and form other compounds, and this process absorbs some of the available energy and reduces the adiabatic flame temperature. Thus, the above solution in equation (lv) is often called the *adiabatic frozen flame temperature* to signify that it has been assumed that no dissociation effects among the products have been taken into account.

Consider now the same type of combustion reaction using air instead of pure oxygen. The stoichiometric combustion reaction for methane in air is as follows:

(lvi)CH_4 + $2 O_2$ + $7.524 N_2$ → CO_2 + $2 H_2O$ + $7.524 N_2$ + 797,920 joules.
      16 g   64 g   210.7 g   44 g   36 g   210.7 g

This time the energy contained in the reactants must include the diatomic nitrogen. The energy of the reactants is calculated as shown below:

(lvii)

Reactant	C_p	amount	$mC_p(T–T_r)$ enthalphy energy
CH_4	2.21 j/g°K	16 g	954.7 joules
$2O_2$	0.917 j/g°K	64 g	1,584.6 joules
7.524 N_2	1.042 j/g°K	210.7 g	5,927.8 joules
	total energy of reactants		8,476 joules

The equation for determining T is set up as before, except that the diatomic nitrogen is now included.

(lviii) $E_{total} = \underset{\text{carbon dioxide}}{mC_p(T - T_r)} + \underset{\text{water vapor}}{mC_p(T - 373°K)} + \underset{\text{nitrogen}}{mC_p(T - T_r)}$

806,387 joules = (44 g)(1.393 j/g°K)(T – 273°K) + (36g)(2.93j/g°K)(T – 373°K)+(210.7g)(1.298j/g°K)(T - 273°K)

Solving for T in the equation (lvii) above gives:

(lix)   T = 2,128°K or 1,855°C.

Since the temperature is well below 3,000°C, no significant dissociation effects are expected to occur, and the calculated temperature should be close to the actual temperature.

Actual measurements of the adiabatic flame temperature of methane at stoichiometric conditions (as reported in *Bulletin 680, U.S. Bureau of Mines, Investigation of Fire and Explosion Accidents in the Chemical, Mining, and Fuel-Related Industries*, by Kuchta, table 17) found a flame temperature of 1,875°C. The figure derived in equation (lviii), 1,855°C, varies only 20°C or 0.9% on the absolute scale from the actual measured value.

Comparing the adiabatic flame temperature of burning methane in air to that of burning methane in pure oxygen finds that the cooling effect of the nitrogen is substantial. This is, of course, why welding and brazing processes usually use pure oxygen instead of air.

It is noteworthy that the maximum temperature achieved by burning natural gas in air, 1,895°C or 3,378°F, is just barely above the melting point of mild steel, which is about 2,800°F or more. Under normal circumstances, typical heat losses and combustion inefficiencies preclude natural gas from being able to melt mild steel parts. The maximum adiabatic flame temperature assumes stoichiometric conditions, which are rarely even approached in uncontrolled fires. When there is too much air or too little air, the flame temperature drops significantly.

Exceptions to the above occur when the mild steel parts are very thin, which minimizes conductive losses in the mild steel, and the parts are very close to the hottest part of the flames. And the heat from burning natural gas is more than sufficient, even assuming some losses, to melt copper (m.p. 1,083°C) or aluminum (m.p. 660°C) if the flames are in direct contact with the metals.

As has been done with methane, now consider once more the combustion of wood to determine its maximum flame temperature.

As before, the combustion reaction of wood is modeled as follows:

$$
\begin{array}{cccc}
\text{solid} & \text{liquid} & \text{gas} & \text{gas} \\
\end{array}
$$

$$
\text{(lx) } C_6H_{10}O_5 + 1.22H_2O + 6O_2 + 22.572N_2 \rightarrow
$$

$$
\begin{array}{cccc}
162g & 21.96g & 192g & 632g
\end{array}
$$

$$
\begin{array}{ccc}
\text{gas} & \text{liquid} & \text{gas} \\
6CO_2 + & 6.22H_2O + & 22.572N_2 + Q_c \\
264g & 112g & 632g
\end{array}
$$

The heat of combustion for wood is 2,902,400 joules. However, unlike the previous analysis of methane combustion, it will be necessary in this case to deal with both the sensible and latent heats of the water in the combustion products. This is because the heat of combustion given above for wood combustion is the higher heating value. The higher heating value does not include the heat required to turn room temperature water into steam at some elevated temperature.

To make life easy on ourselves, however, if we assume that the reference temperature is room temperature, or 296°K, then the energy of the reactants does not have to be calculated. By definition, it is zero at the reference temperature.

As before, however, an equation is constructed for the energy contained in the combustion products. It is given as follows:

(lxi)
$$
Q_c = mC_p(T - T_r) + mC_p(T - 373°K) + mC_p(73°K) + mh_l + mC_p(T - T_r)
$$
$$
\text{carbon dioxide \quad water vapor \qquad\qquad water \quad latent heat \quad nitrogen} \\
\text{of water}
$$

Substituting numbers and leaving out the units for brevity, equation (lxi) is then:

(lxii) Q_c = (264)(1.393)(T–296) + (112)(2.928)(T–373) + (112)(4.186)–
(73) + (112)(2,260) + 632(1.298)(T–296) = 2,902,400

The reader will note that the C_p values for carbon dioxide and diatomic nitrogen have changed from before. This is because the C_p values for a temperature of 2,222°K have been chosen. Solving for T finds that:

(lxiii)   T = 2,060°K or 1,787°C

Thus, the maximum possible flame temperature of wood, combusted under the most ideal conditions, is just a little less than that of methane. However, wood is a solid fuel; it is usually not pulverized but is burned in large chunks. Thus, wood usually burns in an air-starved condition, because the size of the wood pieces limits the access of air to the reaction which occurs on the surface of the wood. This is in contrast to methane gas which can mix intimately with the air and can react with the air on all sides.

Also, while the reaction itself is air-starved, there is a lot of air near the reaction which soaks up a significant portion of the combustion heat and carries it away without being directly involved in the reaction. This is in part because the combustion of wood proceeds at a slower rate than that of methane, giving more time for heat transfer effects to come into play. A fast reaction, like the combustion of methane well mixed with air, takes place quickly and allows little time for heat transfer to occur. Thus, methane combustion can more closely approach the adiabatic condition than wood combustion can.

A wood fire is then both air starved and air rich at the same time. This means that the flame temperature is reduced due to a lack of air being able to get to the combustion site, and the flame temperature is also reduced because of excess air which "steals" some of the available combustion energy. Thus, a typical flame temperature of wood in open air burning is often in the range of 550°C to 900°C. As a general rule, the more smoke that is produced in a wood fire, the "colder" the flame temperature of burning.

Again, it is noted that the melting points of mild steel, copper and aluminum are respectively 1,538°C or more, 1,083°, and 660°C. Assuming the typical heat losses and combustion inefficiencies, an open-air wood fire will not melt steel, and except for special circumstances, will not melt copper. However, once established, most fires burning reasonably seasoned wood can melt aluminum.

This is why copper wiring will usually survive a house fire with only oxidation and annealing damage, while aluminum wiring is often found melted by the fire in several places where the fire was "boxed in."

Figure 2.4 Fire under highway bridge due to ignition of transient living quarters. Fire caused some spalling of concrete exterior.

O. More Imperfect Combustion — Dissociation

As briefly discussed in the preceding section, when the flame temperature is about 2,500°C or more, a process called *dissociation* becomes significant. Dissociation occurs where there is enough energy to cause breakdown of the carbon dioxide and water in the products of combustion. The carbon dioxide breaks down into carbon monoxide and diatomic oxygen; the water breaks down into diatomic hydrogen and oxygen.

For example, at about 2,000°C, about 10% of the carbon dioxide normally formed in combustion will dissociate into carbon monoxide and oxygen. This will absorb about 10,104 joules per gram of CO formed. At the same temperature, about 3% of the water vapor will dissociate into hydrogen and oxygen. This will absorb about 142,100 joules per gram of H_2 formed.

This is why at high combustion temperatures the actual flame temperature will usually be less than the calculated adiabatic flame temperature, unless terms for dissociation are added to the energy balance. The dissociation process will soak up some of the available energy and reduce the over-all temperature of the products.

As the combustion products cool, the dissociated compounds will reform into their original compounds and the energy once absorbed will be released again. This causes cooling gases to exhibit a quasi-latent heat effect.

P. Pyrophoric Degradation

As briefly noted before, wood is primarily composed of cellulose, lignin and similar organic compounds. About 25% of most types of wood is lignin, and 30% or more is cellulose. The chemical formula for cellulose is $(C_6H_{10}O_5)_n$, where the "n" subscript indicates that the basic chemical unit within the parentheses is repeated in long chains. The basic chemical formula for lignin is variable, but its empirical formula is similar to that of cellulose.

Wood used in construction work is generally kiln dried to a moisture level of about 12% by weight. Most construction-grade woods will ignite at temperatures in the range of 260°C to 430°C (500°F to 806°F).

When wood is exposed over time to a heat source, two effects occur that affect its ignition temperature: the first effect is that the wood directly exposed to the heat source dries out. As the moisture content in the wood decreases, the ignition temperature drops. This is because less heat is used up in vaporizing moisture trapped in the wood.

A fuller explanation of this effect is as follows: wood burns at temperatures well above the boiling point of water. If wood is to be ignited, moisture trapped in the wood must be heated up above its boiling point. The trapped moisture will turn into steam before ignition of the wood occurs, and this change of phase of liquid to steam consumes a large amount of heat. The heat needed for this phase change is "stolen" from the combustion heat. If enough heat is "stolen," the combustion reaction cannot sustain itself and stops.

Of course, most people who have built campfires are familiar with the problem of using "green" wood in a fire. Green wood is wood that has been recently cut and has a high moisture content. If wood is too green, that is if it contains too much moisture, the wood won't burn. If it has had some time to dry or is mixed in with some dry wood, a fire can perhaps be sustained. However, the wood will hiss, pop, and even explode. Steam will blow out the ends of the logs, the fire will burn with a lot of smoke, and the fire will not produce much warmth.

The second effect due to exposure to a heat source over time is a general decomposition of the wood itself. A mild form of destructive distillation or pyrolysis occurs. The side chains are oxidized into wood alcohol and terpene type products, and the long chains of cellulose and lignin are broken apart. As this occurs, the affected area of the wood darkens. If the process continues, the affected area eventually becomes char. This second effect also lowers the ignition temperature. Char or carbonized wood is more easily oxidized than regular wood.

Occurring together or singly, these two effects are often called *pyrophoric degradation.* Wood that has undergone pyrophoric degradation can ignite at temperatures as low as 150°C (~300°F). Fires are sometimes caused by pyrophoric degradation in the following way: wood is placed near a heat source or vice versa. The heat source by itself is not sufficient to raise the temperature of the wood up to the normal ignition temperature range. However, the heat source is sufficient to initiate pyrophoric degradation. As time passes, the ignition temperature of the affected area of the wood drops. When the ignition temperature of the affected wood falls below the temperature produced by the heat source, the wood may ignite.

Fires caused by pyrophoric degradation can be quite insidious. The process can occur over a period of time no longer than minutes when the heat source is continuous and the wood temperature is just below the regular ignition point. However, the process can also occur in a period of time measured in months or even years, when the heat source is sufficiently intermittent and the wood temperature is near the minimum ignition temperature of about 150°C.

In some cases, if the heat source is sufficiently intermittent and the temperatures generated in the wood are relatively low, it is possible that any drying effects in the wood may be reversed by natural diffusion. During the "on" period, the heat from the appliance may dry the wood. But if the drying is slight and no significant pyrolytic effects have yet occurred, it is possible for the wood to replenish its moisture from humid air or other sources during the "off" period. If the usage pattern of the appliance changes to where it is used more often, the wood may then not have a chance to regain its moisture, and pyrophoric degradation may follow. Thus, an appliance that never before caused a problem when occasionally used, may start a fire if used for an unusually long period of time.

One example of a case of pyrophoric degradation involved a combination heat pump and air conditioning unit. Because of certain technical limitations, heat pumps do not function efficiently below about –2°C (~28°F). For this reason, heat pump units are usually equipped with direct resistance heating coils in the supply duct. The coils kick in when the outside air temperature is less than about –2°C (~28°F) and the heat pump is turned off. The heating coils are usually mounted as close as possible to the hot-air supply outlet to minimize losses.

In this case, the combination heat pump and air conditioning unit had been installed so that the direct resistance coils were too close to wood framing around the hot-air supply wall opening.

When operated, the direct resistance heating coils heated the wood up to perhaps 175–185°C by radiant heat transfer. While the heat pump system component was often used, due to the climate, the direct resistance coils themselves were operated only infrequently. Because of these circumstances, pyrophoric degradation proceeded slowly. Ignition of the wood and fire damage to the structure did not occur until nearly 2½ years after the unit had been installed.

Because several identical units had been similarly installed in the building, it was possible to check the unburned units for evidence of "in-progress" pyrophoric degradation. This was done, and it was found that each of the unburned units showed some charring of the wood framing around the hot-air supply wall opening.

Some common places where pyrophoric degradation occur are

- around floor furnaces,
- around fireplaces, chimneys, and hearths,
- around ceramic kilns and similar heat-producing specialty appliances,
- around space heaters placed near walls, wood materials, or drapes,
- in paper-backed insulation improperly laid over fluorescent light ballasts (especially the older types without thermal switches) or high intensity canister type lighting,
- around poultry brooding lamps, heat lamps, and high intensity lighting,
- around high-wattage trouble lights that have been laid on combustible materials,
- around single-wall flue pipes set in wood materials, and
- in utility closets where stored materials are near pilot lights, burners or light bulbs.

Sometimes a floor furnace or flue pipe installed close to wood or combustible materials may give years of service without a problem. Then one day a fire may unexpectedly occur, having begun in the wood around the framing of the furnace or the flue pipe because of pyrophoric degradation. Why does such a fire wait so long to happen? Was pyrophoric degradation occurring all along, but extremely slowly?

In such cases, a little further digging may reveal that a recent storm or high wind moved the flue pipe and shifted it to a new position, slightly closer to the wood frame. Similarly, it may be discovered that furniture was recently moved over the floor furnace grille, causing it to shift slightly closer to the wood framing. The difference between pyrophoric degradation occurring or not occurring may be just a centimeter of additional distance between the wood and the heat source.

In addition to wood-type materials, similar pyrophoric degradation effects can occur in textiles, especially cotton and natural fibers, paper, cardboard, certain plastics, and other types of organic materials. The reader may have noticed that many of the items in the preceding list are composed of large amounts of cellulose, lignin, or cellulose-like polymers.

Q. More Pyrophoric Degradation, or If At First You Don't Fricaseed, Fry, Fry Again

A variant form of pyrophoric degradation sometimes occurs in deep-fat fryers such as are used in fast-food restaurants for french fries or chicken. Most deep-fat fryers thermostatically control the cooking temperature of the oil or fat. In addition to this manually set thermostat, there is also a high heat limit switch imbedded in the bottom of the fryer cooking well.

The purpose of the high-heat limit is to turn off the appliance before the temperature of the oil becomes so high that it boils or ignites. The set point of the high heat limit switch is usually slightly less than the published boiling temperature of the oil or fat substance recommended for the appliance.

However, when oil or cooking fat is heated continuously, the oil eventually breaks down. Large fatty polymer chains break down into smaller ones. As a general rule, small organic molecules boil at lower temperatures than large organic molecules. This is why the smaller-molecule substances are sometimes referred to as "light distillates," or "light ends."

In a distillation process, the light distillate substances boil off first leaving behind the thicker, denser substances sometimes called the "heavy ends." Thus, if a deep-fat fryer has been left turned on at a high cooking temperature for a long time, the oil may break down so that it can boil and possibly ignite at temperatures below the set point of the high heat limit switch.

A typical french fryer fire might occur like this: at closing time, the french fryer is accidentally left on at a high cooking temperature. During the night, the oil is continuously heated at the high temperature and the oil breaks down into lighter organic substances. At some point when the breakdown is sufficient, the boiling point of the degraded oil is the same or less than the thermostat temperature setting. When this occurs, the oil in the fryer well boils out of the fryer. This action may result in a fire in several ways:

- the oil that boils out may stream down onto the burners of the french fryer located underneath and ignite,
- the oil may run laterally over the tops of counters, grills, or other nearby appliances and ignite from contact with their burners, pilot lights, etc., or
- enough oil may boil out of the fryer that the upper sections of the heating coils are exposed to the air. Since air is a poor heat conductor, the coil quickly heats up until the oil boiling up around it is ignited.

The last scenario is interesting and merits additional discussion. The high heat limit switch will usually not stop the fire from occurring in this instance because of the following.

The high heat limit switch is typically located in the bottom third of the cooking well. It senses the temperature of the oil, not of the heating coil. The coil is designed to be surrounded by oil, which efficiently conducts away the heat generated in the coil. Air is a poor conductor of heat. If the coil is surrounded by air and not oil, the coil's temperature quickly rises; it cannot get rid of the heat fast enough to stay cool.

Because the high heat limit switch measures the temperature of the oil, and not the coil, the temperature of the coil can quickly become higher than the ignition temperature of the oil before the oil in the cooking well will heat up enough to cause the high heat limit switch to open the circuit.

When a fire has occurred in a french fryer and the oil boiled out just prior to the fire, this can usually be determined by visual inspection. First, there may be a lot of oil on the floor and surrounding appliances due to the boil-over. Secondly, the fire in the cooking well will burn initially above the oil level, leaving tell-tale blackening on the sides of the well. Thus, the soot and carbonization inside the cooking well will document the level of the oil when ignition broke out.

Chapter 3:
Odorants and Leak Detection

A. General

Certain gaseous fuels like methane, ethane, butane, and propane are colorless and have no readily recognizable odor. If unadulterated methane, ethane, butane, or propane vapors are in a room at explosive concentrations, an unaided person would not be aware of the danger – he could not see, taste, or smell them using only his own senses. Unadulterated hydrocarbon gaseous fuels such as these can be a death-dealing, invisible threat.

Despite this safety problem, gaseous fuels such as methane, butane and propane are very desirable for home, business and industrial use. They burn cleanly, and they have a high energy density, that is, a high amount of combustible energy release per unit of mass. They leave no ash residues that require disposal. They are amenable to "on demand" heating and cooling systems. A gas boiler, gas furnace, or gas stove turns on and off more or less instantly with no waiting time like with wood or coal. Gas appliances do not need pumps like liquid fuels. They also do not have the bulk material handling problems like coal or wood, and they are relatively cheap.

Gaseous fuels such as methane and propane are distributed by pipework made of iron, steel, plastic, copper, or aluminum. It is a given proposition that not all gas pipework and appliances are installed "according to Hoyle." Over time, gas pipework can corrode and deteriorate. Occasionally, gas pipework is inadvertently damaged by induced machinery vibrations, piping movement, and general stupidity.

In the latter category, my favorite stupid gas pipe tricks include the handyman who welds shelving brackets to steel gas pipes, and the electrician who uses gas piping for electrical grounding of high-voltage appliances.

From a safety standpoint, a designer or system manager should assume that installations using gaseous hydrocarbon fuels will eventually develop leaks. Since leaks often occur at joints and connections, consider the following. For a small house, it would not be unusual for there to be perhaps ten separate joints and connections in the pipework serving a simple furnace and hot water tank. If each day one unsafe leak developed in a thousand such connections, a daily quality rate of 99.9%, then every day one house out of every 100 would spring an unsafe leak. One hundred houses is the size of a small neighborhood.

If the quality rate could be improved by a multiple of a thousand, this would cause a daily unsafe leak in one house in each 100,000. Assuming 3 people per house, this is a city about the size of Wichita, Kansas. Thus, even with a quality rate of 99.9999%, a city the size of Wichita, Kansas, would average one house every day that develops an unsafe leak.

Persons familiar with statistics related to manufacturing quality control may recognize that a daily quality rate of 99.9999% corresponds to a "σ" value of nearly 4.0. Many companies involved in implementing the ISO 9000 international manufacturing quality standards strive very hard just to reach a "σ" of 3.08 or 99.9%. It is known that the gas company that services Wichita may be called upon to check out and repair a dozen or more gas leaks a day. From a practical standpoint, we can readily assume that a typical daily quality rate for gas joints and connections is less than 99.9999%, but better than 99.9%. A good guess might be a range of perhaps from 99.99% to 99.999%.

In a city like Wichita, Kansas, with a population of about 300,000, thousands of homes and businesses use methane or propane. There are hundreds of miles of pipework, and many thousands of joints and connections. Gas lines and appliance installations are done by a variety of companies, subcontractors and technicians with varying skills, knowledge, and experience.

Also, these same gas lines and appliances are maintained and looked after with a wide range of vigilance. This includes doing nothing, a popular choice, to making regular checks according to recognized maintenance schedules. It is impracticable, if not impossible, from both legal and economic aspects, to regularly check every installation and joint.

In considering the preceding, a person can assume with some confidence that fires and explosions will occur with some statistical regularity as a result of gas leaks. It is impossible given the above circumstances to have a "leak-free" delivery system that is absolutely safe for everyone and all property involved.

Having now beaten to death the obvious point that gas pipes sometimes leak, the next point to consider is how to send a warning to persons not equipped with technical testing devices that there is a colorless, odorless, and dangerous gas in the area. One way might be to color the gas so that it might appear blue, red, or some other eye-catching color. However, this is not an easy thing to do.

As the reader may recall, natural gas, or methane, has a lower flammability limit of 5%, and propane has a lower flammability limit of 2.4%. To make a naturally colorless gas like methane or propane visible at a concentration significantly less than 2.4% requires either that the gas contain a high percentage of colorant, or that the colorant be remarkably dense and concentrated. Since the point of having a fuel gas is the fuel, having a high percentage of colorant is undesirable.

Further, any colorant added to the gas must not react with the pipe or the gas itself; it ought to burn with the fuel reasonably well, and must stay suspended in the gas. However, dyes and colorants that are dense enough to make low concentrations of gas visible often are too heavy to flow with the gas. They fall out, or react with the gas or the pipework. Because of these problems, to date it has not been demonstrably practical to color methane or propane.

However, it is an easy thing to make methane or propane smell by adding just a little bit of odorant. If the odorant stinks badly enough even when there is only a little bit of gas around, people will notice it. Further, a really stinky, disgusting smell can be noticed in a dark room, in a noisy room, and by blind or deaf people. It may even be stinky enough to wake persons who are sleeping.

In short, since some amount of gas leakage is expected to occur from time to time, people in the area can be alerted to its presence if the vapors stink to high heaven. If the stench is strong enough, people will smell the vapors before the vapors reach the lower limit of flammability, and this allows remedies to be taken before the situation becomes dangerous.

For these reasons, it is generally required by law to odorize gaseous fuels. However, unodorized gas fuels are still allowed to be piped and distributed under certain circumstances. If the addition of an odorant is detrimental to the processing of the fuel gas, or if the odorant serves no useful purpose as a warning agent, then odorization is not required.

As a rule, however, fuel gases such a methane, butane, and propane are odorized when they are put into the commercial distribution system. With methane, this is normally done before the gas is dispatched into a local pipeline distribution system. With butane or propane, this is usually done at the local or regional distribution processing plant.

B. Odorization Levels and Odor Recognition

Normally, fuel gases are odorized so that a normal person can distinctly smell them at a concentration of one-fifth or less of their lower limit of flammability. Thus, a normal person will smell odorant well before the gas has accumulated to dangerous levels. If the gas is accumulating due to a leak, this gives a person some time to get clear of the area and shut off the nearest valve.

Since the lower limit of flammability of methane is about 5% by volume, a normal person will notice the odorant when the natural gas concentration is at about 1% (10,000 ppm) or less. Since the lower limit of flammability of propane is 2.4%, a normal person will notice the odorant when the propane concentration is about 0.5% (5,000 ppm) or less.

The "or less" phrase is added to the above because many distributors of natural gas and liquefied propane use more odorant than is required. It is not unusual for a 25–50% excess of odorant to be used.

In general, the perceived intensity of an odor versus its concentration in the air follows the *Webber-Fechner Equation* given as follows:

(i) $I = k \ln(C)$

where   I = the intensity of the smell,
   k = a constant for the particular chemical odor, and
   C = concentration of the chemical in the air.

Rearranging equation (i) to solve for the concentration gives the following:

(ii) $C = e^{I/k}$

where e = 2.7182.

If equation (ii) is differentiated with respect to I, the smell intensity, the following is obtained, which relates the change in concentration to the change in perceived smell intensity:

(iii) $dC/dI = (1/k)e^{I/k}$

From equation (ii) it is seen that if a person is experienced with odors, an estimation of the concentration of the odor in the air can be done simply by smell. Equation (iii) further shows that at low concentrations the slope of the change in concentration versus the change in smell intensity is low, but at high concentrations the slope is high. This means that estimating the concentration by smell is more accurate at low concentrations than at high concentrations. Once a smell intensity gets to a "strong" level, it is more difficult for a human nose to separate out small variations within "strong."

To see how the above works, consider the following: it is generally expected that the threshold for recognizing the odor of ethyl mercaptan in air is 0.001 ppm. The commonly accepted upper tolerance or exposure limit for humans for ethyl mercaptan in air is 0.500 ppm. Let us consider the lower recognition threshold as the base unit for odor concentration. Thus, 0.001 ppm = 1 odor concentration unit, and 0.500 ppm = 500 odor concentration units. Lastly, let us also define an arbitrary scale for smell intensity where I = 100 for the upper tolerance limit.

If these values are substituted in equation (i), the following is obtained.

$$I = k \ln(C)$$
$$100 = k \ln(500) \text{ @ upper tolerance limit}$$
$$k = 16.09$$

When C = 1, then:

$$I = 16.09 \ln(1) = 0$$

Thus, by definition, the smell intensity at the threshold level is 0, and at the upper exposure limit is 100.

The following table lists a number of representative values showing the relationship between smell intensity, per the arbitrary scale noted above, and concentration levels.

Table 1. Smell Intensity Versus Odor Concentration for Ethyl Mercaptan

Concentration (ppm in air)	Concentration (arbitrary odor units)	smell intensity
0.001	1	0
0.002	2	11
0.003	3	18
0.004	4	22
0.005	5	26
0.010	10	37
0.050	50	63
0.080	80	71
0.100	100	74
0.500	500	100

The average slope of the change in concentration (in arbitrary odor units) versus smell intensity for the first two values in the table is 1/11 = 0.0909. For the second and third values it is 1/9 = 0.1111. However, the average slope between the last two values is 400/26 = 15.38.

As discussed previously, when the concentration is low, a small change in the perceived smell intensity indicates a small change in the concentration. Conversely, when the concentration is high, a small change in the perceived smell intensity can indicate a relatively large change in concentration.

Table 1 can be rearranged into five general smell levels to aid in the estimation of concentration levels. This alternate arrangement is shown in Table 2.

Table 2. Smell Levels versus Concentration for Ethyl Mercaptan

Smell level	Range of smell intensity (as per Table 1)	Range of concentration (in ppm in air)
trace	0–11	0.001–0.002
weak	18–35	0.003–0.009
medium	37–63	0.010–0.050
strong*	63–100	0.050–0.500
overpowering	100+	>0.500

*Note: Mandatory odorization levels for when the flammable gas is at a concentration of 1/5th its lower limit of flammability usually have a smell level at the lower range of "strong." This usually fulfills the requirement for the odorization to be distinctly recognizable by a person with normal smelling ability.

By the use of Table 2, it is possible for even inexperienced persons to roughly estimate concentrations of odorant in the air if their smelling ability is normal.

Similar tables can be generated for the other odorants, and in this way it is possible to roughly estimate an odorant's concentration by simple smell. The technique can be very useful when dealing with statements or interview information.

For example, let us assume that a small explosion occurred in a warehouse. Prior to the explosion, several employees reported that they smelled gas. If the location of the employees when they smelled the gas can be learned, and they can recall how strong the odor was, it may be possible to plot a rough contour map of the gas concentration levels just prior to the explosion over the general plan of the warehouse. This may provide some useful clues in determining the origin of the gas, and its dispersion pathway.

C. Smokers and Other Bad Smellers

From experience it has been observed that some heavy tobacco smokers often do not smell odorized gas as readily as non-smokers. In the same way that smoking sometimes dulls the sense of taste, it also apparently dulls the sense of smell. The following is scenario that has been noted to occur somewhat regularly.

Mrs. Smith, a non-smoker, is doing laundry in the basement when she thinks she smells gas. Because she is not sure, she goes upstairs and asks her husband to check. Mr. Smith, a heavy smoker, goes downstairs and sniffs around. He does not notice any gas smell, and tells his wife that she imagined it, or mistook some other smell for gas.

Some days later, an explosion occurs in the basement. When interviewed, Mr. Smith states that he did not notice any gas smell before the explosion. When similarly interviewed, Mrs. Smith also agrees that there was no gas smell before the explosion. She is reluctant to disagree publicly with her husband, especially since he previously told her she had imagined smelling gas.

Besides smoking, there are other reasons why a person may not readily smell fuel gas odorant. Some people because of disease or injury have lost their sense of smell. Some people, though very few, are born with a diminished sense of smell or no sense of smell at all. Some people may work in processing plants, factories or refineries where their sense of smell is bombarded every day by strong odors, and their noses may not "clear out" until several hours after getting home.

It has been noted in some research work that smelling ability also diminishes with age. In two studies discussed in the August 1987 issue of *Fire Technology*, it was reported that persons in the age group 70–85 years old have a detection threshold for ethyl mercaptan ten times higher than that of persons in the age group 18–25 years old. In fact, some of the people in the 70–85 age group failed to note the presence of odorant at a concentration equivalent to that of the lower limit of flammability.

In another study reported in the same issue of *Fire Technology*, it was found that almost half of the people tested who were over 60 years of age failed to reliably smell ethyl mercaptan in LPG which was odorized according to the current standard (see next section). The logical conclusion of this study is that older persons are at greater risk for LPG accidents.

Additionally, some homes and buildings are subject to strong odors that can mask the smell of fuel gas odorant. The smells generated by pets, animals, fertilizer, rotted grain or similar can mask the smell of fuel gas odorant. Smells associated with medical facilities and nursing homes may also be too strong for a person to notice any fuel gas odorant present.

Odors generated by nearby slaughter houses, feed lots, cesspools, septic tanks, fermentation facilities, etc., can drift over to nearby homes and buildings and mask odorant smell on an occasional or regular basis. Poorly maintained and unsecured tenements can also develop sufficiently foul odors that any smell of fuel gas odorant is lost in the pungent mixture.

While not as well publicized as smoke detectors, home devices are available through mail order houses and resourceful hardware stores that will detect the presence of natural gas or LPG. These devices do not depend on the presence of an odorant, but detect the basic hydrocarbon gas directly. They work in a manner similar to a home smoke alarm. When a certain threshold concentration of gas is detected, an audible alarm goes off. For the hearing impaired, it would be an easy matter to connect the alarm signal to a flashing light. When the occupants of a house have impaired smelling ability, or perhaps cannot physically go to the basement due to wheelchair access problems, these devices might afford some piece of mind.

D. LPG Odorants

Three types of chemicals are specifically listed by the *Code of Federal Regulations* to odorize liquefied petroleum gas or LPG (see CFR 1910.110(b)(1), revised July 1, 1990). They are ethyl mercaptan, thiophene, and amyl mercaptan. The most widely used odorant is ethyl mercaptan.

LPG can be a blend of several hydrocarbon gases. By federal law, LPG is any material that is composed predominantly of any of the following: propane, propylene, normal butane, iso-butane, and butylenes. The exact specifications for LPG are set forth in ASTM D1835, *Liquefied Petroleum Gas Specifications*. Generally, commercial LPG is a combination of propane and butane. For home and farm use where high volatility is needed, most LPG is predominantly propane, with perhaps 5–10% being butane or some of the other gases. For uses where low volatility is needed, usually industrial situations, most LPG is predominantly butane, with perhaps 5–10% being propane or some of the other gases.

Federal regulations allow other types of chemicals to be used as odorants instead of the three listed. Any odorant is acceptable if it has a distinctive odor when gas vapors are at one-fifth the concentration of its lower limit of flammability.

As a practical matter, however, no one makes significant use of this allowance. In the present litigious climate, no gas company would want to use a new type of odorant in place of the standard, government-sanctioned ones.

The term *mercaptan* is somewhat an archaic misnomer. Mercaptan is an older chemical term derived from the Latin *mercurium captans*, which literally means "mercury capturing." Mercaptans react with mercuric oxide to form various crystalline compounds. The mercaptan group of chemicals are also called thioalcohols, sulfur-alcohols, hydrosulfides, and thiols. The last term, *thiols*, is the more current designation for this group, but it also includes thioethers, sulfhydrates, and thiophenals.

In general, a mercaptan is an organic compound similar to an alcohol, but has the oxygen in the hydroxyl group replaced by a sulfur atom. Note the similarity of the empirical formula for ethyl mercaptan, C_2H_5SH, to that of ethyl alcohol, C_2H_5OH.

Ethyl mercaptan is also called ethanethiol, and ethyl sulfhydrate. It is one of the most pungent, stinky and persistent odors known. It is the essence of skunk stench. Physically, it is a colorless liquid that boils at 36°C and freezes at –121°C. It has a specific gravity of about 0.84. It is only slightly soluble in water, but is soluble in both ethyl alcohol and ether. Its closed cup flash point is below 26°C and it autoignites at 299°C. Human tolerance level is only 0.5 ppm in air. Barring time and patience, about the only practicable deodorizing chemical that can remove the stench is tomato juice.

Federal regulations state that 1 pound of ethyl mercaptan is to be used for every 10,000 gallons of liquefied petroleum gas. Since a gallon of propane at 0°C weighs about 4.42 pounds per gallon, this is a weight ratio of about 1 pound of ethyl mercaptan to 44,200 pounds of propane. Since the molecular weight of ethyl mercaptan is 62, and the molecular weight of propane is 44, then the gram molecular weight, or mole, mixing ratio is 1 to 62,282. This computes to a mole solution mixture of about 16 parts of ethyl mercaptan per one million parts of propane or 16 ppm.

If the ethyl mercaptan were to evenly mix with the propane at a mole mixing ratio of 1/62,282 and vaporize at the same ratio (which it does not do), then when propane is at its lower flammability limit of 0.5% in air (5,000 ppm), there would also be about 0.080 ppm of ethyl mercaptan in the air. This would be 80 times the concentration level for threshold recognition. As is noted in Table 1, the intensity of smell at that concentration would be easily recognizable by a normal person.

If the LPG is primarily composed of butane, however, the numbers change. Butane weighs about 4.99 pounds per gallon. Thus, one pound of ethyl mercaptan for every 10,000 gallons of butane would be a weight ratio of 1 to 49,900. Since the molecular weight of butane is 58, this is a mole mixing ratio of 1 to 53,341 or a mole solution mixture of about 18.7 ppm.

Amyl mercaptan is also called pentanethiol. Its empirical formula is $C_5H_{11}SH$. Amyl mercaptan is not a pure substance, but is often a mixture composed of the various isomers of the compound. Physically, it has a slight amber or light yellow color with a specific gravity of 0.83 to 0.84. It is insoluble in water, but soluble in ethyl alcohol. The open cup flash point is 18°C. Because it is a mixture of isomers, its boiling point ranges between 104°C and 130°C.

Federal regulations require that 1.4 pounds of amyl mercaptan be used to odorize 10,000 gallons of LPG. This is a weight ratio of 1 pound of amyl mercaptan to 31,571 pounds of propane. Since the molecular weight of amyl mercaptan is 104, and that of propane is 44, the mole mixing ratio is 1 to 74,623. This computes to a mole solution mixture of about 13.4 ppm.

If the LPG is primarily butane, however, then the weight ratio is 1.4 pounds of amyl mercaptan to 49,900 pounds of butane. This is a weight ratio of 1 to 35,642. The mole mixing ratio is then 1 to 63,909, or a mole solution mixture of about 15.6 ppm.

Thiophane, also called tetrahydrothiophene, is the least frequently used odorant for LPG. Its empirical formula is C_4H_7SH. It appears clear like water, and has the same specific gravity as water, 1.0. Having some isomers, it boils in a range of 115°C to 124.4°C.

Federal regulations indicate that 1.0 pound of thiophane is to be mixed with 10,000 gallons of LPG. This is a weight ratio of 1 pound of thiophane to 44,200 pounds of propane, the same weight ratio as used for ethyl mercaptan. Because the molecular weight of thiophane is 88, the mole mixing ratio is 1 to 88,400. This computes to a mole solution mixture of 11.3 ppm.

If the LPG is primarily butane, the weight ratio using thiophane becomes 1 to 49,900. The mole mixing ratio is then 1 to 75,710 or a mole solution mixture of 13.2 ppm.

E. Natural Gas Odorants

In natural gas systems, odorant is injected into the pipeline stream much like an aerosol spray. Sampling is then done, usually at several points in the pipeline system well downstream of the injection point, to assure proper dispersion and concentration of the odorant within the distribution system (as per ANSI/ASME B31.8, section 871.4).

Unlike LPG odorization requirements, the regulations concerning the odorization of natural gas are less specific. Unless specific state laws apply, natural gas utilities may use any odorant in any amount as long as the following requirements are met (as per ANSI/ASME B31.8, sections 871.1–3):

- "The odorant when blended with gas in the specified amount shall not be deleterious to humans or to the materials present in the gas system and shall not be soluble in water to a greater extent than 2½ parts of odorant to 100 parts of water by weight."

- "The products of combustion from the odorant shall be non-toxic to humans breathing air containing the products of combustion and shall not be corrosive or harmful to the materials with which such products of combustion would ordinarily come in contact."

- "The combustion of the odorant and the natural odor of the gas shall provide a distinctive odor so that when gas is present in air at the concentration of as much as 1% by volume, the odor is readily detectable by a person with a normal sense of smell."

Often, either methyl mercaptan or ethyl mercaptan is used to odorize natural gas; sometimes both substances are used in some type of mixture. Since some of the properties of ethyl mercaptan have already been discussed in the previous section about LPG odorants, only methyl mercaptan will be discussed in this section.

Methyl mercaptan, which is also called methanethiol, CH_3SH, is water-white when liquid, and colorless as a gas. It is slightly soluble in water, and boils at about 6°C. Its flash point is below 0°C. Its lower limit of flammability is 3.9% and its upper limit of flammability is 21.8%, which is similar to that of natural gas.

Methyl mercaptan has a molecular weight of 48, about three times that of natural gas, CH_4, which is 16. This difference is primarily due to the additional sulfur atom in methyl mercaptan. Structurally, methyl mercaptan is simply a methane molecule with a –SH radical substituted for one of the hydrogen atoms.

As a gas, methyl mercaptan is toxic, is a strong irritant, and stinks to high heaven. An upper tolerance level of 0.5 ppm for human exposure in air has been established. The accepted threshold recognition concentration for a person with normal smelling ability is 0.002 ppm in air.

F. Sampling LPG for Odorants

As was noted previously, odorant is added to LPG for safety by the local distributor. Its presence is intended to warn persons who are in the area that there are dangerous LPG vapors present. Some people might even consider odorant to be the first line of defense against gas leaks.

There have been instances of fires and explosions where it was found that the odorization of the LPG was not sufficient for a person in the area of the leak to detect its presence. In some cases, large settlements have been awarded by the courts against LPG distributors based on a finding that the LPG provided by the distributor was insufficiently odorized. The premise is that if odorization had been sufficient, the plaintiff would have smelled it, the leak would have then been detected, and the fire or explosion could have been prevented.

For these reasons, whenever a fire or explosion involves LPG, the parties involved may wish to determine the level of odorization in the LPG. This can be done in three different ways: smelling a small gas release; sampling gas from the lines, and sampling liquid from the tank.

The first method is simple. A small amount of LPG gas is released in a calm area from the gas line and is then smelled by a person or persons with normal smelling ability. The odor can be rated by the smellers as being overpowering, strong, medium, weak, or trace. Of course, since LPG is flammable, is it assumed that only small amounts are released in an area free of sparks and flames. It is further assumed that the small amounts of LPG gas are released in areas where the gas can be easily dissipated with fresh air.

If needed, the "smell" method can actually be set up to be more quantitative in line with the federal requirements for detection thresholds. For example, a large, somewhat air-tight cardboard box can be obtained; an amount of LPG gas can then be released into the box equal to 0.5% of its volume. A person with normal smelling ability can then stick his or her nose into a hole provided in the box for this purpose, to sample the contents to determine if the odorant smell can be detected at the 0.5% level. If needed, several testers can sniff the contents to develop a small sample statistical basis. While this is not an officially sanctioned method of testing the odorant level of LPG, it can roughly indicate whether or not the level of odorization is in line with federal requirements.

A second method of checking the odorant content of LPG is to take a liquid sample directly from the tank. This requires a special container to hold the sample liquid; the special container is lined with materials that will not react with the odorant. Most LPG tanks have a connection at the top, under the protective cap, that will allow a liquid sample to be drawn from the tank. Usually, the local LPG distributor has the fittings which will make the connection between the tank and the LPG liquid sample container. The liquid sample is then taken to a laboratory where the odorant concentration in the liquid is determined, usually by gas chromatography. This is usually considered the most accurate method of determining odorant content.

A third method involves taking samples of the gaseous LPG itself. A special LPG sampling cylinder is connected to the gas line and gas is run through the cylinder until all the air in the cylinder has been purged. The cylinder is then closed off, thus trapping a sample of the LPG gas in the cylinder. The gas sample in the cylinder is then taken to a laboratory and analyzed with a gas chromatograph for odorant content. Due to the fact that odorants often react with plain steel cylinders, it is important to use a cylinder which is designed for this purpose. (See discussion of odorant fade in next section.)

There is also an alternative method of testing LPG gas for odorant which provides immediate estimates in the field without complicated laboratory work. In this method, a field gas detection kit is used. Gas from the LPG tank is released into a sample collection balloon or bag. Enough gas is released into the bag or balloon to ensure that any resident air is purged, so that there is nothing in the bag or balloon but LPG gas. A hand pump, which is like a reverse bicycle pump, is then used to draw the LPG gas through a thin glass vial which contains a chemically treated filter material. As the LPG gas passes through the vial, any odorant present reacts with the chemicals impregnated in the filter, and the filter changes color along a graduated line.

Of course, the more color change there is along the length of the vial, the higher the concentration of odorant in the sample. The concentration of the odorant is then found by measuring the length of color change along the vial, and checking a chart for the corresponding odorant concentration.

In general, the accuracy of this method in a single test is perhaps $\pm 10\%$. Neophytes using this method often underestimate the amount of odorant present in LPG gas because it is a common mistake to not thoroughly purge the bag or balloon of resident air. Any air mixed with the LPG, of course, causes the indicated concentration of odorant to be less. This is because the amount of gaseous odorant present is compared to the total volume of gas drawn through the vial to obtain the concentration per volume.

Considering the ease and cheapness of the test, however, several tests can be done in short order to develop a statistical basis for an accuracy better than a single test. Because this method provides an immediate measurement of the odorant concentration, it is well worth considering, especially when the odorant content is well above requirement concentrations.

A common procedure is to use this method first to estimate the amount of odorant present. If the concentration of odorant is well above the requirements, so that the range of accuracy of the method does not overlap the required odorant concentration, it may not be necessary to take a liquid or gas sample for laboratory analysis. If the indicated concentration is close to the requirement, however, then the more accurate sampling and laboratory methods may be required.

Several companies make these gas sampling devices and vials. "Samplair™" is one brand name. Besides being able to test for the presence of LPG odorants, this equipment is also useful for testing for other gases. The same equipment, for example, can be used to test for concentrations of CO, CO_2, CH_4, aldehydes, or other common gases in air. The only change in the equipment is the vial: a vial sensitive to the particular gas being looked for is used. As before, chemicals in the filter material in the vial will indicate by their color change if the particular gas is present as the sample is drawn through the vial by the action of the hand pump.

There is an extremely important point to remember with regard to evaluating either liquid or gaseous samples of LPG. The concentration of odorant in a liquid sample of LPG will generally be different than its concentration in a gaseous sample from the same LPG, because the evaporation rate of the odorant is not the same as the evaporation rate of the LPG.

For example, it was previously noted that the required ethyl mercaptan odorant for propane LPG computes to a ratio of 16 moles of ethyl mercaptan per 1,000,000 moles of propane. If this were wholly vaporized, this would be a concentration of 16 ppm of ethyl mercaptan in propane, by volume. As measured in the liquid state where no vapors above the liquid have formed, this is a ratio of 12 micrograms of ethyl mercaptan per milliliter of propane.

If vapors form above the liquid, then at equilibrium the ratio within the liquid phase might be 9 micrograms of liquid ethyl mercaptan per milliliter of liquid propane. At the same time, in the gaseous phase (i.e., in the head space above the liquid), the ratio would be 33 nanograms of gaseous ethyl mercaptan per milliliter of gaseous propane, or about 12 ppm. (The expansion ratio is one mole forms 22.4 liters of gas, or one milliliter of liquid volume expands to 270 milliliters of gaseous volume.)

If some of the liquid from within the same tank were then released directly to the outside and were allowed to expand to atmospheric pressure, the ratio would be 11 nanograms of gaseous ethyl mercaptan per milliliter of gaseous propane, or 4 ppm.

Thus, it can be seen that the concentration of ethyl mercaptan in a sample of propane is not a single number; the concentration will depend upon from what phase and state the propane is sampled from the tank.

The matter is further complicated by the fact that as gaseous propane is drawn from the tank, the relative concentrations of the ethyl mercaptan will change. Initially, when no LPG gas has yet been drawn from the tank, the concentrations of ethyl mercaptan will be as discussed above: 33 ng/ml in the head space (12 ppm), and 9.0 μg/ml in the liquid. However, as gas is drawn from the tank, the odorant concentration in the head space will increase. For example, if 50% of the LPG is withdrawn, the concentration of ethyl mercaptan in the gaseous phase over the liquid in the tank will be 55 ng/ml (20 ppm).

In essence, this occurs because as gas is withdrawn, the propane is boiling away and is concentrating the odorant by distillation. The boiling point of the ethyl mercaptan is 36°C, while the boiling point of propane is –42.5°C. Thus, the history of gas withdrawal from an LPG tank can affect the measured concentration of odorant for either the head space or the liquid.

At very cold ambient temperatures, another type of distillation effect can also occur. Because of the difference in boiling points, at very low temperatures the vaporization rate of ethyl mercaptan can be significantly reduced. Some of the odorant "freezes out" of the gaseous solution and stays in the liquid phase. This causes the concentration of odorant in the gaseous phase in the head space to be reduced from usual levels. This effect is most pronounced as the ambient temperature approaches the boiling point of propane.

G. Sampling Natural Gas for Odorants

The amount of odorant in natural gas is normally checked and regulated by the franchise utility, which is itself inspected by a state regulatory body. Thus, the odorant content of natural gas in commercial and residential systems is usually consistent. As noted before, it is required by ANSI/ASME B31.8 (1982), section 871.4, that the utility keep records of the amount and type of odorization employed. If there is some question about odorization levels, these records can be reviewed.

However, from time to time it may be necessary to check odorization levels of natural gas at the point of use. This may be due to a number of reasons, some of which are discussed in the next section about odorant fade. A point of use odorant check can be done in several ways.

The simplest is a *smell test*, which is basically the same as that discussed for LPG. A small amount of natural gas is released in a calm area from the gas line and is then smelled by a person or persons with normal smelling ability. The odor can be rated by the smellers as being overpowering, strong, medium, weak, or trace. Again, since natural gas is flammable, it is assumed that only small amounts are released in an area free of sparks and flames. It is further assumed that the small amounts of gas are released in areas where the gas can be easily dissipated with fresh air.

As with LPG, if needed, the "smell" method can be set up to be more quantitative in line with the federal requirements for detection thresholds. For example, a large, somewhat air-tight cardboard box can be used. An amount of natural gas can then be released into the box equal to 1.0% of its volume. A person with normal smelling ability can then stick his or her nose into a hole provided in the box for this purpose, to sample the contents to determine if the odorant smell can be detected at the 1.0% level. If needed, several testers can sniff the contents to develop a small sample statistical basis. As noted before, while this is not an officially sanctioned method of testing the odorant level of LPG, it can roughly indicate whether or not the level of odorization is in line with accepted standards.

Another method uses field sampling devices like the "Samplair™" device. Natural gas from the supply pipe is released into a sample collection balloon or bag. Sufficient gas is released into the bag or balloon to ensure that any resident air is purged, so that there is nothing in the bag or balloon but natural gas. A hand pump device, like a reverse bicycle pump, is then used to draw the natural gas through a thin glass vial which contains a chemically treated filter material. As the gas passes through the vial, any odorant present reacts with the chemicals impregnated in the filter, and the filter changes color along a graduated line. The concentration of the odorant is then found by measuring the length of color change along the vial, and checking a chart for the corresponding odorant concentration.

In general, the accuracy of this method in a single test is perhaps ±10%. Neophytes using this method often underestimate the amount of odorant present because the bag or balloon is not thoroughly purged of resident air. Any resident air mixed with the natural gas causes the indicated concentration of odorant to be less. This is because the amount of gaseous odorant present is compared to the total volume of gas drawn through the vial.

Considering the ease and cheapness of the test, however, several tests can be done in short order to develop a statistical basis for an accuracy better than a single test. The use of such testing in combination with a basic smell test may be sufficient to provide evidence of adequate odorization, especially if the tests indicate that the odorization well exceeds requirements.

The specific methodology for a "wet chemistry" testing of natural gas odorization is contained in ANSI/ASTM D2385. In this test, a volume of natural gas is bubbled through a neutral cadmium sulfate solution to remove hydrogen sulfide. The same sample of natural gas is then bubbled through basic cadmium sulfate to draw out the mercaptan compounds. The amount of hydrogen sulfide and mercaptan sulfur in the absorbers are then iodometrically determined.

While it is not necessary to repeat the whole methodology here, a few points bear mentioning. First, the test must be done on site. The gas is not to be sampled and transported in a container to another location. This is done to avoid odorant fade or contamination due to the container. Secondly, the test requires a certain expertise in the preparation of reagents and the use of laboratory titration apparatus. Since the point of this method is its accuracy, it is recommended that it be done by persons with laboratory experience.

H. Odorant Fade

The term *odorant fade* denotes conditions or situations in which the odorant concentration in LPG or natural gas diminishes or fades. It was noted previously that one cause of odorant fade in LPG is very cold temperatures. At temperatures approaching the boiling point of LPG, some of the odorant can "freeze out" of the gas in the head space of the LPG tank, causing the odorant concentration in the gaseous portion to lessen.

This effect is one consequence of the fact that an odorized flammable gas, such as propane, is a solution of two gases, each with its own distinguishing characteristics. The odorant fade of LPG associated with low temperatures is a consequence of the different boiling points, vaporization rates, and molecular weights of ethyl mercaptan and propane.

Odorant fade in LPG has also been documented when there is un-treated masonry, such as poured concrete of cement blocks, in an area. While the masonry can adsorb both propane and ethyl mercaptan, the masonry surface preferentially adsorbs the odorant molecules faster. Thus, a basement filled with odorized LPG may lose odorant faster than propane to adsorption by the masonry. This could cause the odorant smell to fade given enough time.

Thus, a gas leak in an unfinished concrete or cement block basement may be harder to smell than the same size leak in the same basement where the walls and floor have been painted or sealed.

Odorant fade has also been noted to occur in new LPG tanks. In a never-before-used LPG tank made of alloy steel, the odorant appears to be adsorbed by the interior surface of the tank, which then reduces the concentration in the liquid and gaseous LPG in equilibrium with each other. With subsequent fillings, however, the interior surface apparently becomes saturated and the odorant fade effects become insignificant. After four or five fillings, the fade effect is generally not noticeable. Rust and scale on the interior surface appear to increase the fade effect.

In using cylinders for sampling gaseous LPG, it has been found that odorant fade occurs in cylinders made of plain steel, aluminum, polytetrafluoroethylene (Teflon™-like plastic), polyethylene-terephthalate (plastic), stainless steel, ceramic coated stainless steel, untreated glass, and silanized glass. However, of the materials noted, silanized glass and stainless steel, especially type 316, caused the least amount of fade. This was followed closely by aluminum. If the storage time is short, say less than 40 hours, the amount of fade may be insignificant with respect to the concentrations under consideration. As the amount of storage time increases, the fade effect generally increases.

Pressure levels were also noted to have an effect on the amount of fade. Silanized glass appeared to cause the least amount of fade at low pressures, about 15 psig, while stainless steel appeared to cause the least fade at higher pressures, about 100 psig.

It has also been noted that when natural gas or LPG diffuses through loose soil, sand or clay, especially zeolite type clays, some or even all of the odorant may be stripped out of the gas. Thus, it is possible for a gas leak underground to be stripped of its odorant.

This effect may be especially important when buried gas pipes underlie or pass close to buildings. If a leak occurs near or under the building, the odorant could be stripped away as the gas diffuses through the soil, perhaps allowing unodorized gas to diffuse into the building.

One reason why ANSI/ASME B31.8, section 871.3 requires that natural gas odorant not have a solubility of more than 2½ parts of odorant to 100 parts of water by weight is to preclude the odorant from being wholly absorbed by low-lying water pockets in the gas lines. These small water pockets often form when pipes from a warm area pass into a cold area and the moisture in the gas condenses.

I. Value of Odorants in Diagnosing Leaks that Cause Explosions or Fires

If a leak has been present for a time and the escaping odorized gas has impinged upon nearby materials or diffused through them, often some of the odorant will have become trapped in or on the material. This causes the material to stink like the odorant, even when the source of the leakage has been stopped or removed for some time. This is analogous to a used sweat sock or t-shirt. Long after the sweaty, stinky body part has been removed from the item, and long after the item has dried out, the lingering odor tells the beholder that it was once worn by someone who had exercised hard.

This is a very handy property in the diagnosis of fires or explosions caused by gas leakage, because the point of gas leakage may be pinpointed by the presence of odorant smell in an adjacent item or material that normally should not have any odorant smell.

For example, suppose that a gas line ran under the wood floor of a ranch style house with a basement. Suppose further that along the pipe was a pipe joint that had leaked natural gas for some time. Given enough time and appropriate conditions, the gas could have collected in the trough created by the floor joists and floor decking, filled it from the top to the lower edge (because natural gas is naturally buoyant in air) and perhaps diffused downward, eventually contacting a hot light bulb and exploding.

Of course the explosion itself would suggest that the cause was associated with a gas leak. However, it might be important to know the specific location of the leak. One way, of course, to check for leaks would be to re-pressurize the lines with compressed air. However, if the force of the explosion was sufficiently severe, it might have caused several new leaks to occur in the line. Thus, the leak test alone might not be sufficient to establish the specific location of the leak.

If the leak had been operating long enough for the wood fibers in the neighborhood of the leak to adsorb odorant, the point of leakage may be found simply by smelling along the length of the pipe, especially at the leak points found by the compressed air test. Generally, the specific point of leakage that was related to the explosion will smell of odorant.

Sometimes when the leak has been severe, the odorant will leave a trail from the point of leakage to the point of ignition. For example, in one particular building explosion case, the point of leakage was a natural gas pipe in the street not far from the building. The pipe corroded and leaked, allowing the natural gas to escape and percolate through a horizontal layer of sand used to bed the gas piping in the trench. The natural gas followed the pipe for several feet, until the pipe made a 90° turn and became a riser which surfaced immediately adjacent to the air intake of the building. The air intake had apparently sucked the errant natural gas into the building, where it eventually collected and exploded.

Upon checking for sources of natural gas leakage in the building, no leaks were found in the building's pipework. However, gas odor was noted around the riser on the outside of the building. When the pipe was dug up, the smell of odorant in the sand led right back to the point of leakage created by the corrosion.

Subsequent chemical testing using gas chromatography confirmed that the odorant in the sand was the same mixture of mercaptans as that used in the natural gas. This was done to eliminate any "sewer gas" odor arguments that might have been deposited. Sewer gas can contain dihydrogen sulfide, H_2S, which can smell like a mercaptan odorant. As in any city, there were sewer pipes located in the same general area under the street. As a further comparative test, along a similar section of pipe which was known to have not leaked, no odorant in the bedding sand was found using similar smell and chemical testing.

Besides sand, odorants will often leave a trail of smell through materials like insulation, wood chips, dirt, fabric, masonry, wood, and other porous or fibrous materials.

When the source of the gas leak has been removed or the leak has stopped, the smell of odorant in the adjacent materials may fade with time and exposure to fresh air. Thus, it is important to check for such pockets of odorant smell as soon as possible after a fire or explosion.

It also happens that such pockets of residual odorant smell can be destroyed or lost in the ensuing fire, or in the overhaul after the fire. Water from a fire hose may wash it away. The materials containing the residual odorant smell may be part of the fall down which is shoveled out. Nearby materials damaged in the fire may have created masking odors. Thus, there can be a lot of reasons why residual odorant pockets can go undetected after a fire, even if they have survived the fire itself.

J. Leak Detection

Having just spent several pages talking about odorants, I would be remiss if I did not note that one of the simpler ways to detect leaks is by smell. However, smells can sometimes be confused. While our sniffers are reasonably sensitive, they are often not discriminating. The smell of chicken droppings, cat box vapors, decayed grain, gasoline, and similar are sometimes confused with natural gas or LPG odorants.

A simple and sensitive method for finding leaks in piping where the gas is still operating is a bubble test. In this test, a soap solution capable of making bubbles is sprayed or dabbed on joints along the pipe. Where there is a leak, the soap solution will form bubbles filled with the escaping gas.

It is usually convenient to use an empty Windex™ spray bottle for this purpose, or perhaps an empty dishwashing liquid squeeze bottle. Persons whose childhood experiences include making soap solutions for bubble pipes will have no difficulty in mixing up a satisfactory soap solution. For those whose childhood was deprived of this experience, I recommend that a small bottle of soap solution for bubble blowing be purchased from the local toy store. It works very well, is cheap, and will save the embarrassment of having to admit to colleagues that you don't know how to blow bubbles.

If needed, the volumetric leak rate can be estimated with a stop watch and a small ruler or scale. As the bubble grows, its diameter can be measured. Assuming that the bubble is a sphere, and knowing the time it takes to reach the measured diameter allows an estimate of the leak rate to be made.

(iv) $Q = (1/6)(\pi)(D^3)/t$

where Q =   leak rate, volume per time,
      D =   diameter of bubble at time t, and
      t =   lapsed time to form bubble of diameter D.

When available, a video camera is very useful in recording bubble growth in real time, so that time-versus-diameter measurements can be made at leisure. This is a real advantage when the piping being checked runs through the crawl space of a house. Of course, it is still necessary to provide a scale on the video tape against which the bubble diameter can be measured.

A traditional way in which "yard lines," the small gas pipes which run from the main gas line to a residence, or other buried gas pipes are checked for leaks is by "walking the lines." A person simply walks along where the pipe is buried and notes the vegetation from time to time. Where gas is leaking from a pipe, the surface vegetation will often die, become stunted, or turn yellowish. Usually, the affected vegetation will follow closely the strike of the buried pipe. When the buried pipe has no dip, the point of leakage will usually be near the center of where the vegetation has been the most affected.

This is because when there is no significant dip or slope to a buried pipe, gas emanating from a leak will normally flow horizontally in either direction along the pipe, and then will diffuse upward. This is due to several reasons. The pipe is often bedded in sand or loose fill dirt; this provides a very porous pathway for the gas as compared to the undisturbed soil located outside the trench which had been dug to bury the pipe in. Also, over time the pipe will often move slightly in the dirt because of expansion, contraction, vibrations, pressure variations, or soil settlement. This may hollow out a small space between the sides of the pipe and the surrounding dirt or sand. The resulting eccentric annulus of empty space around the pipe provides an easy path through which gas can flow.

If the buried pipe does have a significant dip, it is often the case that the gas will flow upward to the first point where the dip is zero, or near zero, and will then diffuse upward at that location. Thus, if the pipe has significant dip, the "dead" spot in the grass may be an elbow joint where the pipework with a dip connects into a horizontal run of pipework.

The advantage of "walking the lines" is that it only costs time and labor. It is simple to do, and nearly anyone can be trained to do it in a short time. The disadvantages include:

- It does not work well in non-growing seasons, when the ground is snow covered, or in city areas where there is little vegetation for comparison.

- There can be a significant time delay between when the leak initiates, and when the vegetation begins to show signs of stress.

- It may not show small leaks. The gas may be too little to cause stress in the plants, especially if there are other types of stress around.

- It may fail to show leaks when there is an unusual soil pattern where the pipe has been buried such that the gas preferentially diffuses to an offset location. For example, a leaking gas pipe buried close to an old fashioned brick-lined storm sewer duct may be close enough to the sewer line that the gas may flow into it rather than diffuse upward. Or, in the case of a leaking gas pipe under an asphalt street, the gas may diffuse upward and collect under the asphalt cap, which acts as a barrier. The gas may then follow the slope of the street and come out at the first opening or crack, which may be located some distance from the actual leak.

- Other types of plant stress can be mistaken for gas leakage. Some types of plant stress may even follow the buried line. For example, when a sewage pipe that runs parallel with the gas line leaks, it may cause plant stress to occur along the same strike as the gas line. For cost reasons, sometimes contractors will dig one trench to a residence into which all the buried pipework will be laid.

A common method used for leak detection is "sniffers" or combustible gas detectors. These devices detect combustible gas vapors, and are not only useful in locating gas leaks, but can also be useful in finding accelerant vapors from petroleum distillates.

The devices come in a variety of forms. Some have internal electric pumps that suck up and sample gas at the end of a probe, and conduct the gas into the test chamber of the instrument. Other types rely upon manually operated pumps or squeeze bulbs to sample the air. Most of them work by igniting the sample of air containing the combustible gases, and then sensing the heat, light, or degree of ionization generated by the combustion. The output may be a meter indicator, a digital readout, or an audible signal. In the latter case, the signal beeps more frequently when the concentration is high.

Often, aerosol cans of premixed combustible gases can be purchased so that the various "sniffers" can be calibrated for a particular gas.

Sniffers can be used in many different ways. For example, they can track down leaks along pipework. By trial and error sampling at many locations, the trail of a leak can be followed by its increase in concentration back to its source. They can be used for surface gas detection surveys, especially in conjunction with walking the lines. Sometimes the sniffer can detect gas at the surface over buried lines before the vegetation has had time to react. However, they lose their usefulness for surface surveys when it is windy, the ground is covered with ice, or there is excessive soil moisture.

With the use of drilling equipment, sniffers can also be used for subsurface surveys. Sometimes these are called bar hole surveys. A hole is drilled down into a pipe bed trench or some other subsurface space suspected of containing gas and some time is allowed for any subsurface gas to diffuse into the hole. Air from the hole is then sampled for combustibles. Usually, the sniffer will have a bar attachment at the end for this purpose, which is basically a long hose or pipe extension to the sniffer so that only air from the hole is sampled.

The main disadvantage of sniffers is that they are usually indiscriminate with respect to the type of combustible gas detected. While most are calibrated for methane, they will also respond in varying sensitivities to most flammable gases, sometimes including ammonia. I have observed gas utility personnel think they have located a subsurface gas leak, to only find upon digging that they had located a buried cache of decaying cat dung. They also respond in varying degrees to fine, airborne carbon particulants, or fine grain dust.

Further, it is also possible to "poison" some types of sniffers with heavy metals. For example, tetraethyl lead in older types of gasoline can coat the catalyst, usually platinum, within the test chamber. Thus, after exposure to vapors containing heavy metals, the sniffer sensitivity can be significantly reduced. Some of these problems can be mitigated by the use of pre-sampling filters at the bar end. Such filters may keep out some of the particulants, dust particles, or heavy metal particles.

Pressurized escaping gas usually produces a sound. Most of us have heard the hissing noise associated with escaping air from an air hose or similar. Sound is also produced in the ultrasound range, that is in the spectrum above human hearing. The top end of human hearing is usually given as 20,000 Hertz. Using this basic principle, above-ground pipes can often be checked for leaks using ultrasound detectors. As a rule, as the magnitude of the gas pressure increases, the ultrasound energy generated by the leak increases also.

The effectiveness of this method depends upon the quietness of the piping, and the amount of attenuation of ultrasound by piping components. For example, a broad spectrum of white noise created by machinery directly or indirectly connected to the pipework can mask the ultrasound signal from a leak. Pitot tubes, venturis, or small valves partially open can also produce ultrasound similar to that of a leak. In fact, having several simultaneous leaks may create sufficient background noise to make detection work difficult.

Some piping systems contain components that may damp out the ultrasound created by the leak. Other piping systems may "ring" or "reflect" so that a single leak appears to come from several directions. A combination of damping, ringing and reflection in the pipework can cause the operator to be misdirected as to the location of the leak, unless a thorough survey of the pipework is done.

Generally, it is required that when the point of leakage is determined using ultrasound, a second method is used as confirmation.

A "shut in test" is where a section of pipe is isolated from the system and is pressurized with air or a purgative gas such as nitrogen. The pressurized pipe section is then checked periodically for pressure loss.

Usually, the pressure used for the test is no less than what the pipework would normally carry; often it is higher. Usually, the same basic test parameters for pressure and lapsed time used to certify newly installed pipework are used to test the shut in section for leaks. If there is a pressure drop indicating leakage, the rate of drop per lapsed time can be used to establish the size of the leak(s) from basic gas law considerations.

For example, suppose that pipe of length L with an inside diameter of D were shut in at both ends, and pressurized with air to pressure P_2. The section of pipe is then allowed sufficient time to come to equilibrium with the ambient conditions.

The volume of the section of pipe is:

(v) $V = \pi(D^2/4)L.$

At pressure P_2 the amount of gas, in mass units, in the shut in section of pipe would be:

(vi) $m_2 = (P_2 V)/(RT) = (P_2)\pi(D^2/4)L/(RT)$

which is just a simple application of the ideal gas law, where R is the gas constant for air (or whichever purgative gas is used), and T is temperature.

After a certain time t has elapsed, the pressure drops to P_1. Thus the mass in the shut in section of pipe lost by leakage during this period is determined as follows:

(vii) $m_2 - m_1 = (P_2 - P_1)V/(RT)$

The above assumes that the temperature within the pipe section has not changed significantly during the time leakage has occurred, and that the amount leaked is small with respect to the volume within the pipe so that equilibrium of the gas inside the pipe is maintained with the ambient, in essence, an isothermal process.

The leak mass flow rate is then as follows:

(viii) $(m_2 - m_1)/t = (P_2 - P_1)V/(RT)t = [(P_2 - P_1)\pi(D^2/4)L]/[(RT)t]$

If it is necessary to convert this mass flow leak rate to a volumetric leak flow rate at standard conditions, the ideal gas law can then be reapplied for standard conditions.

(ix) $[(m_2 - m_1)/t]RT_s /P_s = Q$

where Q = volume of gas leakage at standard conditions per time, and the subscript s denotes standard conditions.

By taking the limit of equation (viii), it is seen that the following holds:

(x) $dm/dt = [\pi(D^2/4)L / (RT)][dP/dt]$.

By substitution, the following is obtained:

(xi) $Q = [dm/dt] RT_s / P_s$

$Q = [\pi(D^2/4)L(Ts)/P_s(T)][dP/dt]$.

The size of the hole(s) causing the leak can then be estimated by applying the continuity equation:

(xii) $[dm/dt] = Av\rho$

where A = area of hole,

   v = velocity of gas escaping through hole, and

   ρ = P/RT or density of gas at the hole, which in this case would correspond to the conditions within the pipe section.

Now, the velocity of escaping gas at the hole is derived from Bernoulli's Flow Energy Equation for a compressible gas:

(xiii) $v = C [2J(h_2 - h_1)]^{1/2}$

where h_2 and h_1 are the enthalpies of the gas respectively inside the pipe, and then outside the pipe,

  J = enthalpy conversion factor to convert thermal units to work, and

  C = orifice factor, usually taken to be 0.98.

By substitution then, the area of the leak hole can be estimated from the following:

(xiv) $A = [dm/dt] [1/v][RT/P_2]$

  $A = [\pi(D^2/4)L/(RT)][dP/dt][RT/P_2]/C[2J(h_2 - h_1)]^{1/2}$

  $A = [\pi(D^2/4)L][dP/dt]/P_2 \, C[2J(h_2 - h_1)]^{1/2}.$

The above estimation for the leak size can be useful in deciding to which classification the leak belongs (see next section).

It is useful if a pressure reading just above the normal working pressure is taken, and another just below the normal working pressure. This supplies the "$P_2 - P_1$" which can be used to determine the specific mass or volumetric leak flow rate between those two pressures, i.e., at the working pressure. This can be important in establishing whether or not this particular leak could have caused the fire or explosion, given the resulting damage and the amount of time involved.

Shut-in tests are most effective for testing buried pipework, or for testing large, complex systems of pipework. If there are no leaks, a single shut-in test can provide a clean bill of health to pipework that would otherwise be expensive to dig up, or labor-intensive to check using bubble testing or a combustible gas detector. The main disadvantage is that a shut in test does not by itself specifically locate the leak; it just indicates whether leaks are present and is specific about the leak rate. Shut in testing also requires ancillary equipment and preparation.

After a fire or explosion, a shut in test can be very useful if it verifies that there are no leaks in a specific section of pipework. If no leaks are found after a fire or explosion, it can be concluded there were none prior to the fire or explosion. However, if a shut in test does indicate that there are leaks, it cannot be concluded that the leaks were present prior to the fire. Especially in an explosion, it is possible that the movement of the building during or after the accident event caused leaks in the pipework. In such cases, it will be necessary to examine the specific leak sites to determine from other evidence whether the leaks occurred before or after the accident event.

In concluding this list of methods for detecting leaks, let me add one methodology which should **not** be used: *flame testing.* Some of the older plumbers and HVAC technicians, and some of the younger stupid ones, may use a small flame to check for gas leaks. The idea is that the flame will ignite any errant gas and cause a flame to flash back to the point of leakage. The point of leakage can then be spotted by the flame, or by the direction of the flash back along the pipe.

While this method can work, it is stupefyingly unsafe. First, if the technician comes across a bigger amount of leakage than expected, he may set off the explosion he was seeking to avert. Of course, during the post-explosion investigation, the position of the technician's body can be used to determine the approximate location of one point of the gas pocket boundary.

Secondly, often natural gas may burn nearly clear. It is possible by this method to accidentally ignite gas emanating from a leak point, and then not be able to find it. Given time, the flame may cause the leak hole in the pipe to get larger by melting, or it may cause a low-temperature soldered joint close by to come loose due to heat conduction through the pipe. If the flame is not discovered and put out, it may eventually cause a general conflagration. Of course, since there may be some time delay from when the technician was present in the facility to when the fire was discovered, the technician will claim it was not his fault.

The flame test reminds me of a certain WWII era animated cartoon. The cartoon character checked for dud bombs by periodically striking live bombs with a hammer. Those which did not explode were labeled duds. I think checking for leaking gas with an open flame is not much different from the premise of that cartoon.

K. Leak Classification

ANSI/ASME B31.8, Appendix M, establishes a classification system in which flammable gas leaks are classified. The classes are as follows:

- Grade 1: This is a leak that is an existing or a probable hazard to persons or property. A grade 1 leak requires immediate repair or preventive measures until it is no longer hazardous.

- Grade 2: This is a leak that is currently nonhazardous, but could develop into a hazardous condition given time. A grade 2 leak requires scheduled maintenance prior to the leak becoming hazard-ous.

- Grade 3: This is a leak that is nonhazardous, and can reasonably be expected to remain nonhazardous.

Some grade 1 leak examples are given below:

- Escaping gas that has been ignited.
- Gas which has migrated into or under a building.
- Any combustible gas concentration measurement which shows flammable gas at 80% of its lower flammability limit in a confined area.

Some grade 2 leak examples are given below:

- A combustible gas concentration measurement which shows flammable gas at 40% or more of its lower flammability limit under a sidewalk in a wall-to-wall paved area.
- A combustible gas concentration measurement which shows flammable gas at 80% or more of its lower flammability limit in gas associated substructures.
- Any combustible gas concentration measurement which shows flammable gas at 20%–80% of its lower flammability limit in a confined area.

Some grade 3 examples are given below:

- Any combustible gas concentration measurement which shows flammable gas reading of less than 20% in a confined area.
- Any reading under a street or sidewalk in areas without wall-to-wall paving where it is unlikely that gas could migrate into a building.

Of course, not all leaks found in pipework can automatically be associated with the cause of the fire or explosion being investigated. Some leaks may simply be coincidental. It is therefore important to determine if any leaks found during an investigation are grade 1 leaks or not. By definition, it would take a grade 1 leak to cause a fire or explosion.

Consider the following. An arsonist sets fire to his house using the tried and true method of pouring gasoline on the floor. During the course of the post-fire investigation, it is found that the LPG system has a number of leaks in its pipework. The attorney for the arsonist uses this information to posit that the fire was caused not by his client, but by a leak in the LPG system. He may even perhaps file suit against the local LPG distributor.

The important point in this scenario is that the attorney for the arsonist now has some facts he can show to a jury to give credence to his theory of how the fire started, i.e., the fire was accidental and was caused by the LPG system. At the minimum, the attorney can use this information to confuse the jury. It is important to remember that the defendant does not have to prove exactly what *did* occur to be found innocent; all he has to do is show that there is significant doubt as to what occurred.

Thus it is very important, when such leaks are found, to investigate whether or not the leaks were caused during or after the fire, as opposed to having been there prior to the fire. If the leaks were present before the fire, it is important to establish which grade of leak they were.

*"To the trained eye there is as much difference
between the black ash of a Trichinoply and the white fluff
of bird's eye as there is between a cabbage and a potato."*

Sherlock Holmes, *The Sign of the Four*

Chapter 4: Determining the Point of Origin of a Fire

A. General

As noted in Chapter 2, fire is a type of chemical reaction. It is a rapid, self-sustaining oxidation reaction where heat, light and by-products are produced. While it may seem trivial to repeat, in order for fire to take place there must be three things present:

- combustible fuel in sufficient quantity,
- sufficient air or an oxidizing agent to react with the fuel, and
- an energy source, agent or action sufficient to facilitate ignition.

These are the fundamental principles for determining the point of origin of a fire. The point of origin must be where all three components necessary to initiate fire were present at the same time and place when the fire began.

Admittedly, some types of fires can be self-starting in terms of activation energy. Simply bringing certain materials into contact with one another, like air and white phosphorus at 30°C, can initiate burning. In such cases, the fire is not started by a spark or flame, but by some type of action which allows the reactants to come into physical contact with each other.

There are also materials that can self-ignite when a third chemical or agent is added to the first two, which are already in contact with one another. The third chemical, or catalyst, does not react with either of the other two chemicals to itself initiate burning; it does, however, react with them in a way that lowers the activation energy threshold between the two. Because of this, the oxidation-reduction reaction between the two materials can start at a lower temperature, or with significantly less initial energy input than otherwise. Thus, two chemicals that would not ordinarily self-ignite with one another can self-ignite if a certain catalyst or agent is added to the mix.

However, returning to the basic point, there is ample oxygen in the air to support combustion nearly everywhere where there are buildings and people. Thus having enough oxygen to support burning is usually not a problem, except perhaps in vaults, vacuum chambers, or other unusual airtight structures.

Similarly, most buildings, homes and manufacturing facilities contain ample amounts of combustible materials. At one time, it was popular to advertise that a warehouse or hotel was "fire proof." This claim was made because the building itself was made of masonry, steel, and other noncombustible materials. However, these buildings still contained large amounts of furniture, clothing, decorations, papers, boxes, and other materials which themselves could burn.

Of course, just because a material does not burn does not mean it is "fire proof." Masonry and steel are both adversely affected by fire. It is amazing how many of the so-called "fire proof" hotels and warehouses have burned down over the years. For this reason, the designation "fire proof building" is no longer used.

Thus, two of the three components necessary for a fire to occur are typically already present in most places, and they have likely been present for a long time without fire occurring. Consequently, the key to solving the point of origin of a fire and its causation often revolves around determining the nature of the third component necessary for fire: the ignition energy.

B. Burning Velocities and "V" Patterns

From casual observation it is apparent that fire propagates at different rates depending on the material and its orientation. With respect to orientation, for example, it is common knowledge to anyone who has used matches that a fire burns *up* a match faster than it burns *down* a match. It is also common knowledge that when a match is held horizontally, its burn rate is somewhere in between.

Consider the following simple experiment. A common wooden kitchen match is about 50 mm long, excluding the match head, and about 2.5 mm × 2.5 mm square in cross section. If timing is begun after the match head has ignited and the wood stem begins to burn, it takes about 30 seconds for the match to burn to the end when held horizontally. Similarly, it takes 6 seconds for the match to burn to the end when held vertically with the ignited end at the bottom. When the ignited end is held at the top, in most cases the match goes out after fire travels 15 mm downward from the head in an average lapsed time of 35 seconds.

Using parametric equations, the above information can be expressed as follows.

(i) $z = (50 \text{ mm}/6 \text{ sec})t = (8.67 \text{ mm/sec})t$

$x = (50 \text{ mm}/30 \text{ sec})t = (1.67 \text{ mm/sec})t$

$$z_d = (15 \text{ mm}/35 \text{ sec})t = (0.43 \text{ mm/sec})t$$

where z = fire travel distance in upward vertical direction,
 x = fire travel distance in horizontal position, and
 z_d = fire travel distance in downward vertical direction.

Figure 4.1 Downward fire spread pattern from ceiling.
No obvious "V" pattern is visible.

Inspection of the above three equations for fire velocity on a wooden match finds that:

- burn velocity is about five times greater upwards than laterally,
- burn velocity is about four times faster laterally than downward, and
- burn velocity is about twenty times faster upward than downward.

Because of the above, when fire is allowed to burn on a vertical wall surface, it will generate a "V"–shaped burn pattern; this is because as the fire burns upward, it will at the same time also spread laterally, but at a slower rate. If the lateral burn rate were equal to the upward burn rate, the angle of the "V" with the vertical would be 45°, and the angle at the notch of the "V" would be a right angle, 90°. For this reason, upward moving fires have a "V" angle of 90° or less. Due to convection processes, lateral burn rates do not equal or exceed upward burn rates. If the "V" angle is more than 90°, the fire was not upward burning.

Consider what happens if the fire is downward burning instead. Let us suppose that a fire begins somewhere in the ceiling, and then spreads downward along a vertical wall. The initial point of burn on that wall begins at the top of the wall, in the middle.

Because the burn rate is several times faster laterally than downward, the shape of the downward burn pattern is an oblique angle, and not an acute angled "V." For example, using the previous numbers for burn rates in thin wooden match sticks, the lateral burn rate is about four times faster than the downward burn rate. This would cause the fire to spread laterally 4 length units to the left, and 4 length units to the right, as it descended one length unit downward. This is an angle of 76° with the vertical, and would create a "V" with an angle of about 152° at the notch of the "V."

Thus, downward burning fires do not create "V" patterns with an acute angle; they create burn patterns that have oblique angles at the notch of the "V."

By measuring the angle of the "V" burn pattern, the ratio of the upward burning rate to the lateral burning rate can be determined. For example, if the angle at the notch of the "V" were 45°, the angle with the vertical would be 22.5°. The tangent of 22.5° is 0.414. Thus, the average burn rate in the lateral direction would be 41% that of the burn rate in the upward direction, or the upward burn rate is 2.4 times the lateral burn rate.

Because there will also be some downward burning, the actual point where the fire began is not always located exactly at the notch of the "V." It will often be located slightly above the lowest burned area of the "V" pattern.

For example, using the fire velocity numbers noted previously for the dry, thin wood used in matches, if there were a vertical wall made of the same material and a fire were begun at some point on that wall and allowed to burn for 5 seconds, the resulting burn pattern would appear something like that depicted in the following figure.

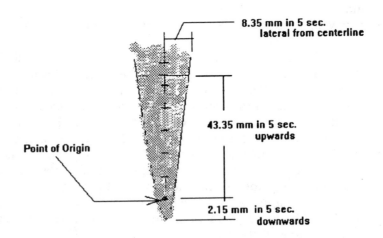

Figure 4.2 Typical "V" burn pattern on thin, dry wood veneer in vertical position.

In this case, the ratio of upward to lateral fire velocity is 5.2 to 1. This creates an angle of 11° with the vertical, or an angle at the "V" notch of 22°. Because there was some downward burning, the actual point of origin of the burn is located 2.15 mm above the lowest point of the "V."

Of course, the specific flame velocity parameters will change from material to material. However, the general principle is the same: fire propagation upward is significantly faster than lateral propagation, and lateral propagation is significantly faster than downward propagation. It is not unusual in some materials for upward burn rates to be as much as 20 times faster than lateral burn, or upward burn rates to be as much as 50 times that of downward burn rates.

It is for these reasons that fire investigators often look for the lowest point of significant burn damage, often called the *low point*, and observe whether fire damage appears to fan out laterally and upward from that point. Sometimes the point of origin of the fire is located at the low point.

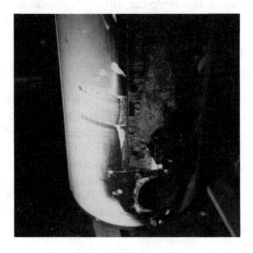

Figure 4.3 Any question about this "V" burn pattern?

C. Burning Velocities and Flame Velocities

There is an important exception to the previous discussion of "V" patterns, and that exception involves the use of liquid accelerants. When a liquid accelerant, especially one whose flash point is below room temperature, is splashed on a wall and ignited, the fire travels quickly throughout the contiguous area wetted by the accelerant: downward, upward and laterally. With respect to burn within the wetted area, the directional fire velocities are nearly the same for all practical purposes.

This is because the fire actually spreads by deflagration of the flammable vapors clinging close to the liquid layer of the accelerant. This is why, when the vapors of a flammable liquid accelerant are ignited, they often catch fire with a sudden "whoosh" or "whomp" sound as the flame front quickly spreads in an explosion-like way. Unconfined vapor "explosions" of this type are often called "puffers."

As vapors are given off by the liquid accelerant and mix with the available air, there will be five basic zones of flammability close to the surface of the wetted area:

1. The outermost zone is where the vapors are too thin or diffuse to support combustion. No combustion occurs here even though some flammable vapors are present.

2. The next zone, closer in, is where the vapor concentration is more than the lower limit fuel-to-air ratio necessary for combustion to occur, but is less than stoichiometric conditions.

3. The third zone is where the air-to-fuel ratio is at stoichiometric conditions, and combustion effects are maximum. This is not a continuous line or boundary, but usually is a thin, unstable region subject to the ambiguities of diffusion and convective turbulence between the air and the fuel vapors.

4. The fourth zone is where the fuel-to-air ratio is more than stoichiometric conditions, but not so high as to "choke off" combustion by exceeding the maximum limit of flammability.

5. The fifth zone, which is right up next to the wetted surface, is where the fuel to air ratio is too high for combustion to occur. It is for this reason that in a pool of highly volatile flammable liquid, sometimes the flames seem to burn slightly above the surface of the pool.

Of course, once the vapors are ignited, the heat released during combustion causes the gases to expand and push away from a vertical wall which then expands the zones. The gases first move outward into the room, and then also upwards due to convection effects. Thus, the burning vapors of a flammable liquid can extend well beyond the perimeter of the area wetted by the accelerant.

As noted before, the burning velocity of the thin wood used in match sticks is about 1.67 mm per second when the match stick is held horizontally. Under similar horizontal burning conditions, the maximum burning velocity of acetone is 425 mm per second. Similarly, methanol burns at 570 mm per second, and ethylene oxide at 890 mm per second. Respectively, the burning rates of these accelerants are 254, 341, and 533 times the burning rate of match wood.

Figure 4.4 Propane water heater. Note melted gas control valve and "V" pattern emanating from gas pipe hose inlet.

However, a simple comparison of burning velocities is not the whole story. The definition of "burning velocity" with respect to gaseous fuels is: the speed at which a laminar combustion front propagates through the flammable mixture relative to the unburned mixture. In essence, burn velocity is measured with the fuel itself as the reference point. Expansion or convection effects upon the gas mixture itself are ignored.

In other words, the "burning velocity" of a gaseous fuel does not take into account the fact that the whole gaseous mixture may be expanding or moving upwards, downwards or sideways relative to a stationary object, such as a wall.

When such expansion or convective effects are taken into consideration, the term used is *"flame speed."* Flame speed is the velocity at which the fire itself is seen to travel relative to stationary objects.

The fire or flame velocity associated with deflagration of the flammable liquid vapor are much faster than the burn velocity of the underlying solid fuel which has been wetted by the accelerant.

Figure 4.5 "V" burn pattern on hot-water heater emanating from gas control valve area.

This is to be expected since fire velocities are a function of several factors, including: the activation energy needed to initiate combustion; the amount and rate of heat given off during combustion; and the resulting expansion and convection of hot, burning gases away from the point of ignition. When the activation energy required for combustion ignition is low, when the heat of combustion per gram is relatively high, and the rate of combustion energy release is high, the flame velocity is correspondingly high.

In general, the flame speed is related to the burn velocity in the following way:

(ii) $V_f = V_b + V_g$

where V_f =   flame speed,
      V_b =   burn velocity, and
      V_g =   the velocity of the gas mixture itself relative to a stationary object.

If stoichiometric conditions are assumed, and it is also assumed that the flames are not turbulent, the maximum flame speed of most combustible gases is roughly eight times the burn velocity. The number eight comes from the fact that this is the average amount of expansion of a combustible gas when it burns in air at optimum conditions. (Most deflagration type explosions reach a maximum pressure of "8 × atmospheric pressure" at stoichiometric conditions.)

Thus, the vertical flame speeds of combustible gases can be as much as eight times their burning velocities. This would mean, for example, that the vertical burning rate of a wooden match of about 8.67 mm per second, would be nearly 392 times less than the vertical flame speed of acetone, which is about 3,400 mm per second at stoichiometric conditions.

Essentially, the accelerant burns so much faster than the wood or whatever, that the fire spreads throughout the wetted area before any of the underlying solid can significantly ignite and burn on its own. Thus the fire in the underlying solid seems to have begun basically all at once in the accelerant-wetted area. The entire wetted area appears to be the point of origin, which when a person thinks about it, is exactly true.

Once the underlying solid has begun to burn and the accelerant is largely consumed, the fire will once again follow the "normal" rules with respect to "V" patterns. This is one of the reasons why when a fire does not appear to follow the normal rules, it may be because of human intervention in those rules. This topic will again be discussed in Chapter 8, "Arson and Incendiary Fires," and especially in section H of that chapter.

D. Flame Spread Ratings of Materials

The relative burning rates of materials used in buildings are often given in certain building codes and specifications, especially with regard to interior finishes. This, of course, is done to prevent the use of materials that allow unusually rapid and deadly spread of fire into living areas. The terms used in connection with the relative burning rates of materials are *"flame spread rating"* or *"flame spread index."*

One of the more common tests used to determine the flame spread rating of a material is the *Steiner Tunnel Test.* The specific testing procedures for this test are contained in ASTM E84, *Standard Method of Test for Surface Burning Characteristics.* A sample of material 0.565 m wide by 7.32 m in length is burned and timed, and the time required to burn the material is correlated to a relative rating. Some common interior finish materials rated by this method are listed in Table 1.

As noted in Table 1, items that do not burn at all are given a 0 rating. Some items which ordinarily are not thought of as flammable, such as enameled metal surfaces, can surprisingly burn and propagate fire, albeit poorly compared to items like wood paneling.

Because it is not easy to obtain about 7.32 meters or 24 feet of continuous sample from a fire scene, an alternative type of test is often done with materials taken from fire scenes. ASTM E162, *"Standard Method of Test for Surface Flammability of Materials Using a Radiant Heat Source"* requires a piece of material only about 15 cm by 46 cm. ASTM E162 can be correlated loosely with the findings of ASTM E84; however, the fire investigator should be aware that the correlation is not exact. Since some building codes rely specifically on test results according to ASTM E84, there may be some legal problems if a proceeding depends precisely on whether a particular material meets the fire code flammability spread rating per ASTM E84.

For carpets and rugs there is a specific test, often called the *"pill test,"* used to determine their relative flammability. The pill test is more formally titled, *"Standard for the Surface Flammability of Carpets and Rugs, FF I-70,"* (Federal Register, Vol. 35, #74, page 6211, April 16, 1970). This test measures the ignitability of carpets and rugs from small ignition sources such as dropped cigarettes and matches. Sometimes a carpet material that passes the pill test can still contribute to fire spread because of general chemical decomposition due to exposure to large sources of heat. When this is suspected to have occurred, the carpet should be tested according to ASTM E648.

Table 1. Flame Spread Ratings as Per ASTM E84

material	rating
gypsum plaster in ceiling	0
enameled metal in ceiling	0–20
wood base ceiling tile with flame proofing	20–75
wood base ceiling tile without flame proofing	75–300
brick, concrete, or plaster walls	0
enameled metal walls	10–20
gypsum board	20–75
½-inch thick wood	70–200
cork sheets	100–250
untreated fiberboard	200–500
plywood paneling	70–300
shellac finish on paneling	>500
concrete floor	0
linoleum*	50–600

*In general, the use of the Steiner Tunnel Test is not recommended for floor coverings like carpet, linoleum and such. For floor coverage, ASTM E648 or NFPA 253, *"Standard Methods of Test for Critical Radiant Flux of Floor Covering System Using a Radiant Heat Source"* is generally used. (See Section F, Radiation, discussion of radiant heat flashovers.)

With respect to the structural elements of a building, the fire resistance or endurance of those materials is given in "hour" ratings in accordance with testing procedures contained in ASTM E119, *"Standard Methods of Fire Tests of Building Construction and Materials."* This procedure is also contained in NFPA 251.

In this test, structural materials or elements, such as a beam or column, are put into a special test furnace and the temperature of the materials on the protected side or space is plotted against lapsed time. The resulting curve is called the *"fire endurance standard time-temperature curve."* The test is continued until failure occurs. Failure would be one of the following:

- inability to carry rated load,
- cracking, bending or other significant dimensional failure in the material,

- loss of surface continuity such that flames or hot gases can pass through the material; it is easily pushed aside by a stream of water, or
- loss of insulation capacity such that the temperature on the other side rises to more than 250°F.

It has been found experimentally that a one-hour fire rating per ASTM E119 corresponds to a fire load of about 10 pounds of ordinary combustible materials (like wood) per square foot of floor space in a building, or about 80,000 BTU/sq.ft.

It is emphasized to the reader, however, that the hour fire rating of ASTM E119 is not to be considered how long a particular material or structural member will actually endure in a fire. A "2–hour" rated column will not necessarily endure two hours of an uncontrolled fire; it may endure much less than two hours, or perhaps more than two hours. The hour fire rating of ASTM E119 is simply an arbitrary rating system. To avoid the confusion it would have been well if the ASTM officials had used a different term. Unfortunately, the term has become ingrained in many building codes and legal descriptions, and is with us to stay.

While some materials such as wood and natural textiles are intrinsically flammable, often they can be chemically treated to reduce their flame spread rating. Cellulose and textile fibers, for example, can be treated with a boric acid solution to reduce their rate of burning. Wood is often treated by pressure impregnation with mineral salts to reduce burning rates.

When these treatments are done, the material is often labeled as being *fire resistant* or *fire retardant.* Sometimes fire treated materials can be substituted for all or a portion of gypsum board fire rated barriers when a certain hour fire rating is required by code. For example, in some jurisdictions the use of fire retardant treated wood trusses with a one-hour rated ceiling of gypsum board underneath might be substituted for a two-hour rated ceiling of gypsum board with untreated trusses.

However, when fire retardant chemicals are used, sometimes the basic properties of the material are altered. For example, when wood is treated with certain fire retardants, its structural strength may be significantly reduced, and this loss of strength must be considered and allowed for in the initial design. A simple substitution of fire retardant trusses or columns for untreated trusses or columns without proper design consideration could result in unacceptable structural weakness in a building. Thus, the use of such fire retardant treated materials should be a design decision by the responsible architect or engineer.

Due to the effects of some fire retardant chemicals on wood, there even may be geographic or ambient temperature limitations placed on the use of such treated wood. For example, wood trusses treated with one type of fire retardant might be restricted to areas where the average humidity is low, away from coastal areas, or where attic temperatures do not exceed 140°F.

Lastly, fire retardant chemicals can sometimes be lost from a material by exposure to water or solvents, by repeated washing, or by inadvertent exposure to other chemicals which may react with them. When this occurs, it is possible that the protection thought to be present by the use of fire retardant-treated materials has been lost.

With fire-treated wood, for example, high humidity and high ambient temperatures can leach out the impregnated mineral salts. With fire retardant treated clothing for children, repeated washing in hot water or in chlorine-containing bleaches can leach out or react with the fire retardant chemicals. This is why such clothing must carry tags to caution the owner against improper washing, and provides recommended washing instructions.

Figure 4.6 Fire was in the wall and traveled up the wall cavity, which acted as a chimney

E. A Little Heat Transfer Theory, Conduction and Convection

To more fully understand how fire propagates, it is first necessary to understand some basic principles of heat transfer. In general, heat can be transferred from one point to another by only three means: *conduction, convection,* and *radiation.* In any of the three modes there must be a temperature difference or gradient between the two points for heat transfer to occur. Heat will flow from the area or point where the temperature is higher to the area or point where the temperature is lower.

A useful analogy between heat flow and water flow can be made. Let temperature be analogous to elevation, and heat be analogous to water. In the same way that water will flow down the elevation gradients and collect in the low spots, heat flows down the temperature gradients and collects in the cool spots. Like elevation, temperature is a measure of potential. When there is no difference in potential, there is no flow of either water or heat.

Conduction occurs when heat is conducted through a material by diffusion of the thermal kinetic energy through the material. The equation which describes one dimensional conduction through a material is given in equation (iii) below.

(iii) $q = -kA[dT/dx]$

where q = rate of heat conduction (energy per time),
  k = thermal conductivity of the material (energy / time × distance × temp),
  A = area of the path perpendicular to the direction of heat flow, and
dT/dx = temperature gradient in the x direction, that is, the direction of heat flow.

From equation (iii), it is seen that:

- when the area A is increased, the heat transfer increases,
- when the thermal conductivity k increases, the heat transfer increases,
- when the temperature difference dT rises, the heat transfer increases, and
- when the thickness of the material dx decreases, the heat transfer increases.

In general, materials that have high electrical conductivity also have high thermal conductivity. Thus, materials like copper and aluminum which are excellent electrical conductors are also excellent thermal conductors. Similarly, materials like concrete or porcelain which are poor electrical conductors are also poor thermal conductors.

The second mode of heat transfer, convection, is actually a special type of conduction which takes place between a solid material and a moving fluid. As with regular conduction, in order for heat to be transferred, there must be a significant temperature difference between the solid material and the moving fluid. The fluid heats up or cools down as it passes over the surface of the solid material. By its motion, the fluid then transports the heat or cold to another point downstream. New fluid then replaces the old fluid which has moved on, and the process is repeated.

In natural or free convection, the fluid is set into motion by buoyancy effects. The density of nearly every fluid depends on its temperature.

When a small portion of the fluid is either heated or cooled, that small portion becomes either more buoyant or less buoyant with respect to the rest of the fluid. Buoyant forces then cause the fluid to move away from the surface, and the old portion of fluid is replaced by a new portion of fluid.

When a portion of fluid is passed over the surface of the solid material, flows away, and then is returned to the surface to repeat the process over and over, the repeating pattern is called a *circulation cell.* If the system is in equilibrium so that the temperatures at specific locations in the system stay about the same over time, stable convective fluid circulation patterns develop.

For example, consider an old-fashioned steam radiator in a closed room when it is cold outside. When the radiator is hot, the air that comes into contact with the radiator heats up and rises. As it rises to the ceiling, the air begins to cool. When it meets the ceiling, it moves laterally across the ceiling, spreads out, and cools some more. When it has sufficiently cooled, it gets heavy and begins to sink to the floor. As it sinks, it is drawn into the current of air flowing towards the radiator. The air then again contacts the radiator, and the process is repeated.

In *forced convection*, the natural convection effects are enhanced by fans or pumps which force the flow of fluid over the surface of the solid. In forced convection, usually the velocity of the fluid is such that free or natural convection effects are not a factor and are neglected. In other words, the velocity of the fluid, as set into motion by a fan or pump, is usually many times greater than the velocity of the fluid as set into motion by natural convection effects.

Since fire in a house or business structure generally spreads more by convection than the other two modes, sometimes an arsonist will turn on fans, blowers, or strategically open windows to deliberately set up strong drafts to help the spread of the fire. In essence, he is attempting to set up forced convection rather than depending on free convection. Forced convection will not only cause the fire to spread more rapidly, but can be used to direct the spread of the fire to specific areas in the building.

An important characteristic of free convection is that there is always a thin layer of fluid next to the surface of the solid surface which does not move. Essentially, this thin layer is "stuck" to the exterior surface of the solid. This thin layer is called the *boundary layer.* Heat from the solid surface is actually conducted through this thin boundary layer into the stream of moving fluid. In forced convection, however, this boundary layer is usually in a constant state of removal and replacement, especially when the flow is extremely turbulent.

The equation describing convection type heat transfer is

(iv) $q = hA \, (\Delta T)$

where q = rate of heat flow,
    A = area involved in heat transfer,
    ΔT = temperature difference between solid surface and fluid, and
    h = convection heat transfer coefficient.

The heat transfer coefficient h for forced convection is given by the following equation:

(v) $h[D/k] = K[Du\rho/\mu]^{\alpha}[C_p\mu/k]^{\beta}$

where D = dimension associated with the length of the heat transfer area; with pipes, it is diameter; with plates it is the length of contact across the flat surface,
    k = conductivity of fluid,
    K = an experimentally determined constant,
    ρ = density of fluid,
    u = velocity of fluid,
    C_p = heat capacity of fluid,
    μ = viscosity of fluid,
    α = experimentally determined exponential coefficient, and
    β = experimentally determined exponential coefficient.

It is noteworthy that the above equation has been arranged in groups of dimensionless parameters in the manner consistent with the Buckingham Pi Theorem for similitude modeling of fluid systems. For those readers who may be interested in simulating fires and fire damage by the use of laboratory models, knowledge of similitude and the Buckingham Pi Theorem is a must (see bibliography, *Similitude in Engineering*).

In fluid mechanics and heat transfer, each dimensionless parameter in equation (v) has its own name. This is because these same groupings of variables come up routinely in the mathematical description of fluid flow. The names of the parameters are noted below:

    $h[D/k)]$ Nusselt Number,
    $[Du\rho/\mu]$ Reynolds Number, and
    $[C_p\mu/k]$ Prandtl Number.

In like fashion, the heat transfer coefficient h for free or natural convection is given by the following equation:

(vi) $h[D/k] = K[D^3ga(\Delta T)/\mu^2]^{\alpha}[C_p\mu/k]^{\beta}$

where g   = gravity, and
       a   = density temperature coefficient.

As before, equation (vi) has been arranged in groups of dimensionless parameters. The new parameter, the one in the middle of the right term which replaced the Reynolds number in the forced convection equation, is called the *Grashof* or *free convection number*. Comparing equations (v) and (vi), only the middle parameter is different.

In general, the above equations can be reduced to the following typical relationships.

(vii) $q = C_1 A(\Delta T)u^{6/5}$ forced convection.

(viii) $q = C_2 A(\Delta T)^{5/4}$ free convection when the Reynolds number is less than 2,000 (laminar flow).

(ix) $q = C_3 A(\Delta T)^{4/3}$ free convection where the Reynolds number is more than 4,000 (turbulent flow).

where C_1, C_2, and C_3 are arbitrary constants determined by experiment, and A is the heat transfer area.

It is left up to the reader to solve for C_1, C_2, and C_3 in terms of the other variables listed in equations (v) and (vi).

Examination of equations (v), (vi), (vii), (viii), and (ix) finds the following general principles at work:

1. Increasing the temperature difference increases the heat transfer.

2. Increasing the heat transfer area increases the heat transfer.

3. Increasing the fluid flow in forced convection increases the heat transfer.

4. Increasing the turbulence in free convection increases heat transfer.

In most fires, convection effects are responsible for much of the fire spread. As the reader may have already surmised, the reason why the burning velocity up a wall is several times greater than down a wall is because the primary mechanism for upward fire travel is convection, while the primary mechanism for downward fire travel is conduction.

Since most walls are made of insulating materials, the conduction of heat through the wall material is poor. In fact, most of the common materials that burn in a fire like wood, paper, textiles, and such are poor conductors of heat. This is why downward fire travel is generally so slow, except when accelerants or similar faster burning materials are involved.

F. Radiation

The third mode of energy transfer, radiation, is where heat is transferred from one point to another by electromagnetic waves, typically in the wavelength range of 0.1 to 100 microns. No intermediate material is needed. In fact, when there are intermediary materials such as gases or suspended dust, the amount of heat transferred by radiation is decreased due to absorption of heat by the gas or dust.

In this method of heat transfer, the amount of energy radiated by a body into space is proportional to the fourth power of its surface temperature. The amount of heat or energy emitted this way is governed by the *Stefan-Boltzmann Law*, given in equation (x) below.

(x) $\qquad q = \sigma \varepsilon A T^4$

where q = the amount of heat or energy emitted,
$\quad \sigma$ = 5.67×10^{-8} watts / m^2 ($^\circ$K^4), the Stefan-Boltzmann constant,
$\quad A$ = area of the radiating surface,
$\quad T$ = surface temperature in absolute units, and
$\quad \varepsilon$ = emissivity, that is, the efficiency of the surface with respect to a black body or perfect radiator.

For perfect radiators or *black bodies,* the ε value equals one. This means that the radiating surface is 100% efficient in allowing the energy to be radiated from the surface. Alternatively, another definition of a black body is one which absorbs all the radiant energy which falls on it; it does not reflect away any radiation.

Absorptivity and emissivity are essentially the same thing; the only difference is the direction of the flow of radiation. *Emissivity* typically refers to radiation leaving the surface while *absorptivity* refers to radiation being received by the surface. Numerically, the two parameters are the same, which is known as *Kirchoff's Identity.* More formally, it is stated: the emissivity and absorptivity of a body are equal at the same temperature.

When radiation strikes a surface, there are only three things that can happen to it. It can be absorbed; it can be reflected away as occurs with a highly polished, mirror-type surface; or it can be transmitted through the material, as occurs with glass.

Table 2 lists some representative values for the absorptivity of some common materials at room temperature except where noted. The specific emissivity of a material does change with temperature.

Table 2. Absorptivities of Some Common Materials

material	absorptivity
water	0.96
rough red brick	0.93
concrete	0.63
aluminum foil	0.087
polished silver	0.02
hot tungsten filament, 6,000°F	0.40
lampblack	0.97
well rusted steel	0.95
enamel paint, any color	0.90
fire brick	0.70
molten steel	0.30
polished sheet steel	0.55
hard rubber	0.95
roofing paper	0.92
steam @ 540°F @ 1 atm, 1 ft thick	0.28

When two radiating bodies "see" one another, both will transfer energy to one another. Assuming no energy losses due to absorption of energy by air, water vapor, etc., the net energy exchange between the two bodies is given by the solution of the Stefan-Boltzmann equation for both radiating bodies:

(xi) $q_{net} = \sigma\varepsilon CA[T_1^4 - T_2^4]$

where C = factor which accounts for relative position and geometry of the two surfaces relative to one another,

A = area of the surface at which heat flow measurements are being made, and

ε = relative emissivity/absorptivity of the surface at which heat flow measurements are being made.

For example, consider a small electric heater which is used to provide "spot" warmth in a chilly room. The heater uses 1,500 watts. If we assume that the that the area of the heating coils is $0.01m^2$, that the emissivity is 0.55, and that the surface temperature of the resistance coils is about 1,000°K when operating, then the proportion of input energy converted to radiant energy can be estimated by the application of the Stefan-Boltzmann relationship.

$$q = \sigma \varepsilon T^4$$

$$q = [5.67 \times 10^{-8} \text{ watts/m}^2 \ (°K^4)][0.55][0.01 \text{m}^2][1,000°K]^4$$

$$q = 312 \text{ watts.}$$

Thus, 312 watts or $312/1,500 = 21\%$ of the energy input to the heater ends up as radiant heat. The rest of the energy is dissipated convectively.

Consider also the following example of radiant heat transfer from the ceiling of a room to its floor. Let's say that the whole ceiling is on fire, so that the flames form a deep, luminous layer across the ceiling. The ceiling is 7 m by 10 m, and the distance from the floor to the layer of flames is 2.25 m. Under these conditions, the factor C which accounts for geometry and position is equal to 0.7.

If the luminous flames are relatively hot and are burning at a temperature of about 1,350°K, and it is noted that the paper items on the floor which burn at a temperature of 550°K have been ignited, then the heat transfer from the ceiling to the floor is as follows:

$$q_{net} = \sigma \varepsilon CA[T_1^4 - T_2^4]$$

$$q_{net} = \ [5.67 \times 10^{-8} \text{ watts/m}^2 \ (°K^4)][0.65][0.70][70 \text{ m}^2][(1,350°K)4 - (550°K)^4]$$

$$q_{net} = 6,163,000 \text{ watts or}$$

$$q_{net}/A = 88,100 \text{ watts/m}^2.$$

Thus, in order for fire in the ceiling to "flash over" and cause items on the floor to ignite by radiant heat, it is necessary for the fire in the ceiling to be at 1,350° Kelvin, which is about 1,970°F, or almost as hot as is needed to melt copper, and the rate of radiant heat transfer to be 88,100 watts/m².

This is a heat rate roughly equivalent to burning 120 grams of liquid octane type gasoline per minute per square meter of ceiling and having all the released energy be in the form of radiant energy. Of course, in actuality, it would take five to twenty-five times as much fuel as this because only a small fraction of the released energy becomes radiant heat; most of the released energy will be soaked up by convection and conduction effects.

An interesting point to note with respect to radiation "flashovers" is that they often occur when there is a luminous fireball or layer of luminous flames in the ceiling rather than on the floor. In other words, flashovers more often occur when radiant heat transfer is going from the ceiling to the floor rather than vice versa. Why is this? A check of Table 1 provides the answer.

When most fires burn, the flue gases contain ample amounts of water vapor and unburned particles; these are mostly soot. Both of these materials are very good absorbers of radiant energy. Thus, when viewed from above, a hot, luminous fire on the floor is "cloaked" by its flue gases of water vapor and soot particles which soak up much of the radiant energy before it can reach the ceiling.

On the other hand, when the fire is located in the ceiling, the "butt" of the flames can poke through the cloud of flue gases. This is, of course, because the flames are actually hot expanding gases which are pushing away from the ceiling. When the expansion is exhausted, the fumes then simply turn and begin their convective rise back towards the ceiling.

When radiation leaves a hot, luminous object, unless it is guided, confined or otherwise directed in some fashion, it will lose intensity according to the inverse square law.

(xii) $I_1 / I_2 = r_2^2 / r_1^2$ or $I_1 r_1^2 = I_2 r_2^2 = K$

where I = radiant energy intensity in watts/m^2,
     r = distance from source of radiant energy,
     K = constant equal to the radiant energy output at the source.

Thus, if the radiant energy intensity measured at 1 meter from the source is 100 watts/m^2, then at 4 meters the radiant energy intensity is:

$[100 \text{ w/m}^2] / I_2 = 16 \text{ m}^2 / 1 \text{ m}^2$

$I_2 = 6.25 \text{ w/m}^2$ and $K = 100 \text{ w.}$

Luminous fire is actually a cloud of burning flammable particles. The temperature of a burning cloud and its emissivity can be measured at a distance by the use of an instrument called an *optical pyrometer.* In general, when temperatures are more than 600°C, pyrometers are used to measure the temperature.

The optical pyrometer works by comparing the color of the flames with that of a hot incandescent filament. The filament is viewed against the luminous cloud and the current through the filament is adjusted until the color of the filament matches the color of the cloud. The current through the filament is calibrated to correspond to the various temperatures of the filament.

In total radiation type pyrometers, the radiation is directly measured by a solar-cell type semiconductor. The amount of radiant heat falling on the semiconductor is converted to a current, and the current is calibrated to indicate the amount of incident radiation being absorbed and the temperature of the radiating body.

When steel is heated to a temperature of about 1,000°F, it begins to glow with a very dull red color. As the steel is heated further, the color shifts from red to orange, and then to yellow. Near the melting point at about 2,800°F, steel will radiate with a nearly whitish color. Thus, given the right circumstances, the temperature of some substances like steel can be estimated from their apparent, visible radiant color.

G. Initial Reconnoiter of the Fire Scene

In observing a fire scene for the first time, it is often best not to rush directly into the fire-damaged areas in search of the origin. Most fire investigators will first reconnoiter the fire scene to observe which areas did not burn.

This is important for two reasons: first and obvious is the fact that the areas which did not burn do not contain the point of origin. Often, knowing what was not burned by the fire allows the elimination of many theoretical point-of-origin possibilities. The second reason is to determine the extent of fire damage to the building and to examine it carefully for structural weakness before entering it; a crippled building can be a death trap for the unwary investigator.

This last point cannot be emphasized too much. *It is very prudent to first examine the fire-damaged structure before entering it to see where it has been structurally weakened, or is in danger of collapsing.* Then, if needed, the proper equipment can be secured to do the job safely. Generally, with a little thought and imagination, every building, no matter how damaged, can be safely examined without putting people's lives in jeopardy. No fire diagnosis is worth dying for.

As noted previously, many investigators will search for the "low point" of the fire. This may be evident by conspicuous two-dimensional V patterns on walls, or perhaps less recognizable three-dimensional V patterns (or cone patterns) in stacks of materials. As discussed, fire spreads generally more by convection than conduction. Thus the lowest point of burn in a building will often be the point of origin.

However, as noted in the previous section, when a flashover from radiant energy transfer occurs, it can produce a false low point. For example, if the ceiling were to fill up with hot, luminous flames sufficient to radiate heat downward onto the tops of furniture and rugs, fires could break out in those places.

Fortunately, radiant heat flashovers are usually easy to recognize. They have the following characteristics:

1. There will be a source point or area for the radiant heat. This will be an area which has sustained very hot fire usually over an extended area, like a ceiling or wall.

2. There will be several radiant heat "low point" areas of ignition, and they will be positioned so that they can "see" the source point or area for the radiant heat.

3. Other evidence indicates that these areas began burning well after other parts of the building or structure had already burned.

Other false low points can be caused by fall-down debris. *Fall down* is the general term used to indicate materials that have become displaced to new locations, generally to floor areas, because of fire damage.

For example, in a particularly severe fire, burning roof shingles might fall into the basement space because fire has consumed the supporting structures between the roof and basement. The burning shingles may ignite small, secondary fires in the basement, perhaps even causing obvious V patterns. These secondary burn patterns, even though they may technically be the lowest burn patterns in the structure, are not the point of origin of the fire; they are simply secondary points of fire origination caused by burning fall down debris. However, sometimes they can mistakenly be taken for the primary point of origin.

In general, such secondary points of origin can be distinguished from the primary point of origin by the following:

1. Since they occur later in the fire, the lateral spread from them is smaller and more limited. The fire spread from the secondary source may not even be contiguous with the main portion of the fire damage.

2. Sometimes the piece of fall down which caused the secondary fire is located nearby and is recognizable.

3. The fire at that point will have no other source of ignition except for the piece of fall down, which would not normally be associated with ignition. For example, it is not logical that timbers found in the attic could be the primary source of ignition for a fire which started in the basement.

4. The secondary fire pattern does not meet the conditions necessary for it to be the point of ignition: The point of origin must be where all three components necessary to initiate fire were present at the same time and place when the fire began.

H. Centroid Method

Imagine that a large piece of cardboard is held horizontally. Now imagine that some point in the plane of the cardboard near the center is ignited. The resulting fire will burn away from the initial point of ignition more or less equally in all directions in the plane. If the fire is extinguished before it reaches the edges of the cardboard, the fire will burn a circular hole in the cardboard. Of course, the center of the hole is the point of origin of that fire.

The above is an example of the underlying principle of the *centroid method* for determining the point of origin of a fire. This method is particularly useful in single-story structure fires, where the building is made of more or less the same materials and has the same type of construction throughout. This homogeneity of materials and construction means that lateral fire spread rates will be similar in all directions.

Basically, the method works as shown in the above example. The extent of burn damage in the structure is noted and perhaps even drawn to scale on a plan drawing; then the center of damage is determined. This can be done by "eyeball," for those with calibrated eyeballs, or by more sophisticated methods including graphic integration and mathematical analysis.

Graphic integration involves the use of a drafting instrument called a *planimeter*, along with a detailed scaled sketch of the fire-damaged areas. The sketch is done on a Cartesian x-y plane and a convenient point of origin is selected. The sketch of the fire-damaged area is then sectioned off into smaller areas. The planimeter is used to measure the plane area encompassed by fire damage in the various sections. The distances from the center of these smaller areas to the respective x and y grid origins are then measured.

The position of the fire damage centroid is calculated using the equations for determining the center coordinates for plane centroids, which are given below. The origin of the fire is then near or at the location of the centroid of the fire damaged area. The indefinite integral equations for determining the centroid are as follows:

(xiii)

$$X_c = \frac{\int (x)\,dA}{\int dA} \qquad Y_c = \frac{\int (y)\,dA}{\int dA}$$

where dA = differential of burned area,
      (x) = distance from y axis,
      (y) = distance form x axis,
      X_c = x coordinate of centroid, and
      y_c = y coordinate of centroid.

Since most fire burned areas are not regular and easily modeled by an integratable function, a plot of the burn pattern can be made over a grid system, and the areas can be determined by counting grid squares, or portions thereof. The integrals can be approximated by numerical evaluation as follows:

(xiv)

$$x_c = \frac{\sum x_i \, (\Delta A_i)}{\sum (\Delta A_i)} \qquad y_c = \frac{\sum y_i \, (\Delta A_i)}{\sum (\Delta A_i)}$$

where x_i = distance from y axis to area section,
y_i = distance from x axis to area section, and
ΔA_i = incremental area section.

Some discretion must be used in applying the centroid method to allow for fires that start near an "edge" or "corner." In the example using a piece of cardboard, the fire had plenty of material to burn in any direction of travel in the plane, and was put out before it reached an edge. Thus, the fire was able to move laterally away from the point of origin in all directions.

However, if the fire had begun at an edge or corner, it would have burned away from that point in a skewed symmetric fashion. The edge or corner would prevent the fire from burning further in that direction; the fire then could only burn in directions away from the edge or corner. For example, a fire that begins at an edge will burn away from that edge in a semi-circle pattern. A fire which begins in a corner burns away from the corner in a quarter-circle pattern. In short, the radial symmetry produced by a more or less equal fire travel rate in the lateral direction is affected when the fire must stop at a boundary for lack of fuel.

This shortcoming can be overcome by the use of mirror symmetry. For example, suppose that a fire began at the center of the east wall of a square shaped building, and was put out before it spread more than half-way to the west wall. The fire pattern in the building would then appear roughly half-moon shaped in the plan view. By placing a mirror alongside the east edge of the building plan, the burned area "reflects" to the mirror and a round burn pattern is observed. The centroid method is then applied to both portions: the "real" side and the "virtual" or mirror side. For a corner fire, two mirrors or two mathematical reflections are needed.

When a fire begins near a wall or corner, but not exactly at the wall or corner, the mirror symmetry technique described above has shortcomings. In such an instance, the virtual portion of the fire damage must be estimated. The virtual fire damage is that portion which would have burned if the building or material was infinitely continuous in the horizontal plane. In essence, the fire damage which would have occurred had the fire continued is estimated, and a centroid is determined taking into consideration both the actual and the virtual damage. See Figure 2 in following section J for an example of the virtual damages due to a fire.

I. Ignition Sources

When the centroid method has been completed, and the point or area of fire origination has been determined, that area must then be examined and inventoried for potential ignition energy sources. Such energy sources commonly include pilot lights, space heaters, electrical appliances, fluorescent light fixtures, fireplaces, chimneys, smoking materials, cooking equipment, lamps, electrical wiring and outlets, and so on.

Occasionally, the ignition of combustibles can be spontaneous, but this usually involves organic oils or materials that can readily undergo decomposition. It is commonly assumed that a pile of oily rags can catch on fire by itself; this is not true when the oil is a petroleum-based product. In fact, it is only true when the oil comes from an organic source, like linseed oil, tung oil, spike oil, and the like. These organic oils contain large amounts of organic acids which can react with air at room temperature. Motor oils and lubricants generally do not ignite spontaneously and are very stable.

As mentioned in Chapter 1, decaying fecal matter covered with straw and without ready access to air can spontaneously ignite. Also, wet hay or undried vegetative material can also spontaneously ignite when stored in bulk. However, spontaneous combustion is a multi-step process initially involving bacterial decay. It typically occurs in barns, feed silos, or animal pens which have not been cleaned out in a while. The occurrence of such spontaneous combustion in one- or two-family dwellings is relatively rare compared to other causes.

The flaring up of smolders is often mistaken for spontaneous combustion. In a smolder, the combustible materials are sometimes starved for air, and thus the combustion reaction proceeds slowly. This effect usually occurs in a woven or porous material.

However, some types of smolders are simply a function of the material. Despite sufficient air, the combustion for some materials proceeds very slowly. This is typical of some plastics and man-made organic materials and fibers.

In general, a *smolder* is any type of combustion process where the leading edge of the combustion zone moves only about 1–5 cm per hour. Because of this, a smolder produces modest heat and smoke, and is hard to detect when in progress. Smolders can be dangerous not only because of their obvious fire hazard, but also because while going undetected, they can release toxic gases such as carbon monoxide or even cyanide, which can slowly poison the atmosphere of an occupied room.

When an oxygen-starved smolder reaches a place where there is ample air, it may burst into flames. Similarly, when the leading edge of fire in a smoldering material reaches a more readily flammable material, it also may suddenly flare up. In both cases, the resulting fire may appear to have "spontaneously started" where the smolder finally burst into flames.

Some materials, when heated to relatively low temperatures, decompose and then react to produce more heat which eventually causes ignition of the material. This effect is also mistaken for spontaneous combustion. Polyurethane foam is a material that exhibits this behavior. When heated, perhaps by hot wiring or a hot flue pipe, polyurethane foam undergoes chemical decomposition. The chemicals present after decomposition occurs react with one another and give off heat. If the heat cannot escape, it may accumulate sufficiently to ignite the rest of the foam.

J. The Warehouse or Box Method

Figure 2 shows a typical fire damage pattern which often occurs in single-level warehouse type buildings. The fire spreads in a radial pattern in the ceiling area and reaches first one perimeter wall, and then another. The perimeter wall which the fire reaches first will exhibit the most damage along its length. The wall which the fire reaches second will exhibit the second most fire damage, etc. The "virtual" fire damaged areas, where fire would have spread had the building been larger in the horizontal plane, are also shown in Figure 2.

It is seen that if a person simply bisects the wall damage on the right side and extends a line perpendicular to the wall into the building, the line will intersect the point of origin. By doing this also on the left side, and on the bottom, three lines can be drawn which all intersect at the point or area of origin. If the fire had spread to the top wall, a fourth line could also have been drawn.

In warehouses and similar rectangular buildings, the point of origin can be quickly, and usually very accurately, estimated by this method. This technique is sometimes called the "box" method or the "warehouse" method for determining the point of origin. It works especially well in buildings where the fire has reached the ceiling area, and the ceiling area is generally open to fire spread.

In essence, the method simply requires observation of the fire damage along the exterior of the perimeter walls, and the generation of perpendicular lines which bisect the damaged area. This is especially easy

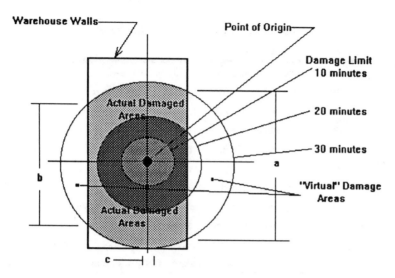

Figure 4.7 Warehouse fire: Actual and "virtual" damaged areas

to do when the exterior walls are metal sheeting, and the paint has blistered away where the fire has directly impinged on the interior side.

The warehouse method of determining the point of origin of a fire and the centroid method are essentially the same technique. Both assume that the lateral burn rate is about the same in all horizontal directions, and that the fire would burn out a circular pattern of damage with the point of origin at the center. It is left up to the reader to prove the equivalency of the two methods.

K. Weighted Centroid Method

This method is similar to the basic centroid method except that this method assumes that the point which has been subject to the longest duration of fire, and has consequently sustained the severest damage, is the point of origin. To this end, areas which have been more severely damaged by fire are given more weight in determining the centroid than areas which have less severe damage. As before, the method assumes a generally homogeneous structure in terms of material flammability and construction.

For example, the various fire damaged areas can be divided into severity zones, with the most severe areas of burn damage given a weighted factor of 10. Areas with less severity of fire damage are assigned lower-weighted factors as shown below. Areas with no fire damage are assigned a weighted factor of 0 and drop out of any equations.

Table 2. Weighting Factors for Fire Severity

factor	description
10	materials are gone, wholly burned away
9	materials are mostly gone, some residual
8	materials are partially gone, recognizable residual
7	materials are burned all over but shape intact
6	materials are mostly burned
5	materials are partially burned
4	materials are slightly burned
3	materials are heat damaged from nearby fire
2	materials are heavily smoke damaged
1	materials are slightly smoke damaged
0	materials exhibit no significant fire damage

A sketch of the building can be made with the various damaged areas drawn in. When the weighting factors are applied to the various areas, the resulting burn damage sketch will appear somewhat like a topographic map with contour lines. Whereas the contour lines in a "topo" map indicate elevation, the contour lines in the fire sketch indicate fire severity.

The centroid of the fire damaged area can then be found by applying the weighting factors to the various areas affected. The equations for the determination of the centroid coordinates would then be as follows:

(xv)

$$X_c = \frac{\sum x_i (\Delta A_i) f_w}{\sum (\Delta A_i)} \qquad y_c = \frac{\sum y_i (\Delta A_i) f_w}{\sum (\Delta A_i)}$$

where f_w = weighting factor,
x_i = distance from y axis to area section,
y_i = distance from x axis to area section, and
ΔA_i = incremental area section.

As with the basic centroid method, this method is often done by eyeball by an experienced fire investigator. However, the method also lends itself to more sophisticated computational analysis. In fact, several inexpensive computer-assisted drafting and design (CADD) programs are available that allow the building plan to be laid out on a computer screen and the fire-damaged areas to be drawn in as an overlay. Some of the programs can then automatically find a centroid of an area.

It is also possible to scan in actual photographs of the fire scene and work directly from them in determining the point of origin, burn severity areas, etc. This, or course, requires that the photographs be taken from strategic vantage points. However, the use of actual photographs in conjunction with computer generated overlays indicating the significance of the damage patterns visible in the photographs can be a very powerful demonstrative tool.

The 10-point system listed in Table 2 is somewhat arbitrary. Actually, any reasonable method of rating fire damaged areas can be used as long as the area of severest damage is assigned the highest weighting factor, and the area of least damage is assigned the lowest weighting factor. A simpler system, using 1–2–3 is more practical for hand calculations. In that system, 3 is severe, 2 is moderate, 1 is light, and 0 is a no-damage area.

One note of caution should be observed when using this method: not all buildings burn homogeneously. For example, if a fire started in a kitchen and then spread to a storage area where an open 55-gallon drum of oil was stored, the most severely damaged fire area would be the storage area, not the kitchen. Thus, the initial reconnoiter of the damage should note where there were fuel concentrations that might skew the weighting.

L. Fire Spread Indicators — Sequential Analysis

The point of origin of a fire can also be found by simply following in reverse order the trail of fire damage from where it ends to where it began. Where several such trails converge, that is the point of origin of the fire. In essence, this method involves determining what burned last, what burned next to last, etc., until the first thing that burned is found.

In the same way that a hunting guide interprets signs and markers to follow a trail of game, a fire investigator looks for signs and markers which may lead to the point of origin. For example, a fast, very hot burn will produce shiny type wood charring with large alligatoring. A cooler, slower fire will produce alligatoring with smaller spacing and a duller-appearing char. Fire breakthrough or breaching of a one-hour rated firewall will likely take longer than fire breakthrough of a stud-and-wood-paneled wall.

As noted, wood char and alligatoring patterns are useful indicators. The reader may recall that commercial wood is about 12% water by weight. As heat impinges on a piece of wood, the water in the surface material will evaporate and escape from the wood. The rapid loss of the water at the surface is also accompanied by a rapid loss of volume, the volume which the water formerly occupied. The wood surface then is in tension as the loss of water causes the wood to shrink. This is the reason why wood checks or cracks when exposed to high heat or simply dries out over time.

Of course, if the heat is very intense, more of the water "cooks" out, and the cracking or alligatoring is more severe. When the heat is quickly applied and then stopped, there is just enough time for the surface to be affected. When the heat is applied for a long time, there is enough time for the wood to be affected to greater depths.

Other indicators of temperature and fire spread include paint, finishes, coatings and the condition of various materials (e.g., melted, charred, burned, warped, softened, oxidized, annealed, etc.).

For example, the paint finish on a furnace is a valuable indicator of the temperature distribution on the furnace. As the temperature increases to perhaps 250–400°F, the first thing to occur is discoloration of the paint. As the temperature rises over about 350–400°F, the paint will bubble and peel off, exposing the underlying primer. As the temperature rises again to more than 400–450°F, the primer will come off, and the undercoat, often zinc, will be exposed and oxidized. And as the temperature increases still more, perhaps beyond 786°F, the undercoat will melt away leaving only the bare steel metal, which itself oxidizes.

Often it is easier to visually determine the hottest point on the furnace or appliance several days after the fire. The areas where all the paint, primer, and galvanized undercoating have been removed by high heat exposure will be bright red where the bare sheet steel has rusted since the fire.

Another example is metal ventilation ductwork. Metal ventilation ducts are often made of galvanized steel, that is, steel with a thin coating of zinc. The galvanization which is normally shiny will first dull and darken on exposure to heat. When temperatures rise above 500°F, the zinc begins to oxidize significantly and turns whitish. As the zinc is heated past 500°F, it whitens more and more. However, when the temperature approaches 786°F, the unoxidized zinc melts and sloughs off, leaving bare steel exposed. (The zinc oxide itself will not actually melt until a temperature of about 3,600°F is reached, but usually sloughs off with the unoxidized zinc under it.) Thus, the hottest spots on ventilation ductwork are also the red spots, where the exposed steel has oxidized to rust.

The interpretations of many such markers, V patterns, etc. are then combined into a logical construct of the fire path. One favorite test used in the sequential analysis method is the question: "Which is burned more, the material on this side or that side?" The answer to this question then supplies a directional vector for the fire spread, and the vector is back-tracked to another position where the question is again posed. In a sense, following a trail of indicators is like playing Twenty Questions.

Figure 4.8 Copper propane pipe frayed and melted at end due to "blow-torch" effect.

In order to avoid a false trail due to fall down, it is common to backtrack several fire trails from finish to start. When several such trails independently converge to a common point of origin, the confidence in the answer is greatly increased.

The advantage of the sequential method is that no special assumptions need be made concerning structural homogeneity. The disadvantages are twofold. First, it relies on the individual skill and knowledge of the investigator to find and properly interpret the markers. Not all fire investigators have the same knowledge about materials, fire chemistry, heat transfer, etc. One fire investigator may spot an important marker that another also saw but ignored.

Figure 4.9 Heat pattern in sheet metal cover of buss duct. Note the distinct "banding" effects.

Secondly, it assumes that enough markers are present to diagnose the fire and can be found; this is not always the case. Sometimes the severity of the fire or the fire fighting activities destroy significant markers and indicators. Also, sometimes the markers may be present but are lost in the jumble of debris. Thus, sometimes there are gaps in the evidence, and the resulting sequential analysis is discontinuous.

M. Combination of Methods

Few fires lend themselves to complete analysis by only one of the methods described; many require a combination of methodologies. For example, it is common to determine a general area where the fire began using one of the centroid methods, and then determine a specific point of origin using a combination of fire spread indicators and an examination of available ignition energy sources.

Properly applied fuses and circuit breakers protect branch circuit conductors from reaching ignition temperatures of ordinary combustibles, even under short circuit conditions. However, lamp cords, extension cords, and appliances of lower rating than the branch circuit conductors may reach higher temperatures without blowing the fuse or tripping the breaker if there is a malfunction in the appliance or the cord.

Section 2-3.3, NFPA 907M

Chapter 5: Electrical Shorting

A. General

A significant proportion of all fires that occur in structures are caused by electrical short circuits. The building's wiring system, lighting fixtures, appliances, installed machinery, and extension chords are the some of the more common items in which shorting occurs.

The shorting components themselves usually do not directly catch fire. Most electrical components contain insulated metal conductors, and except in very unusual circumstances the conductors themselves are not flammable. The insulation around the conductors doesn't ordinarily ignite or burn except in some older types of wiring where the insulation material may be flammable.

Shorting causes electrical conductors to excessively heat up. This may cause the plastic insulation material coating the conductors to melt and slough off, leaving the conductors bare; fire can then begin when flammable materials come into direct contact with the hot conductors.

If the short circuit produces enough heat, the metal conductor itself may melt, flow, and drip onto flammable materials located below it. The melting temperature of conductors such as copper and aluminum is usually higher than the ignition temperature of common construction materials such as wood, paper, and textiles. Sufficient heat transfer between the conductor drippings and the flammable materials during contact can result in the initiation of a fire.

Fire can also ensue when there is high-voltage electrical arcing. In such arcing, molten conductor droplets may spatter onto nearby flammable materials. Since spattering can cause molten material to be thrown off above, below, and to the sides of the short, it is possible that fire from arcing can be initiated in places other than directly below the short.

Lastly, fire can also start when a flammable material is close enough to the shorting component that it ignites due to radiative, conductive, or convective heat transfer directly from the electrical arc plasma. The arc plasma created by electrical shorting is the same type of plasma created during arc welding, which can reach temperatures ranging from 2,500°F to 10,000°F. In fact, a significant number of accidental fires associated with arc welding occur each year, usually because the welder did not follow proper safety procedures. One common situation is when flammable vapors drift over to and collect in an area where arc welding is being done.

While shorting is indeed a common cause of fires, unfortunately some fires not caused by shorting are conveniently blamed on electrical shorting. It is the case that electrical shorting is the "cause of last resort" for some investigators. This is because nearly all inhabited buildings in the U.S. have electrical wiring of some type. When a building catches fire and burns, it is probable that the fire will cause something electrical to short out, no matter what actually caused the fire. Thus, an investigator who cannot determine the specific cause of the fire can always find some evidence of shorting to blame as being the cause, and close out his paperwork.

Because of this, it is necessary to discriminate between *primary shorting* and *secondary shorting.* Primary shorting is shorting which causes the fire; secondary shorting is caused by the fire. Of course, both types can and do occur in the same fire. Primary shorting can occur at one location and cause a fire to start. The fire can then burn up live electrical equipment at another location, resulting in secondary shorting within that equipment.

In general, primary shorting has the following characteristics:

- It occurs at or close to the point of origin of the fire. There are indications of fire spread away from it, and the point of shorting is often in the area of severest burn damage.

- Heat damage to the conductor is more severe at the interior than at the exterior (inside to outside damage pattern).

- Significant movement or travel of the short has occurred, i.e. the short appears to have been active for a relatively long time. Ample beading may be present.

- The severest damages in the electrical item which shorted are limited to a small area proximate to the short, rather than being spread over a large, general area.

- In consideration of the whole body of evidence, it is the short which must have occurred first in the time line of the fire.

Secondary shorting has the following general characteristics:

- It occurs in locations away from the point of origin of the fire. There are indications of fire spread to the short from other locations. The short may be in a general area where, except for the short itself, there is little difference in fire damage severity. This indicates that the area had been approached by a fire front spreading from another area.

- The conductor interior may not be as severely damaged as its exterior (outside to inside damage pattern).

- Little movement or travel of the short has occurred. The short appears to have been active for only a short time. Beading effects may be limited.

- In consideration of the whole body of evidence, it is a short which may have occurred at any time during the course of the fire.

It should be noted that the above characteristics cited for both primary and secondary shorting are generalizations; they may not all apply to a specific case.

For example, consider a situation where a fire begins in one short extension cord due to shorting, and the ensuing fire then engulfs a second short extension cord plugged into the same outlet, causing secondary shorting to it. Both shorts would have occurred near the point of origin of the fire, and both might be located in the area of severest burn.

Similarly, consider the situation where a short causes a fire, which then spreads to where flammable fuels are stored. When ignited, the fuels cause very severe damage in their general area, including very severe damage to some electrical wiring; more severe, in fact, than what occurred at the point where the fire began.

B. Thermodynamics of a Simple Resistive Circuit

Consider a simple circuit that has only a resistive element and an alternating-voltage source, such as shown in Figure 5.1. Like in most household circuits, the voltage varies sinusoidally.

In this circuit, the instantaneous current flowing through the resistive load follows Ohm's Law.

(i) $\qquad E_{max}(\sin \omega t) = I(R_L) \qquad$ Ohm's Law

where I = current,

E_{max} = maximum voltage amplitude,

    t = time, and
    ω = frequency of alternating current in radians per second (1
        Hertz = 2π radians/sec.)

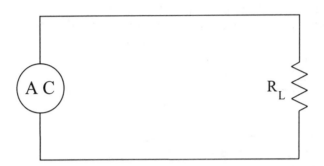

Figure 5.1 Simple resistive circuit

Given that the resistive load is constant, then the current varies as follows:

(ia) $I = (E_{max} / R_L)(\sin \omega t)$

If it is assumed that the root-mean-square values for current and voltage are substituted for the instantaneous values, equation (i) becomes simply

(ii) $E = I R.$

The energy consumed by the resistance in the circuit per unit of time is given by

(iii) $P = E I = I^2 R = E^2/R.$

where the E and I terms are understood to mean root-mean-square values for voltage and current, respectively, and the circuit is either d.c., or single-phase alternating current.

The above is usually referred to as the *power* of the circuit, and the common units of electrical power are watts. One watt is the product of one volt of potential and one ampere of current. In other units, one watt is equivalent to one joule of energy per second, 3.413 BTU per hour, or 0.7376 lbf-ft/sec. A kilowatt, 1,000 watts, is equivalent to 1.341 horse-power in English units.

In the circuit shown in Figure 1, since the load is purely resistive, the power consumed by the load becomes heat. As power is consumed, the temperature of the resistive load will rise until its cooling rate, or heat transfer from the load, equals the electrical power being consumed. When that occurs, the circuit is in thermal equilibrium with the environment and the temperature of the resistive load will stabilize.

In less technical terms, the above situation is analogous to a large holding tank that has a water input valve and a drain valve. The input valve is like the power being consumed by the resistive load, the cooling rate is like the drain valve, and the holding tank is like the resistive load. If the drain is closed and the input valve is open, the tank will fill, and the water level (or temperature) will rise. If the drain is opened a little, the tank will fill more slowly. If the rate of drain is set equal to the rate of water input, the tank will neither fill nor empty, and the water level in the tank will stabilize.

Mathematically, the above situation is described by the following linear differential equation.

(iv) $\quad P - (dQ/dt) = mC_p(T - T_o)/t$

where P = power input to the component,
$\quad dQ/dt$ = rate of heat transfer from the circuit to the environment,
$\quad\quad m$ = mass of the resistive load,
$\quad\quad C_p$ = specific heat at constant pressure of the resistive load,
$\quad\quad T_o$ = ambient temperature (in absolute units),
$\quad\quad T$ = temperature of resistive load (in absolute units), and
$\quad\quad t$ = elapsed time.

In the above equation, the first term P is the amount of energy coming into the resistive load that is converted into heat. The second term, dQ/dt, is the amount of heat removed from the resistive load by cooling. The right-hand term in the equation, $mC_p(T - T_o)/t$, is the rate at which heat is being stored in the resistive load. As more heat is stored, the temperature of the load or resistance increases.

In equation (iv), the mass of the wires connected to the resistive load has been ignored to keep things simple. It is assumed that the only item heating up is the mass of the resistive load.

Despite the above simplifying assumption, equation (iv) is still fraught with other complications. First, the resistance of the load changes with temperature. For most common materials used in electrical conductors, as temperature increases, resistance increases. However, there are notable exceptions, such as carbon film resistors, which actually lose resistance with rising temperature within certain ranges. In either case, the relationship between resistance and temperature is typically described mathematically as follows:

(v) $\quad R = R_o(1 + \alpha(T - T_o)) = R_o + R_o\alpha(T - T_o)$

where R = resistance,
     R_o = resistance at ambient temperature T_o,
     a = temperature coefficient of resistance, and
     T = temperature.

When the material resistance increases with increasing temperature, α is positive. When the material resistance decreases with increasing temperature, α is negative.

To complicate matters just a bit more, the coefficient of resistance α also varies with temperature. With common conductor materials, like copper or aluminum, it diminishes slowly in absolute value as temperature increases. For example, for aluminum at 0°C, α has a value of +0.00439/°K. At 25°C, the value decreases to +0.00396/°K, and at 50°C the value decreases further to +0.00360/°K. However, for this "simple" model of a resistance circuit, it is assumed that the average coefficient of temperature between the two end point temperatures is used.

Another complication to equation (iv) is that the rate of heat transfer also depends on temperature. As the temperature difference between the hot resistive load and the ambient increases, the rate of heat transfer increases. This is shown in equation (vi) below.

(vi) $dQ/dt = UA(T - T_o)$

where U = heat transfer coefficient for convection and conduction around the resistive load, and
    A = heat transfer area.

And now to be really ornery, the U term in equation (vi) is also dependent upon temperature. In fact, in some regions, especially the transition zone between laminar and turbulent convective flow, U can be decidedly non-linear. However, again to keep things simple, it will be assumed that in the range under consideration, the U value is constant.

If equations (v) and (vi) are substituted back into equation (iv), then an expression is obtained that approximately depicts the relationship of temperature and electrical power consumption in a simple resistive circuit.

(vii) $P - (dQ/dt) = mC_p(T - T_o)/t$

    $I^2R - UA(T - T_o) = mC_p(T - T_o)/t$ substituting equations (iii) and (vi)

    $I^2[R_o(1 + a(T - T_o))] - UA(T - T_o) = mC_p(T - T_o)/t$ substituting equation (v)

Collecting terms and simplifying gives the following.

(viii) $I^2R_o + I^2R_o\alpha T - I^2R_o\alpha T_o - UAT + UAT_o = mC_p(T)/t - mC_p(T_o)/t$

$T[I^2R_o\alpha - UA - mC_p/t] = T_o[I^2R_o\alpha - UA - mC_p/t] - I^2R_o$

$T = T_o + [I^2R_ot] / [(mC_p) + UAt - I^2R_o\alpha t]$

The above expression allows the increase in temperature of the resistive load to be calculated, provided that the following factors are known: the applied current, the heat capacity and mass of the resistive load, the initial resistance at ambient temperature, ambient temperature, and the heat transfer coefficient and area.

In the derivation of equation (viii) above, the expression I^2R was substituted for P, the power term, in equation (iv). However, an alternative substitution, E^2/R, can be made for P the power term, as follows:

(ix) $P - (dQ/dt) = mC_p(T - T_o)/t$

$E^2/R - UA(T - T_o) = mC_p(T - T_o)/t$

$[E^2/R_o(1 + a(T - T_o))] - UA(T - T_o) = mC_p(T - T``o)/t$

Collecting terms and simplifying gives the following:

(x) $E^2 - UA(T - T_o)[R_o + R_o\alpha(T - T_o)] = [mC_p(T - T_o)/t][R_o + R_o\alpha(T - T_o)]$

$[E^2] / [R``o(mC_p/t + UA)] = (T - T_o) + \alpha(T - T_o)^2$

Equation (x) allows the calculation of the temperature of the resistive load if the following is known: the applied voltage, the initial resistance, the ambient temperature, the heat transfer coefficient and area, and the heat capacity and mass of the resistive load. Unfortunately, equation (x) is not as easy to work with as equation (viii). While equation (viii) is a linear equation in T, equation (x) is quadratic in T. Thus, equation (x) could have two solutions, one real and one extraneous.

Of course, it is possible to take equation (viii), and substitute E^2/R_o for the I^2R_o terms, and obtain the following:

(xi) $T = T_o + [E^2t/R_o] / [(mC_p) + UAt - a^E2t/R_o]$.

Equation (xi) is useful in that it does not have the quadratic form of equation (x) and closely resembles the linear equation (viii).

In equations (viii), (x), and (xi), there are terms included to account for the variation of resistance with temperature. Table 1 below lists some common values for a, the coefficient of resistance with respect to temperature.

Table 1. Some Temperature Coefficients of Resistance at 20°C, or 293.15°K*

material	α in dimensionless unit per °K
aluminum	0.00403
brass	0.0036
copper wire	0.00393
steel	0.0016

*Standard Handbook for Mechanical Engineers, 7th Ed., p. 15–8

To determine how important these terms might be, consider the following. Given a 40°K rise in temperature from 0°C to 40°C, a copper wire has an increase in resistance of

$$[1 + (0.00393/°K)(40°K)] = 1 + 0.157 = 1.157 \text{ or } 16\%.$$

A similar 100°K rise in temperature, from –30°C to 70°C, would result in a 39% increase in resistance. Thus, the increase in resistance caused by increased temperature is a significant factor, and should not be neglected when significant temperature increases are involved.

In some electrical circuits the applied voltage can be considered constant within certain ranges. Consider what theoretically occurs in that situation due to the change in resistance with temperature.

(xiia) $E = IR = I[R_o + R_o\alpha(T - T_o)]$

(xiib) $P = EI = E^2/[R_o + R_o\alpha(T - T_o)]$

As the resistance increases due to increased temperature, in order to maintain a constant voltage, the current must drop proportionally. Likewise, as the resistance increases with increasing temperature, the power expended drops. This is sometimes called "heat choke" of the current. (This is analogous to a negative feedback loop.)

Similarly, in some electrical circuits the applied current can be considered constant within certain ranges. In that case, the following applies.

(xiiia) $I = E/[R_o + R_o\alpha(T - T_o)]$

(xiiib) $P = I^2[R_o + R_o\alpha(T - T_o)]$

As the temperature rises, the resistance rises and the voltage must also increase to maintain a constant I. In turn, this causes the amount of power being consumed to increase linearly. Thus, in constant-current applications, heating of the resistive load will cause the applied voltage to increase, and the power to increase. (This is analogous to a positive feedback loop.)

Sometimes, equipment is designed to ensure that the power of the system remains constant within certain operating ranges. In those types of circuits, the product of voltage and current will be constant. In such a circuit, if there were a low voltage condition, the current would correspondingly increase to maintain constant P. Similarly, if the current were to drop, the voltage would increase accordingly. These circuits, theoretically, will neither increase nor decrease in power as the temperature of the resistive load increases.

While very idealized, the basic principles noted in the foregoing analysis of a simple resistive circuit have wide general application: they apply to many types of electronic equipment, lighting equipment, and resistance-type heating equipment. These appliances for the most part convert electricity to heat like a simple resistive load.

In fact, in determining the internal heat load of an office space or building, it is common practice to simply sum the various power consumption ratings of the appliances in a given space. This includes copying machines, lights, telephones, computers, coffee makers, etc. Whatever electricity they consume is eventually converted to heat and released into that same space.

However, when electricity is converted into mechanical work, such as in an electric motor, a modification of the basic thermal energy equation is needed. An additional term is added to account for the conversion. When electricity is converted into mechanical work, significant amounts of energy can leave the component without causing the component itself to heat up. Eventually, the mechanical work is also converted to heat. But it is possible that the conversion to heat will not be associated with the electrical component which originally generated the work. In other words, the mechanical work produced by the component can cross the boundary of the system, and the eventual conversion to heat can occur somewhere else. For this reason, mechanical work is considered an energy loss term in the same way as heat transfer from the component.

To account for mechanical work, equation (vii) is modified as follows:

(xiii) $\quad P - (dQ/dt) - W/t = mC_p(T - T_o)/t$

where W = work output of the equipment.

By substituting as was done in equation (vii) to obtain equation (viii), the following is obtained:

(xv) $T[I^2R_o\alpha - UA - mC_p /t] = T_o[I^2R_o\alpha - UA - mC_p /t] - I^2R_o + W/t$

$$T = T_o + [I^2R_ot - W] / [(mCp) + UAt - I^2R_o\alpha t]$$

Similarly, by substituting as was done in equation (ix), the following is obtained:

(xvi) $$E^2 - [UA(T - T_o) + W/t][R_o + R_o\alpha(T - T_o)] =$$

$$[mC_p(T - T_o)/t][R_o + R_o\alpha(T - T_o)]$$

$$[E^2t - WR_o]/[R_o(mC_p + UA_t + W\alpha)] = (T - T_o) + \alpha(T - T_o)^2.$$

It is left up to the reader to incorporate a mechanical work term into equation (xi) and derive the results.

The efficiency of a motor or machine, that is, the conversion of electrical energy to useful mechanical work, is given by:

(xvi) $$h = W / Pt$$

If the machine loses efficiency due to wear or other forms of deterioration, then less of the input energy is converted into work. In inspecting equations (xv) and (xvi), it is seen that if the work term W decreases, then more of the input energy is converted to heat. When this occurs, the machine will heat up, and the over-all load resistance will increase due to the higher operating temperatures. If the heat increase is sufficient, it may cause damage and eventual failure of the item.

This is what occurs when a motor wears out. As it wears out, it becomes less efficient; more of the input energy becomes heat instead of work, and the motor runs hotter. Given time and further deterioration it may become hot enough for general failure to occur. The bearings may overheat or the dielectric in the windings may fail, allowing internal shorting to occur. If there is no internal thermal protection, such as a bi-metallic thermal switch in the windings, the motor may burn out and catch fire. (Often, the dielectric insulation covering the windings is flammable.) If there is internal thermal protection, the motor will turn itself off when the local area around the switch reaches the set point temperature.

Some thermal protection switches will reset when the motor cools down, others may stay tripped. If it is the former, the motor may restart when it cools and run a short time until the temperature again builds up. This start-stop-start behavior is often encountered in air-conditioner compressors that are in the last stages of operational life. Eventually, the motor will draw enough current to cause the breakers servicing the unit to trip. (This, of course, assumes that the breakers have been properly sized.)

*Figure 5.2 Industrial bus bar which internally shorted
at 90° turn piece.*

C. Parallel Short Circuits

In an electrical circuit, conductor pathways are provided so that electricity can flow to and from an appliance or component to perform some function. A short circuit happens when the electrical current flows through an unintended pathway, i.e. a shortcut electrical pathway, between the conductors.

There are two basic types of short circuits: shorts which create parallel pathways for the electricity, and shorts which create series pathways for the electricity. In the former, the short can be considered as a parallel resistive load, and in the latter, the short can be considered as a series resistive load.

Consider the parallel resistive load first. A simplified schematic of a parallel, short circuit resistive load is shown in Figure 5.3 below.

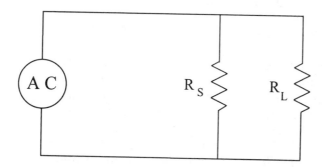

Figure 5.3 Parallel short circuit

The equivalent resistance for two resistive loads in parallel is given below.

(xviii) $[1/R_{Eq}] = [1/R_S] + [1/R_L]$

   $R_{Eq} = [R_S][R_L] / [R_L + R_S]$.

When there is no short, the value for R_S is infinite and $R_{Eq} = R_L$. Consider the following example of a short circuit in the cord of a toaster. The resistance of the heating elements in the toaster is 20 ohms. The electric cord for the toaster is rated for 15 amperes of current. If the toaster is plugged into a 120 v.a.c. source of electrical power and the toaster operates normally, the current and power to the toaster is:

   $I = 120 \text{ v} / 20 \text{ ohm} = 6 \text{ amperes}$,

   $P = (120 \text{ v})(6.0 \text{ a.}) = 720 \text{ watts}$.

Assume now that an internal break has developed in the toaster's electrical cord due to the cord being bent in an excessively tight radius. The break is such that the insulation is much thinner there than elsewhere. Assume also that because of this break the resistance across the insulation to the other wire is 100,000 ohms instead of the typical 10,000,000 ohms.

In this case, the equivalent resistance of the toaster and the short circuit in parallel is 19.996 ohms. Assuming that a constant voltage is being supplied to the circuit, that is, there is a constant voltage applied across the equivalent resistance, then the current and power consumed by the equivalent resistance is given by:

   $I = (120 \text{ v} / 19.996 \text{ ohm}) = 6.001 \text{ amperes}$, and

   $P = (120 \text{ v})(120 \text{ v} / 19.996 \text{ ohm}) = 720.14 \text{ watts}$.

Now, within the parallel circuit, the toaster resistance is consuming the same 6 amperes of current and 720 watts of power. However, the resistance in the short circuit is consuming 0.001 amperes of current, and 0.14 watts of power. Since the short circuit is a pure resistance, this power is being converted to heat and is concentrated in the area of the insulation break. The concentrated heat then causes further deterioration to the insulation. The deterioration may involve melting, charring, or just general degradation of the dielectric properties of the insulation. This results in further breakdown of the insulation.

Because of the damage caused by heating effects, the short resistance now drops to 1,000 ohms, a factor of one hundred less than before. In this case, the equivalent resistance is now 19.608 ohms. This causes a current consumption of 6.12 amperes, and a power consumption of 734.4 watts. Again, the toaster is still consuming 720 watts, but the short is consuming 14.4 watts. As before, the heat produced by the short is concentrated in the area of the short, which further degrades the insulation.

In the final stages of the short, assume that the resistance has dropped to 1 ohm. The concentrated heat has melted away nearly all of the insulation between the wires and the wires are essentially conductor to conductor now. Assuming that the toaster has not yet been separated from the circuit due to melting, the equivalent resistance of the toaster and short circuit in parallel with each other is 0.952 ohms. This results in a current consumption of 126 amperes, which well exceeds the 15-ampere rating of the cord. Hopefully, this would cause the breaker for the branch circuit to trip. If not, it is likely that the conductor in the wire will melt away, as the theoretical power input is now 15.12 kilowatts.

If the breaker or fuse does not open the circuit, often the short will "follow" the conductor back to its source of power as far as it can while the circuit is intact. That is, the conductor will melt, spark, arc, and burn along its length back towards the source of its electrical power. The effect is somewhat like the older type dynamite fusee. When lighted, the burning follows the fusee cord back to the stick of dynamite. Of course, the short does not move away from the source of power, because the short itself has cut off any power in that portion of the conductors.

In the above example, several generalizations are of note:

- As the resistance in the short drops due to heat degradation, the over-all resistance of the combined parallel circuit drops.

- Until the short causes enough damage to sever the circuit, the operating appliance that is parallel to the short will continue to operate as it had, consuming its usual amount of power.

- As the resistance of the over-all parallel circuit decreases, the amount of current consumed increases proportionally. This occurs despite the fact that the circuit has a constant voltage source. Heat choking of the current does not occur because of the parallel resistance arrangement.

It is apparent from the parallel resistance equations that a parallel short will proceed and allow electrical current flow whether or not the appliance is operating. If the appliance is operating, the current is divided, with some of the current flowing through the appliance and some through the short. If the appliance is turned off, and R_L is therefore infinite, the circuit simply reverts to a simple single resistance circuit, where the resistance of the short is the only resistance consuming power.

For example, if the short-circuit resistance were 10,000 ohms and the same toaster is considered, the equivalent resistance is 19.96 ohms. The current consumption for the circuit is 6.012 amperes: 6 amperes through the toaster and 0.012 amperes through the short circuit. The power consumption is 721.4 watts; 720 watts in the toaster and 1.44 watts in the short circuit.

With the toaster turned off, the resistance of the circuit is simply 10,000 ohms. This will result in a current consumption of 0.012 amperes through the short circuit resistance and a power consumption of 1.44 watts. Thus, when the electrical source supplies constant voltage to the circuit, it does not matter if the appliance is turned on or off. The short will proceed unaffected in either case.

This is one reason why so many cases of electrical shorting seem to occur at night or after work hours. If the work day is 8 hours long, then the non-work day is 16 hours long. With the short proceeding whether the appliance is turned on or off, there is a 33% chance the short will cause a fire during work hours, and a 67% chance it will cause a fire during non-work hours. Under these circumstances, the chances are far more favorable for a short circuit caused fire to occur during non-working hours.

Thus, to avoid a short occurring and causing a fire when no one is around, it is good practice to unplug appliances and extension cords when they will not be needed for extended periods. Most fire departments recommend this practice to homeowners to reduce the risk of fire when they are away on vacation.

D. Series Short Circuits

A series short circuit might occur, for example, in an appliance where there is an off-on switch in series with the appliance resistance. This is schematically shown in Figure 5.4.

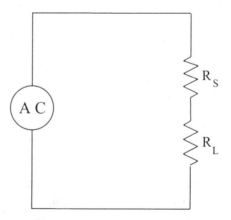

Figure 5.4 Series short circuit

The equivalent resistive load for resistances in series is given below:

(xix) $R_{Eq} = [R_S] + [R_L]$.

The current used in this circuit is then:

(xx) $I = E / (R_S + R_L)$

The voltage across the whole circuit is, of course, E. However, the voltage across each of the resistances is given by the following:

(xxi) $E_S = I(R_S)$ and $E_L = I(R_L)$

where I = the current calculated from equation (xix).

Thus, the power consumed by each resistance is given by

(xxii) $P_S = I^2(R_S)$ and $P_L = I^2(R_L)$

$$P = P_S + P_L = I^2(R_S) + I^2(R_L) = EI$$

where P = total power consumed by the circuit,
    I = current calculated from equation (xix),
    P_S = power consumed by short circuit,
    P_L = power consumed by the load of the circuit.

Under normal circumstances, when the switch is in the closed position (the appliance is "on"), the value for R_S is typically very small, perhaps only a fraction of an ohm. Thus the resistance associated with the switch is trivial, and is generally ignored in circuit calculations.

Consider the same example as before, a toaster that has a 20-ohm heating element with a 15-ampere rated electric cord. The toaster is plugged into a wall outlet rated at 120 v.a.c. Assume that the resistance of the switch is 0.01 ohms. Thus the total resistance of the toaster and switch is 20.01 ohms. When the toaster is operating normally, this results in a current and total power consumption as given below:

I = (120 v) / (20.01 ohms) = 5.997 amperes, and
P = (120 v)(5.997 a) = 719.6 watts.

When the toaster is turned off and the circuit is open, the switch has infinite resistance. Thus no current can flow and no power is consumed.

However, if the switch is damaged, cracked, improperly assembled, deteriorated by the environment, or perhaps subjected to a high-voltage surge such as a lightning stroke, its "off" resistance can be reduced from infinity to some lower value. Assume that the resistance is lowered to 100,000 ohms.

If that is the case, the total resistance of the circuit is now 100,020 ohms, and this results in a current of 0.0012 amperes, and a power consumption of 0.144 watts. Of the total power, the switch is consuming 0.144 watts and the toaster element is consuming 0.0000288 watts. The power consumed by the toaster is trivial, because the voltage across the switch is 119.98 volts, while the voltage across the toaster is 0.024 v. Thus nearly all the power being consumed is concentrated at the point of shorting in the switch, and this power is converted into heat.

As the switch heats up, its resistance drops further due to heat-related deterioration. If we assume the resistance drops to 1,000 ohms, then the total circuit resistance is 1,020 ohms. This results in a current of 0.118 amperes, and a total power consumption of 14.1 watts. Of the total power, the short in the switch is taking 13.84 watts, and the toaster is consuming 0.28 watts. The voltage across the switch is 118 v, and the voltage across the toaster is 2 v. As before the power consumed by the switch is being converted to heat, which causes further deterioration.

When the resistance of the switch drops to 20 ohms, the total resistance is 40 ohms, and this results in a current of 3 amperes, and total power consumption of 360 watts. Of this, the short in the switch is using 180 watts and the toaster is consuming 180 watts. At this point, when the resistance of the switch and the resistance of the toaster are equal, the switch will be consuming the maximum power it can as long as the circuit remains intact.

In series shorting, as shown in the above example, the current consumed often does not exceed the rating of the cord, at least initially. However, if the heat build-up is sufficient to damage the circuit and sever the appliance load out of the series, a second shorting phase may occur where the short is simply a *dead short*, one where the short is the only load in the circuit. This most likely happens when the cord supplying electricity to the appliance has both the "hot" and the "cold" conductors in the same casing, or if the "hot" conductor comes in contact with a ground, e.g. a grounded metal conduit.

With respect to series shorting, the following generalizations can be made:

- When it initiates, most of the power is consumed in the area of the short; very little power is consumed by the appliance or load.

- As long as the series circuit is intact, the current consumed by the short will normally not exceed the current normally consumed by the appliance or load. Thus, series shorts may often not cause breakers to trip.

- When the resistance of the short equals that of the load, the power consumption of the short will be maximum, assuming that the series circuit remains intact. The power consumed by the short at this stage will generally be half that which would be consumed by the appliance or load when operating.

- If the heat causes enough damage, it is possible for the series circuit to degenerate into a "dead" short circuit, i.e. a simple circuit where the short is the only load.

Series shorting such as has been described in the above example occurs even if the switch to a particular appliance is in the "off" position, because when the switch is on, the resistance through the switch is too low for any significant heating to occur.

This is another reason why it is good practice to unplug appliances when people plan to be out of the house for an extended period. Even when the switches are turned off, an appliance can short circuit.

Figure 5.5 Shorting (ground fault) in conduit.
Note how localized the damage is.

E. Beading

One of the more classic visual methods of detecting shorting after a fire has occurred is the observation of *beading*. This term refers to a melted conductor that has re-formed into droplets, or beads, near or at the point of shorting. The heat of the shorting melts the metal wire; once melted, the material's surface tension causes it to form drops or beads. Once the bead of metal is out of the electric current loop it cools and solidifies in the droplet shape.

The two most commonly used metals for conductors are aluminum and copper. Copper melts at 1,892°F and boils at 4,172°F. Aluminum has a melting point of 1,220°F and a boiling point of 3,733°F. Electrical solders, which are usually composed of lead, antimony, zinc and silver, typically melt and flow at temperatures well below 1,000°F; for example, a standard solder composed of 48% tin and 52% lead melts at 360°F. Most electrical solders contain at least 40% tin for good conductivity.

In typical building fires the temperatures of burning wood, cloth, paper and such are ordinarily not high enough to melt copper wires. Such fires will typically cause copper wires to anneal and oxidize in varying degrees, but do not usually cause them to melt. However, electrical shorting can supply sufficiently concentrated energy to cause localized melting of copper in the immediate area of the short. For this reason, the finding of beaded copper conductors in a typical building fire is a strong indication of electrical shorting.

It should be noted, however, that fires involving flammable liquids or gases, some types of combustible fuels, and some combustible metals can reach temperatures that will readily melt copper. Also, in confined areas where there is excess oxygen or air flow to "fan the flames", like a blacksmith's bellows, a fire which normally might not be able to melt copper *may* be able to do so (see note below). Thus it is important to note if any of these fuels or unusual conditions were present in an area where beading copper conductors was observed.

> Note: It is even possible to melt iron with wood fire under the right circumstances. In Africa, iron ore was smelted into iron using large vertical stone towers. These towers were filled with layers of wood, iron ore and limestone. The wood would be burned, causing some of it to pyrolyze into charcoal. The large fire would also set up a high convective draft through the tower, which would supply excess oxygen to the process. The oxidation of the charcoal would provide sufficient temperatures to melt high carbon content iron, and the carbon monoxide from the charcoal helped to reduce the iron oxides. The limestone acted as a flux to remove the impurities from the iron, which would drop to the bottom in pig-like lumps. A check of an iron-carbon diagram of iron shows why this process works. While steel does not melt until a temperature of about 3,000°F is reached, an iron containing 4.3% of carbon, which is the eutectic point, will melt at a temperature as low as 2,200°. Thus, the "trick" is to chemically reduce the iron oxide to iron carbide, and then control the amount of carbon. This is pretty slick stuff when you consider that it was done over 4,000 years ago without the benefit of a single college graduate!

However, in the same typical building fire where there is burning wood, paper etc., the temperatures are often high enough to melt aluminum wires. For this reason, the finding of beaded aluminum conductors is not, in itself, a strong indicator of shorting, especially if the beading is observed in an area corresponding to a "hot" fire area. It is possible that the fire alone can cause the aluminum conductors to bead. Thus, other indicators have to be considered to determine if the beading is due to shorting.

One of the "other" indicators used to determine whether or not beading is the result of shorting is spreading of the strands of multistrand conductors. In large-current carrying conductors, a short circuit may cause a momentary large overcurrent transient. As predicted by Maxwell's Equations, this transient then causes a correspondingly large magnetic field to momentarily develop in the area of the short. These magnetic fields can warp, dishevel and distort the strands of the conductors. Often, a multistrand conductor will have its strands unwind and spread out in the area of the short due to these magnetic effects; a fire by itself will not cause this to happen.

The amount of beading around a short can often be a crude indicator of how long the short was operating. This is because

- the heat input to the short is often a function of the fuse size, breaker rating, or wire size. The one with the lowest current-carrying ability will set the limit for maximum sustainable current.
- a specific amount of heat is needed to raise the temperature of a conductor to its heating point. Thus, given the mass of the beads or amount of "missing" conductor, the amount of electric energy needed to affect formation of the beads can be estimated.

For example, consider a #14 copper wire. This conductor, due to its diameter and material properties, has a resistance of 2.525 ohms per 1,000 feet at room temperature, i.e. 68°F. Its weight is 12.43 pounds per 1,000 feet. Copper has a heat capacity of 0.0931 BTU/lb°F, and a heat of fusion of 75.6 BTU/lb.

Given these facts, consider a two-wire copper conductor 60 feet long. It is fused at one end for 15 amperes, as per *National Electrical Code* standards, and has a dead short at the other end. Under these conditions,

- the resistance of the conductor loop at room temperature is 0.303 ohms.
- the short will draw the maximum current of 15 amperes when the combined resistance of the short and conductors is 8 ohms. If the combined resistance drops below 8 ohms, the fuse will blow, in accordance with its time delay characteristics.
- the amount of heat necessary to raise the temperature of the conductor loop to melting is 254 BTU, assuming no heat losses.
- assuming a power rate of 120 v.a.c. at 15 amperes, the electrical input to the short could be 1,800 watts, or 6,143 BTU/hr. To heat the conductor to near melting would need about 150 seconds under those conditions (assuming no heat losses). Assuming a current of 7.5 amperes it would take about 300 seconds, or five minutes, to heat the conductors up to the melting point.

- assuming a current of 15 amperes, after the conductor reaches melting, it would melt away and form beads at the rate of 13.2 in/sec. along the length of both wires in a direction towards the source of power. The whole 60-foot long section would melt away in 66 seconds.
- assuming a current of 7.5 amperes, the conductor would melt away at a rate of 6.6 in/sec., and the whole 60-ft section would melt in 132 seconds.

In considering the above example, a number of items are worth noting.

- If the fuse were found to be blown, then it could be concluded that the combined resistance of the short and conductors was less than 8 ohms.
- Even momentarily, the resistance of the short circuit would be no less than 0.303 ohms. Thus, the maximum momentary current would be 396 amperes. This could be used to set a limit as to the response time of the fuse if the time response function is known.
- If the fuse did not blow, and the wires were found melted all the way back to the fuse box, then it could be concluded that the combined resistance was 8 ohms or more.
- The minimum warm-up time of the whole 60-foot section of wiring to reach the melting point would be 150 seconds, or 2½ minutes. This, of course, assumes that the short begins fully developed.
- The minimum time needed for melting the wiring, assuming it was already at melting temperature, would be 66 seconds. Thus the minimum combined time for both warm up to melting point, and then melting of the whole 60 feet is 216 seconds, or 3.6 minutes.

The above example demonstrates an important point: it does not take long for a fully developed short to melt a lot of conductor material. In the example, which assumed many ideal conditions, it took less than 4 minutes to heat up and melt 60 feet of two-wire, #14 copper conductor with a dead short at one end. This is 1.49 pounds of molten copper at 1,829°F. Since wood and paper typically ignite at 500°F, this is more than enough to start a fire. In fact, many fires begin with the melting of just an inch or less of copper wire.

An item of note with respect to beading is that in a two- or three-wire insulated conductor which carries single-phase alternating current it is generally the "hot" wire that will bead the most. Sometimes this fact is handy when the wires have not been correctly color coded.

Beading also occurs in steel. In electrical systems steel is often used in conduits, electrical boxes and other components. Occasionally it is also used as a conductor. Shorting can occur between the "hot" copper or aluminum conductor and the conduit or metal box. Normally the conduit and metal boxes are grounded, which allows them to complete the circuit. Typically, the shorting will produce a burn-through pattern in a metal box or conduit similar to that of a cutting electrode stick used by welders. When the arcing melts through the steel, the steel may form beads which then solidify just below the penetrations.

Since typical residential and light commercial fires cannot melt steel, and since only a few types of flammable materials can cause steel to melt in an open fire, the observation of steel beads in an electrical box or conduit in association with a "burn hole" is a very strong indicator of electrical shorting.

Further, even if there were fuel in the vicinity that could melt steel, it would be difficult to explain how the burning of the fuel could produce concentrated and specific points of melting in the conduit or electrical box. Only electrical shorting, and welding-type effects can do this. The fire front developed by a burning fuel load is broad and general; it tends to affect large areas rather than specific points.

F. Fuses, Breakers, and Overcurrent Protection

It is a common but mistaken notion that fuses or circuit breakers will completely protect a building against fire caused by electrical shorting. Fuses and common circuit breakers do not specifically protect against fires or shorting; they protect against overcurrent. They are not specifically short-circuit detecting devices.

In other words, a fuse or circuit breaker simply opens an electrical circuit when that circuit uses more amperes than the current-carrying capacity or trip point of the fuse or breaker. If a short circuit occurs and does not use more current than the trip point, the short will not be suppressed, but will continue to operate as long as its current usage is below the trip point.

In fact, the *National Electric Code* states that the purpose of overcurrent protection, i.e. fuses and circuit breakers, is to open the circuit if the current reaches a value that will cause an excessive or dangerous temperature in conductors or conductor insulation. In residences and light commercial buildings where there is no special-purpose equipment, fuses and breakers are sized to protect the particular branch circuit wiring from getting hot enough to damage its insulation. In sum, if the wiring isn't carrying enough current to get hot, the breaker or fuse won't trip.

*Figure 5.6 Electrical shorting of feeder lines to breaker box.
Note the melted conductor and melted sheet steel in box.*

It is for this reason that an oversized breaker or fuse is a fire hazard. While it allows a person to avoid the aggravation of changing fuses or resetting breakers in an overloaded system, it can allow a short circuit to proceed unchecked, or allow an overload to heat up the wiring until the insulation melts and a short develops.

A fuse is basically a small strip of metal encased in a tube or housing, which is connected to terminals. The metal strip is made of a low melting point alloy, sometimes called a fusible alloy. Fusible alloys generally have melting points in the range of 125°F to 500°F, and are usually made of some of the following materials: bismuth, lead, tin, cadmium, or indium. Usually the alloy's composition is eutectic so that the melting point is well defined.

The electrical resistance of the fusible metal strip is low, so it normally acts as a conductor in series with the circuit. However, when the current in the circuit reaches the set point, the metal strip heats up due to the I^2R effect and melts away, thus opening the circuit.

The rating or set point of the fuse is the amount of current it will allow to flow on a continuous basis without tripping. Under actual operating conditions, however, the trip point may vary from the rating due to localized air temperature around the fuse. In general, as the air temperature around the fuse rises, the trip point drops. This, of course, is because of the temperature-sensitive nature of the metal strip; less electrical energy is needed to melt a hot metal strip than a cold one.

For example, a Fusetron™ dual-element fuse has a carrying capacity of 110% of its current rating at 32°F, 100% at about 86°F, and 90% at about 130°F. At 212°F, its current carrying capacity will be only 63% of its current rating.

The above is very noteworthy. When heat from a nearby fire impinges on a fuse box and causes the fuses to get hot, the fuses may trip even if there has been no short or unusual overcurrent in their circuits. A fire near the fuse box will often cause the fuses to trip (even when there is no short) which then cuts off the electricity to the circuit. This can prevent secondary shorts from occurring as the fire spreads to wiring and equipment.

Circuit breakers are similar in function to fuses. They open the circuit when the current exceeds the set point of the breaker. However, while fuses are not reusable, breakers can be reset after tripping open the circuit. In general, a circuit breaker is a spring-loaded switch which pops to an open circuit position when the current is too high.

In smaller and medium sized circuit breakers, the unloading or tripping mechanism is likely a bimetallic strip through which the current flows. When the strip heats up sufficiently by I^2R effects, the strip overcomes the spring load and opens the circuit. A "snap through" type mechanism is typically used.

In medium and larger sized circuit breakers, the tripping mechanism may be a solenoid. The switch contactors on the solenoid will likely be held in place by a spring load. When the current is at the set point, the current flow through the solenoid produces enough magnetic field build-up in the solenoid to cause the contactors to overcome the spring load. Like the bimetallic version, a snap-through type mechanism is typically used to open the contactors.

In many circuit breakers, both bimetallic and solenoid type current sensing elements are used. The bimetallic element is used to sense the lower overcurrents, typically in the "1 times rating" to "10 times rating" range, and the solenoid element senses the higher level overcurrents, typically in the range of more than ten times the rating. The latter often occurs when the short circuit or ground fault resistance is very low. Most circuit breakers used in residential and light commercial buildings contain both the bimetallic and solenoid sensing elements.

When circuit breakers contain bimetallic elements, they are sensitive to the ambient temperature conditions in the same way that fuses are. If a circuit breaker containing a bimetallic element is put into a hot environment, it may trip at lower overcurrent levels. For this reason, when circuit breakers must be placed in hot or varying temperature environments, dual solenoid type breakers are used. One solenoid is set for the low overcurrents, replacing the bimetallic, and the other for high overcurrents. This substitution is made because solenoid elements are less sensitive to ambient temperatures.

Both circuit breakers and fuses exhibit *inverse time characteristics* with respect to overcurrent protection. In other words, as the applied current above the set point increases, the time required for opening the circuit decreases. Table 2 below lists a typical time current, or minimum melt, curve for a Bussman, 200-ampere, 600-volt, low peak dual element fuse, at standard temperature.

**Table 2. Opening Time vs. Applied Current
for Bussman[TM] Low-Peak LPS-RK 200 (RK1) Fuse**

applied current, amperes	opening time, seconds
2,000	0.01
1,500	0.20
1,000	10.0
600	55
400	150
300	450

The plot of applied current versus circuit opening time is called the *"time current curve"* for the particular fuse or circuit breaker. Usually the plot is on a log-log graph. Figure 5.7, which follows, shows sample time-current plots for both fuses and breakers.

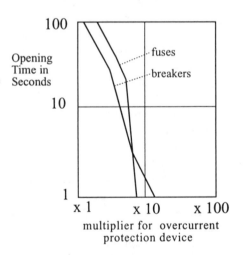

Figure 5.7 Time-current plots

In large power applications, some circuit breakers are not only designed to trip when there is an overload current condition, but they may also trip when there is an underload condition, that is, when the current (or voltage in some instances) flow is too low. Underload-type circuit breakers are typically used when a low current condition would cause damage to a particular piece of machinery or equipment.

In other large power applications, automatic reclosing circuit breakers may also be used. These are circuit breakers designed to automatically reset themselves after tripping. They are often used to guard against unnecessary nuisance trips which generally are quickly taken care of by smaller circuit protection devices located downline or elsewhere in the system. If the overcurrent (or undercurrent) condition persists after two or three attempts at reclosing, the device will lock itself in the open circuit position.

To protect against nuisance trips which occur during large motor start-ups, some breakers are equipped with time delay devices. These devices allow the circuit breaker to handle large but temporary current surges without tripping. The time delay devices are usually calibrated to operate in the zone where electric motor current on-rush normally occurs.

When there are very high voltages, high voltage circuit breakers are employed which either open in an oil immersion, or use a blast of air. These techniques break the electrical arc between the contactors as the contactors open.

With high voltages, even if the contactors are separated, it is possible for the electricity to arc from one contactor to the other and still maintain the circuit, especially if the air pathway has already been ionized by arcing at smaller separations. Once the air pathway is ionized, it is easy to increase the separation without breaking the arc because the air has lost much of its insulating property. (This is the principle which allows the operation of fluorescent lights and neon signs.)

Since most oils are poor conductors, opening the electrical contacts while immersed in oil stops the arcing. Likewise, in the air blast type, air is used to blow away the ionized air pathway; in essence, the air blast simply blows out the electrical arc.

The above brief discussion of circuit breakers and fuses mentions only the more common types; manufacturers offer a wide range of fuses and circuit breakers that are tailor-made for specialty applications, or that enhance or minimize various characteristics of the equipment. For this reason, the design of switch gear and protection equipment has become an engineering sub-specialty shared by both electrical and mechanical engineering disciplines.

In general, manufacturers have done a good job of designing overcurrent protection products that are reliable and long lasting. Most have in-house testing and quality controls to ensure that the products that leave the factory work as specified. When the equipment is installed properly and used appropriately, it will normally provide the required overcurrent protection.

However, as the complexity of the equipment increases, the opportunity for failure also increases. Manufacturers and designers are not omniscient. Sometimes unforeseen conditions develop that were not anticipated by the designers. Damage sometimes occurs in transit or storage. Also, the equipment must be installed correctly and be appropriate for the specific application. If the application is inappropriate, or the installation is incorrectly done, even the best equipment will not do a good job. The more complex overcurrent protection equipment requires preventive maintenance and periodic inspection. The lack of this may allow premature failure of the equipment. And, of course, there are failures caused by sabotage, vandalism, floods, fires, earthquakes, and other mayhem.

In short, for all kinds of reasons, overcurrent protection equipment sometimes does not work right. Sometimes it may not open the circuit properly when an overcurrent condition occurs. It may "hang up" or only open one of the phases in a three-phase system. Sometimes it may not work at all. It may wholly fail and not respond at all to the overcurrent condition. And, sometimes the overcurrent protection equipment itself may be the cause of an overcurrent problem. The equipment may itself develop an internal short circuit. Because of these possibilities, it is important to check the overcurrent protection that may have been present in the system when the cause of the fire is suspected of being electrical in nature.

G. Example Situation Involving Overcurrent Protection

Consider the following situation. In an older house, the branch wiring to a kitchen wall outlet was rated for 15 amperes. The fuse protecting that circuit was the older, screw-in type household fuse. To dispense with the aggravation of frequent fuse replacement, the home owner had inserted a 30-ampere fuse in the socket which was supposed to only have a 15-ampere fuse[1].

One day the homeowner left an automatic coffee maker unattended. Initially, the coffee pot was full. However, after a time all the coffee boiled off and the coffee maker overheated. The overheating of the coffee maker caused the plastic shell of the appliance to soften, collapse, smoke, and char; it also caused the appliance's electric cord to heat up. Where the cord entered the appliance, the plastic insulation broke down and the cord shorted. The short then followed the cord back into the wall outlet and caused the branch circuit wiring to overheat near the outlet.

Because the branch circuit wiring had old-fashioned, flammable fiber insulation wrap, the insulation around the wiring caught fire. The fire

---

[1] Note: In the older type fuse blocks, 5, 10, 20 and 30-ampere rated screw-in types of fuses are physically interchangeable. In most current codes, this type of fusing is no longer acceptable in new installations.

spread through the wall interior and then breached the wall. The resulting fire caused great damage to the house.

In the above situation, what was the primary cause of fire? Was it:

- negligence of the homeowner who left the coffee maker unattended?
- a design shortcoming of the appliance maker who did not include a safety device to account for a dry pot, or overheating situation?
- the 30-ampere fuse in a 15-ampere socket?
- the old-fashioned wiring which was insulated with flammable fiber insulation?

Further, if the correct fuse had been used, would the fire have been prevented, or the damages at least mitigated? Can the manufacturer of the coffee maker correctly assert from an engineering safety point of view that proper branch circuit fusing obviates the need for any internal safety device to protect from a dry pot situation?

H. Ground Fault Circuit Interrupters

A *ground fault circuit interrupter* (or GFCI) is a device which de-energizes a circuit when the current flow in a current-to-ground type short circuit exceeds some predetermined current. The current flowing to the ground which would cause a ground fault circuit interrupter to trip is often much less than the current flow required to trip breakers or fuses on the supply side of the circuit.

In other words, if the current in a short circuit flows over to the safety ground, the GFCI will shut off the circuit. However, if the current from the short circuit flows over to the "cold" wire and not the safety ground, the GFCI will do nothing. In that case, it will be up to the over-current protection to take care of that short.

In single-phase, residential type applications, ground fault circuit interrupters monitor the current passing through the "third" wire or the safety ground wire of the system. The NEC requires that GFCI devices be installed in bathrooms, kitchens, garages, and other areas where people are exposed to electrocution hazards.

For example, one such hazard might be created when a person drops an electric razor into a sink full of water, and then reaches into the water to retrieve the razor. When the razor enters the water, the current from the "hot" line bleeds out into the water and is grounded through the chassis of the razor into the safety ground, i.e., the "third" wire ground. When this occurs, the GFCI senses the current flowing through the safety ground and opens the circuit.

While GFCI devices are generally intended to reduce the risk of accidental electrocution, they sometimes can arrest shorting that would have otherwise resulted in fire. They can be very useful in detecting and arresting shorts that occur on the downline side of the load, from the "cold" wire to the safety ground. This is a type of series short, as discussed before in Section D, except that the ground is now included in the circuit. In essence, the ground completes the circuit from the point of shorting, and substitutes for the "cold" conductor of the circuit.

Shorts of this type can be relatively slow in developing and might not be detected by standard fuse or breaker overcurrent protection. This is because if the resistance at the point of shorting is relatively low, the current flow may not be noticeably higher than normal. In effect, the short would be equivalent to a wire-to-wire splice. However, if the placement of the GFCI in the circuit is in line with the current flow through the ground, it will detect that current is flowing through the ground instead of the "cold" wire, and open the circuit.

I. "Grandfathering" of GFCIs

In residences built before the GFCI requirement of the NEC, it is usually not required that GFCIs be installed, although it is recommended. The original electrical installation is generally allowed to stay in place if it meets three conditions: 1) that it continues to meet the standards current at the time it was installed; 2) that there have been no undue changes made to the original installation; and 3) that its continued operation creates no undue risk.

If significant modifications are made to the house, such as extensive remodeling and rewiring, it is likely that local code enforcement officials will require that the remodeled portion be upgraded to comply with current code requirements, which may include the installation of GFCIs where appropriate. If the remodeling constitutes a basic re-construction of more than a certain percentage, often more than 50 percent of the residence, local code enforcement officials may require that whole house be upgraded to meet current code requirements.

However, while such "grandfathering" is allowed for private residences, this is usually not the case for commercial buildings or public buildings. Usually, such places are required to adhere to the current code in effect with respect to GFCI's, to protect public safety.

As a reminder to the reader, the above references to code enforcement are mere generalizations, and as with any generalizations, they may not apply to your specific area or jurisdiction. To be sure what the requirements are for your area, check with your local code enforcement officials.

J. Other Devices

A variety of other electrical devices are used to sense electrical problems in the lines. Lightning arresters and surge arresters sense high voltage or high current transients and shunt the transient to ground. In some such devices, when the voltage of the transient exceeds a set amount, sometimes called the *clamping voltage*, the line momentarily connects to ground to discharge the transient. In more sophisticated devices, the device may monitor the increase per time of the transient. If either the current or voltage climbs faster than a set amount, the device shunts over to ground momentarily.

Within some appliances with electric motors there are embedded bi-metallic switches; these switches open the circuit in the windings of the motor if the motor windings get too hot. The idea is to shut off the motor before it gets hot enough to short out and catch fire. Some of the bi-metallic switches reset when the motor cools down; other types may stay permanently in the open position once a problem has occurred.

In some appliances, notably some types of coffee makers, there is a thermally sensitive resistor or diode. If the circuit gets too hot, the resistor or diode opens the circuit. These devices do not reset. In many ways the device is like a fuse, except that it is not strictly an overcurrent device. Such devices are usually added to protect against "dry pot" situations.

Some types of electrical equipment "treat" the incoming power received from the utility. Undesirable harmonics, transients, and static are filtered from the line. This may be done by the use of sophisticated circuitry and solid state devices, or by the use of motor-generator sets. In the latter, the power from the utility is used to operate an electric motor, which powers a generator. The idea is that the harmonics, static and transients coming from the utility power lines are smoothed out by flywheel inertia effects within the motor and generator set. Also, there is no direct circuit link between the incoming power from the utility, and the outgoing power produced by the generator. Thus, the power coming from the generator is "cleaner," that is free of harmonics and spikes, than the power received by the motor from the utility.

Another type of "treatment" device is called an UPS device; the UPS acronym stands for *uninterruptible power supply.* Such equipment not only filters out undesirable static, harmonics, and transients, but also switches over to batteries or alternative power generation equipment if the utility suffers a power failure, low voltage condition, or similar.

In any case, it is worth noting that these special-purpose devices which "treat" the incoming power often contain special purpose electrical protection devices. In case of an overload or underload, they may not simply open the circuit and stop everything. They may contain relays which switch over circuits to new lines, or cause certain components to operate that were previously off-line. They may even shed certain circuits or operating equipment in an orderly sequence until the problem is isolated from the rest of the circuit. These special-purpose protection devices may, in addition to overcurrent or undercurrent, sense ground faults, voltage variance, power factors, or relative loading between phases.

K. Lightning Type Surges

While it is possible for lightning to cause electrical shorting problems which may result in fire, more frequently lightning causes circuit components to blow apart which then opens the circuit. This is especially true in circuits that contain non-linear components like inductors, capacitors, transistors, diodes, and IC (integrated circuit) chips. In inductive components like motor windings, lightning or high voltage surges can cause shorting between the windings and the chassis ground. This occurs when the transient voltage is large enough to cause dielectric breakdown in the winding insulation.

Typically, a lightning type surge or transient will not directly cause fuses or breakers to trip. Since a lightning stroke will often occur in less than 50 microseconds, most fuses and breakers do not react fast enough to arrest it. A quick check of the generic current-time plot shown previously in Figure 4 of this chapter shows that as the lapsed time decreases, the amount of overcurrent allowed to pass through the overcurrent protection device increases. Thus, generally, a lightning surge will not be stopped by a breaker or fuse.

In cases where the fuse or breaker provides significant impedance to the surge, the surge may simply arc across the fuse or breaker from terminal to terminal, or terminal to ground. It is not unusual to observe that a lightning-magnitude surge has simply "jumped" around a fuse.

When a lightning-magnitude surge passes through a fuse or breaker box, it may cause damage in a component well downline from the fuse or breaker box. For example, if the component is a motor, it may short out as previously discussed. Because of this shorting damage, the current overprotection of that branch circuit will eventually come into play. Thus, while lightning does not normally cause a fuse or breaker to trip directly, it may cause damages that eventually result in a fuse or breaker tripping.

Figure 5.8 Electrical shorting in meter box.
Feeder line abraded on edge of knock-out hole in bottom of box.

L. Common Places Where Shorting Occurs

The following is a list of items or locations where electrical shorting leading to fires often occurs. The list is not intended to be exhaustive, but represents items that in my own practice seem to occur regularly.

Staples. In residences and light commercial buildings it is common practice in some areas to simply staple Romex type conductors to wood members. If the staple is applied too tightly, the insulation around the conductors can be crushed, cracked or even torn. In some cases, the staple itself may bite or cut into the insulation. Over time, the damaged insulation may further degrade because of tears and penetrations in the protective sheathing. Current may leak from one conductor to another due to the damaged insulation and precipitate shorting.

Corners. When nominally straight conductors are bent at a sharp angle, the conductor cross sectional area may be deformed. When the bend is sharp enough, the conductors may develop a crease, or otherwise become distorted and lose some of their effective current carrying cross-sectional area.

The resistance of a conductor with uniform cross sectional area is given by:

(xxiii) $R = (\rho l) / A$

where ρ = the specific resistance of the conductor usually given in ohms per cm^3,
     l = length of the conductor, and
     A = cross sectional area of conductor.

From inspection of equation (xxiii) it is apparent that if the cross sectional area is halved, the resistance is doubled. And if the resistance is doubled, then the amount of heat generated by the resistance at that point is doubled, as per the power equation given below.

(xxiv) $P = I^2R$

In addition to deformation of the conductor itself, sharp bending of a conductor may cause the insulation on the outside radius of the bend to become stretched. This will reduce its thickness, and may even cause small holes or tears to develop. When such microholes develop in plastic materials, it is often the case that the color of the plastic will "whiten." Clear plastic will often become milk white — opaque where the microholes are concentrated.

Figure 5.9 Electrical ground fault in clothes dryer.
Cord abraded on sharp edge of hole.

When the insulation wrap around the conductor stretches and becomes thin, or develops microholes due to excessive strain, the insulation will lose some of its dielectric properties. Because multiple conductors are often in common casings, the insulation between the "hot" and "cold" conductors may be sufficiently damaged for a current leak to develop between conductors.

Skinning. When wiring is installed, it is often pulled through conduit, weather heads, holes, or box openings. Sometimes as the conductors pass over edges, around corners or over rough spots, the exterior insulation around the conductor is "skinned," that is, some of the exterior insulation is abraded away. This causes the insulation to be thinner at that location; as such, the "skinned" area is an insulation weak spot in the conductor. If the thinning is sufficient, it is possible that current can leak across the weak spot.

Conductors have to handle not only the normal voltage supplied by the utility, but also the voltage spikes and transients commonly generated by switching activities within the utility system. If insulation is "skinned," it may be able to withstand the nominal voltage, but may not be able to stand up to large spikes and transients. Breakdown of the "skinned" insulation may occur after repeated spikes, or after a single spike if it has sufficiently high voltage.

Edges. Wires and conductors are not immobile, although they may appear to be wholly static. First of all, they expand and contract with temperature change. Also, they often slightly jerk in response to large current rushes, such as occur when a motor is turned on. (The amount of jerk can be calculated by the application of Maxwell's Equations.) Because the conductors are often fastened to various portions of a structure, portions of the conductor will move as the structure moves in response to wind, temperature, and/or loads. Thus, conductors in contact with a

*Figure 5.10 "Pigtail" cord on window air conditioner which abraded
on edge of sheet metal and shorted out. There was no safety
grommet in the slot provided for the cord to pass through.*

sharp edge may have their insulation cut after a period of time due to
small relative motions between the conductors and the sharp edge.

Whenever conductors or other types of wiring are run through boxes,
walls, or other items which have sharp edges, the NEC requires that
smooth bushings be provided. (See NEC 410-30; 410-27(b); 370-22;
345-15; and 300-16.)

Flexible Cords. Flexible electric cords typically have stranded conductors, which are composed of many individual hair-like strands of
conductor bundled together. Over time, the cord may be bent back and
forth at a particular point in the cord causing fatigue damage to the
individual strands.

As the strands break apart, the ability of the conductor to carry
current diminishes. If enough of the strands break apart, the cord will
develop a "hot" spot at that point for the same reasons as discussed
under "corners" in the previous paragraphs: loss of current carrying cross
sectional area.

From experience, the two most common points in a flexible cord
where fatigue damage to the strands occurs are where the cord exits the
appliance, and where the cord connects to the male plug; these are the
two points where the cord will often be bent the most.

Some people have the habit of disengaging a plug from a wall outlet
by pulling on the cord. When this is done, the force needed to disengage
the male plug from the outlet is carried by the conductor, since the conductor is usually more rigid than the exterior insulation wrap. Not only
can this cause breakage of the electrical connection between the conductor and the male plug, but if the cord were pulled while it was at an angle
with the plug, individual strands may be broken by combined bending

and tensile stresses in the strands. This is why it is recommended that a male plug be disengaged from a wall outlet only by grasping the plug itself.

In addition to fatigue breakage, flexible cords often sustain physical damage to the cord due to mashing and folding. This may occur, for example, when an extension cord is run through a door jamb and the door is closed on it, when a knot in the cord is pulled tight, or when the cord is walked on often. I have observed where extension cords have been laid across the burners of cook stoves, laid across the rotating shaft of a bench grinder (take a guess on this one as to what happened), laid under rugs in busy hallways, and laid across garage floors where a car was regularly driven. I have also seen them nailed to walls with the nails driven between the conductors, stapled to walls and ceilings, tied around nails and hooks, and embedded into wall plaster to avoid having an unsightly cord hanging down the wall.

One of my favorite cases combines several types of abuse all at once: a breeze box type fan was suspended from the ceiling by its own cord, which had been tied with a square knot to a hot steam pipe. The fan had been suspended over the top of a commercial steam cooker which was regularly opened and closed. This all goes to show, of course, that there is simply no end to the creativity a person can apply to the abuse of flexible cords.

Lastly, besides being physically damaged as noted above, flexible cords are often just electrically overloaded. Many light application extension cords are rated for 15 amperes. If a 20- or 25-ampere appliance is plugged into the cord, the appliance may draw more current than the extension cord can safely handle; the cord will then heat up due to I^2R heating effects. There will be some point along the cord where it will heat up a little more than elsewhere, and if left unchecked the cord may in time fail and short at that point.

It is not uncommon for a 15-ampere extension cord to be equipped with three or more outlets. Thus, if three appliances which draw 10 amperes each are plugged into the extension cord and are operated, the cord will be carrying twice its rated load. Unfortunately, few homeowners are cognizant of the current ratings of extension cords; most people simply use whatever extension cord is handy, has the appropriate length, or is the cheapest.

Lugs and Terminals. Lugs and terminals are used to connect conductors together. The ability of the lug or terminal to carry current is a function of the contact area between the two materials, and the quality of the metal-to-metal contact between them. In most cases, the conductors, lugs, and terminals are cleaned before installation, and pressure is applied to the connection to ensure good contact.

Figure 5.11 Connection block mounted on wood.
Wiring overheated and ignited the wood.

If the contact area between the two conductors is reduced or the contact quality is degraded, the connection will lose its ability to carry current. The connection point can then become a "hot spot" due to I^2R heating effects. Two of the commoner reasons for a lug or terminal to lose its ability to safely carry current are *looseness* and *corrosion*.

Looseness of the corrosion can occur because of vibrations, impacts to the panel box, temperature effects, material creep, chemical attack, and a host of other less obvious causes. Looseness can cause a loss of current-carrying area because in most cases, the contact area is partly a function of the compression between the two materials. When the compression is firm, the two materials are in intimate contact. When the compression is not firm, there may be an air space between the materials that acts as an insulator. A firm connection also tends to push through the light layer of oxide that usually forms on the conductors during storage and shipment.

It is not uncommon for some manufacturers of screw-type lugs to recommend that the lugs be periodically checked for tightness. Some manufacturers of industrial-type bus bars have used "break away" type lug connections to ensure that screw-type connections do not back off and become loose. Other manufacturers have used "crushable" threaded lugs to prevent lug back off. Most have specific tightening specifications to ensure a tight connection that will not back off.

Corrosion at a lug or terminal usually causes problems in two ways. First, the products of corrosion are often not good conductors of electrical current. While copper and aluminum are excellent conductors, copper oxide and aluminum oxide are not. A layer of corrosion products between the conductors typically increases the resistance of the connection, which then results in heating of the connection.

Secondly, corrosion may cause material damage to the connection. It may result in material loss, weakening of the material, or even dimensional distortion. In the latter case, the distortion may occur due to a change in material properties while being subject to the same loading or stress.

Corrosion of lugs and terminals is often caused by exposure to water, constant high humidity, or chemicals. A water drip may occur directly over an electrical box, or the humidity in the area may be constantly saturated. Chemical vapors from processes or materials storage may also contribute to and accelerate corrosion. It is important to note if the electrical box and connections have been rated for the specific environment they have been put into. There are many types of electrical boxes which are variously rated for outside use, use in high humidity, use in explosive environments, etc.

The corrosion of lugs and terminals can also be caused by the electricity itself flowing through certain combinations of dissimilar conductor materials. This is called *galvanic corrosion,* and is basically the phenomenon which is used to produce gold or silver plating in jewelry.

In galvanic corrosion, the passage of electrical current literally causes one of the materials to plate out onto the other. This results in material loss to the donor material which can be substantial, depending upon the circumstances. The material receiving the transferred material does not benefit by this plating action either. Typically, the transferred material quickly oxidizes and becomes a non-conducting crust of hoary "fuzz" or "crud" around the lug or terminal.

The formation of this "crud" then further accelerates the galvanic process because the "crud" itself acts as a surface for gathering water moisture to the connection. The presence of moisture around the connection helps to promote galvanic corrosion because the moisture provides a medium, or a chemical solution if you will, in which the reaction can take place.

Thus, the primary factors which influence the rate of galvanic corrosion include:

- the type of materials in physical contact with one another,
- the amount of current flow,
- the voltage across the terminal connection itself (a relatively high resistance connection will help promote the process), and
- the humidity or moisture that may come into contact with the lugs or terminals.

For these reasons, it is not proper to directly connect aluminum conductors to copper conductors. Copper and iron is also a bad connection combination due to its tendency to quickly corrode. It is also not proper to connect aluminum conductors to lugs and terminals that are rated only for copper conductors, and vice versa.

If a "mixed" connection between a copper conductor and an aluminum conductor must be made, a dual-rated connection box should be used. Also, connections between copper and aluminum conductors can be safely made when an intermediary material is used that is compatible with both; tin is often used for this purpose. Thus, copper conductors and aluminum conductors that will be connected together are often tin coated or "tinned" at the point where direct contact will be made. Other types of solder coatings or "tins" have been developed for use as intermediaries.

However, these coatings must be used with great care. Over time the coating may crack, become abraded, corrosively degrade, etc. Breaching of the coating may then allow the two dissimilar metals to come into direct contact with each other and set up a galvanic corrosion cell.

With respect to dissimilar conductors, the NEC (110-14) states in part that:

> "Conductors of dissimilar metals shall not be intermixed in a terminal or splicing connector where physical contact occurs between dissimilar conductors (such as copper and aluminum, copper and copper clad aluminum, or aluminum and copper clad aluminum) unless the device is suitable for the purpose and conditions of use."

When a lug or terminal connection is loose or corroded, often a chattering or buzzing noise can be heard emanating from the problem connection. This noise is generated by the 60-Hertz alternating current arcing across or within the connection. Because there is not enough current-carrying contact area, current is literally arcing across air gaps in and around the connection.

When such arcing occurs, it typically causes pitting of the connection, and scatters tiny blobs of conductor material in the vicinity of the arcing. The area around the "chattering" often is blackened due to the formation of carbon residues from the air by the arcing. The local temperatures of the arcs themselves will range from 2,500°F to as high as 10,000°F, which is the same range of temperatures found in arc welding or lightning.

If the "chattering" is allowed to continue, it usually results in overheating of the connection, electrical shorting and failure, and possibly fire. Sometimes after a fire, an occupant of the building may recall having heard a "chattering" or "buzzing" sound coming from the electrical box.

Motor Burn Out. When electric motors become worn out, or the rotating shaft becomes locked perhaps due to a seized bearing, the windings in the motor can overheat and short out. This is especially true of motors which are not equipped with internal thermal switches. Such switches, also known as high-heat limit switches, shut off the motor if its windings overheat. Some of the older type motors have flammable insulation shellac around the windings which can then catch fire.

For a charm of powerful trouble,
Like a hell-broth, boil and bubble.
Double, double toil and trouble;
Fire, burn; and, cauldron bubble.

The Witches in Shakespeare's *Macbeth*, Act IV, Scene I.

Chapter 6: Explosions

A. General

An explosion is a sudden, violent release of energy. It is usually accompanied by a loud noise and an expanding pressure wave of gas. The pressure of the gas decreases with distance from the origin or "epicenter". Explosions resulting from the ignition of flammable materials may also be accompanied by a high temperature fireball, which can ignite combustible materials in its path.

Explosions caused by the sudden release of chemical energy are classified into two main types: deflagrating explosions and detonating explosions.

A *deflagrating* explosion is characterized by a relatively slow, progressive burn rate of the explosive material. The progressive release and dispersion of energy through the explosive material in a deflagrating explosion is accomplished by normal heat transfer mechanisms. Because of this, the transmission of energy through the explosive material depends on external factors such as ambient pressure and temperature conditions.

Deflagrating explosions cause damage generally by pushing things about because of pressure differentials. This may include walls, ceilings, floors, large pieces of furniture, etc. Higher pressure gas emanating from the explosion hits an object which has a lower pressure gas on the other side, and the pressure difference between the two sides results in a net force being applied, which may be enough to move the item, or tear it away from its anchor points.

Deflagrations generally have low ability to cause fissile or brisance type damages. Small objects near the epicenter of the deflagration are often left undamaged as the pressure wave passes around them. The pressure differences on their surfaces are often insufficient to cause breakage.

A *detonating* explosion is characterized by a relatively rapid burn rate, high energy release rate, and a high peak explosion pressure. The progressive release and dispersion of energy through the explosive material is accomplished by shock waves and their associated pressure forces and stresses. For this reason, transmission of energy through the detonating material does not depend on ambient conditions of pressure or temperature.

Detonating explosions have higher fissile ability than deflagrations. It is this quality that makes them useful for blasting work. Objects near the epicenter of a detonating explosion are torn apart, often like so much smashed and shattered glass, due to the transmission of intense shock waves through their material.

Some detonating materials have high enough fissile qualities that they are even used to cut large pieces of steel. A small amount of the material, in the form of a putty, is simply applied along the "cut line" of the steel beam. The shock wave generated by its detonation is sufficiently intense to cause the steel to break apart where the putty was applied.

A general distinction between deflagrating explosions and detonating explosions is that the former have subsonic pressure propagation rates within the explosive material while the latter have supersonic pressure propagation rates.

In addition to deflagrations and detonations there is a third category of explosion, which involves the sudden expansion of high-pressure gases, as might occur from a ruptured high pressure vessel or pipe. This category also includes the sudden expansion of pressurized liquids into gas, such as would occur when pressurized boiler feed water flashes into steam when the pressure is suddenly lowered. This category of explosion will be considered first.

B. High Pressure Gas Expansion Explosions

The third category of explosion mentioned in the previous section is sometimes classified as a *polytropic expansion.* This type of explosion does not involve the release of chemical energy via a chemical reaction; it simply involves the rapid expansion of pressurized gases to ambient conditions. In essence, it is the conversion of enthalpy energy to irreversible "P–V" work, with the final state of the gas at equilibrium with ambient conditions.

Polytropic expansions involve a change of state which is usually represented by the general expression:

(i) PV^n = Constant

where P = pressure,
      V = volume, and
      n = polytropic gas constant.

When n = 1, the expansion occurs at isothermal conditions, and gas behavior conforms to the Ideal Gas Law. Of course, when this occurs, the release is not sudden. In order to accomplish isothermal expansion, the release must be very slow in a quasi-reversible manner. This is not an explosion; at most, it might be a small, slow leak at a low escape velocity where the pressure difference is slight.

When $n = k$, where $k = [C_p / C_v]$, the expansion occurs at adiabatic conditions (see Chapter 2, discussion beginning at equation (xxxi). The reader may recall that when a process occurs very fast, no time is available for the transfer of heat to the surroundings, and hence the process is adiabatic. This is the mathematical model which corresponds to explosions.

When n is a value intermediate between 1 and k, the corresponding thermodynamic process is also intermediate between an adiabatic and isothermal process, or perhaps some combination of the two. This is also not a model for an explosion, but might model certain processes that occur less rapidly than an explosion. It could also perhaps model a two or three step process where one of the steps involves a quick, adiabatic expansion.

When gas in a reservoir under high pressure is suddenly released into a lower pressure environment through a hole or rupture, the velocity of the escaping gas is determined by equating the change in enthalphy from the high pressure state to the low pressure state at the hole to its kinetic energy equivalent. In essence, this is a simple conversion of energy equation, as shown below.

(ii) Δ(enthalpy) $= \Delta$(kinetic energy) $= \Delta$(energy between states)

$$m(h_2 - h_1) = (\tfrac{1}{2})mv^2 = \Delta E$$

$$v = [2(h_2 - h_1)]^{\frac{1}{2}}$$

where h = specific enthalphy of the gas,
   m = mass,
   v = velocity, and
   ΔE = total energy change.

In the above equation, it is assumed that the escaping velocity V is either equal to or less than the speed of sound. For various reasons, it will not exceed Mach 1, or the speed of sound of the gas at those conditions.

Because the shape of the hole at the point of rupture can affect the "efficiency" of the above process, a correction factor C is often added to the equation as shown below.

(iii) $v = C[2(h_2 - h_1)]^{\frac{1}{2}}$

where C =   coefficient to account for hole shape and venturi constriction effects.

In general, values for C are near 0.6 when the escaping gases pass through a hole. This assumes that the escaping gas has a high Reynolds number, that is, a relatively high rate of flow. When the vessel simply comes apart, and there is no flow through a hole, then C is simply equal to 1.0.

With a little algebraic hocus-pocus, equation (iii) can be converted into the following expression for gases, provided no condensation occurs in the gas during the escape.

(iv) $v = C\{ 2[P_1V_1][k / (k-1)][1 - (P_2 / P_1)^{(k-1)/k}]\}^{1/2}$

where v = velocity of escaping gas,
  C = coefficient for opening,
  P_2 = pressure outside vessel,
  P_1 = pressure inside vessel ($P_1 > P_2$),
  k = gas constant, C_p/C_v, and
  V_1 = specific volume of gas inside vessel at P_1.

Of course, the total expansion of the released gas can be calculated by simply assuming that the total mass is conserved and undergoes a change of state from conditions "(T_1, P_1, V_1), " to "(T_2, P_2, V_2)."

In general, the sudden release of compressed gas affects only the space into which the gas expands to ambient pressure. In many respects, the blast or explosion effects of a polytropic expansion are about the same as a deflagration explosion, given equal initial pressures and temperatures. However, in a polytropic expansion explosion, there are generally no fireball or fire front effects to consider.

C. Deflagrations and Detonations

In the study of fires and explosions, by far the most common type of explosion encountered is the deflagration. Deflagrations often occur when flammable gases or dusts have accumulated to levels above their lower limits of flammability. Examples of deflagrating explosives include:

1. Explosive mixtures of natural gas and air at room conditions.

2. The decomposition of cellulose nitrate, an unstable compound often used in propellants.

3. Black powder.

4. Grain dust.

Detonations are often encountered in arson or sabotage cases. Occasionally, accidental detonations occur, usually in construction work, quarry work, or similar. Examples of detonating explosives include:

1. Dynamite.

2. Nitroglycerine.

3. Mercury fulminate.

4. Trinitrotoluene (TNT).

5. Ammonium nitrate fuel oil (ANFO).[1]

Under special conditions, a normally deflagrating explosive can be made to detonate. Such special conditions include the application of high pressures, strong sources of ignition, and long flame runup distances. With the rare exception of the last condition, in uncontrolled fires and explosion, deflagrations remain deflagrations.

When an explosion occurs in an unconfined, open area, the pressure wave will harmlessly expand and expend itself until the pressure gradient becomes insignificant. When an explosion occurs in a confined space, the pressure wave will push against the confining structure. This is why when a small amount of loosely piled gunpowder is ignited, it simply burns quickly with a moderate hiss. However, if the same amount of gunpowder is wrapped tightly in a paper container and ignited, it becomes an ear-splitting firecracker that bursts apart.

When an explosion occurs within a typical building, the building is generally damaged. While most building codes require that buildings or inhabited structures be able to withstand externally applied downward loads due to snow, rain, ice, and wind, building codes do not require that the structures be able to withstand the outwardly directed loads generated by an explosion located within or adjacent to the structure.

In buildings, many accidental explosions are typically caused by some of the following:

1. Ignition of natural gas leaks.

---

[1] During the trial for the World Trade Center bombing, the type of explosive the conspirators were caught in the act of making at the time of arrest was a type of ANFO. The authorities described is as a "witches' brew". Hence, the quotation at the beginning of this chapter is an obscure reference to this heinous act of sabotage.

2. Ignition of vapors from improperly stored gasoline, cleaning solvents, copy machine chemicals, or other volatile flammable liquids.

3. Ignition of liquid propane vapors (LP) which have leaked.

4. Ignition of grain dust, coal dust, flour dust, textile dust, and other types of dust from combustible materials.

5. Ignition of certain types of fine metal powders, such as aluminum and magnesium.

6. Ignition of atomized flammable liquids.

Casual inspection of the above list finds that most accident explosions that occur in buildings are of the deflagrating type.

The materials involved in deflagrating explosions can be ignited in a number of ways. The most common source of ignition is an electric spark. As was noted in Chapter 2, the smallest spark which can cause ignition of combustible vapors is called the *minimum ignition energy (MIE)*. Usually the spark as measured in laboratory tests is supplied from a capacitor across an air gap to the fuel. The optimum air gap distance which can cause ignition is referred to as the *minimum ignition quenching distance.*

The following table lists the MIE values for the vapors of several fuels at stoichiometric conditions in air.

Table 1. Minimum Ignition Energies For Combustible Gases in Air*

fuel	MIE
natural gas	0.00030 joules
propane	0.00026 joules
ammonia	>1.00 joules
methanol	0.00014 joules
normal butane	0.00026 joules
trichloroethylene	0.300 joules

*Source: U.S. Department of the Interior,
Bureau of Mines, Bulletin 680, page 33.

One of the reasons why extra precautions must be taken around areas where there is concentrated oxygen, such as in hospitals, is that the MIE of pure oxygen can be many times less than that of the MIE in air. Table 2 lists the MIE values for the same fuels at stoichiometric conditions in pure oxygen instead of air.

Table 2. Minimum Ignition Energies For Combustible Gases in Oxygen*

fuel	MIE
natural gas	0.000003 joules
propane	0.000002 joules
ammonia	not available
methanol	not available
normal butane	0.000009 joules
trichloroethylene	0.0128 joules

*Source: U.S. Department of the Interior,
Bureau of Mines, Bulletin 680, page 33.

A comparison of Tables 1 and 2 shows that some of the combustible vapors will ignite in oxygen at MIE levels two orders of magnitude less than in air.

This extreme sensitivity of pure oxygen to even the smallest spark has been a bane to NASA. A small spark in an oxygen-rich atmosphere is what triggered the fire in Apollo 1, when three astronauts were killed. The breathing atmosphere inside the capsule utilized an oxygen-rich mixture; in later missions this mixture was changed to reduce the hazard.

Oxygen sensitivity to spark ignition was also the cause of the explosion which disabled Apollo 13 en route to the moon. There were cracks in the insulation of some electrical wires in an oxygen tank on the side of the command ship. When the tank was utilized and the oxygen contacted the wires, the ensuing explosion blew off an entire side panel. Only by very remarkable teamwork and some smart thinking on the part of people both on the ground and in the spacecraft were the lives of the astronauts saved.

The following is a partial list of common sources of electrical sparks in homes and commercial businesses which can cause ignition of combustible vapors.

Table 3. Common Sources of Electrical Sparks Which Set Off Explosions

Electric motors: the commutator slip ring sliding contact. Sump pumps are famous for igniting propane vapors which have accumulated in basements.

Loose electrical plugs in wall sockets. When the appliance turns on, the plug prongs may arc to the contacts. This occurs in refrigerators and freezers where the appliance turns on and off intermittently.

Static discharge due to frictional action between two electrically dissimilar materials. The effect is called triboelectrification, and can occur between any combination of gas, liquid, and solid. A particularly hazardous situation is the transfer of flammable liquid from one container to another, especially when one is a plastic bucket.

Relays and switches. Both will spark when the contacts open and close.

Lightning.

Electric bug killers. The high voltage needed to zap a bug can also zap an explosion if there are flammable vapors around.

Thermostats. These also have open and close contact points, although most operate at low voltages.

Old fashioned door bells. Essentially, this is simply another version of a relay, except that the spark is more continuous while the bell is operating.

In addition to sparks, deflagrating explosions can also be set off by the following list of common ignition sources.

Table 4. Non-Spark Ignition Sources Which Set Off Explosions

Pilot lights in hot water tanks, furnaces, heaters, ovens, stoves and gas dryers.

Smoking materials: cigarettes, matches, cigars, lighters, etc. In some cases, lighters have been known to fall into tight places, become wedged there, and allow their butane to shoot out into another ignition source like a fan. This has occurred in vehicles where people toss lighters on the dashboard, and the lighters fall through vent openings into the ventilation system.

Sparks from the sliding contact of metals or abrasives. Examples include grinding wheels, gas welding igniters, cigarette lighter flints, metal chisels, and hacksaws.

Stove or furnace electric igniters.

Hot surfaces, such as electric heater elements.

Radiant energy. Some chemicals only need to be exposed to sunlight to explode. These fall into a special subclass of photoreactive chemicals.

Heat from chemical reactions, or between items being mixed.

Running automobiles or other internal combustion engines, especially in confined garages.

D. Some Basic Parameters

In both deflagrating and detonating explosions, the maximum pressure occurs when the explosion is wholly confined, which is a constant-volume process, and the explosive mixture is close to stoichiometric concentrations. The maximum pressure for many hydrocarbon based deflagrating explosion mixtures ranges between seven and nine times the ambient pressure. The typical maximum pressure for a gaseous detonating explosion will be nearly double that of a deflagrating explosion under the same conditions.

Thus, if the ambient pressure is 1,013.3 millibars, 1 standard atmosphere, the maximum pressure for a typical deflagrating explosion could range from 7,100 mb to 9,120 mb. A gaseous detonating explosion maximum pressure might then be 14,200 mb to 18,240 mb.

The following graph in Figure 1 shows the pressure rise versus time as measured in absolute pressure of a methane and air deflagrating explosion at stoichiometric mixture, 1013.3 mb ambient pressure, and 25°C. The explosion was done in a laboratory vessel which was 3.65 meters in diameter and the explosion occurred under constant volume conditions. It is notable that the maximum pressure attained in the explosion, 8,600 mb, occurred in less than one second.

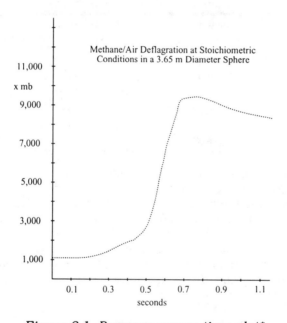

Figure 6.1 Pressure versus time plot*
*Source: U.S. Department of the Interior, Bureau of Mines, Bulletin 680, page 16.

In deflagrating explosions, there is normally a mixture range of fuel and air in which explosions are possible. For example, methane or natural gas will explode when the concentration is between 5% and 15% in air by volume. If the concentration is less than 5% or more than 15%, no explosion will occur. The ratio of air to fuel will be such that the flame propagation will be self-quenching.

While a methane and air deflagration explosion can reach pressures of 8,600 millibars gage pressure when the mixture is optimized for maximum pressure, which usually occurs near or at the stoichiometric mixture, the explosion pressure drops off quickly at mixture concentrations more or less than the optimum point.

For example, at a methane concentration of 5%, the lower limit for methane and air explosions, the explosion pressure will reach only about 3,200 mb. At the upper limit of 15%, the explosion pressure will reach only about 3,900 mb. Similarly, the flame temperature of the explosion, which is maximum at or very near stoichiometric conditions, drops significantly when the mixture is either less than or more than the optimum mixture.

The following table lists some common deflagrating fuels and their explosive limits.

Table 5. Explosive Limits of Some Common Gases

fuel	limits (% v/v)
methane	5.0 – 15.0
ethane	3.0 – 12.4
propane	2.1 – 9.5
acetone	2.6 – 13.0
ammonia	15.0 – 28.0
gasoline	1.3 – 6.0
CO	12.5 – 74.0
methanol	6.7 – 12.0

For dusts such as flour and grain, the lower explosive limits are about 40–50 grams per cubic meter of air. However, some items, such as birch bark wood dust, have a lower explosive limit of 20 grams per cubic meter of air. Bituminous coal and lignite dusts have similar explosive lower limit numbers as agricultural dusts. The upper explosive limits for both types of such dusts are not clearly defined.

Table 6 below lists the lower explosive limits for some metallic dusts. As with the grain dusts, the upper explosive limits for metallic dusts are not clearly defined.

Table 6. Lower Explosive Limits for Metallic Dusts

material	lower limit (grams per cu. meter)
aluminum	80
iron	120
magnesium	30
manganese	120
sulfur	35
uranium	60
zinc	480

E. Overpressure Front

Overpressure is the amount of pressure in excess of the usual ambient pressure. Engineers usually call this the *gauge pressure* and distinguish it from *absolute pressure*, which is the pressure measured from a vacuum. In the English system, gage pressure is measured in pounds per square inch gauge (psig), and absolute pressure is measured in pounds per square inch absolute (psia). When the abbreviation "psi" is used, gauge pressure is often implied.

A reasonable model for calculating the pressure at the explosion front, the boundary where the explosion pressure is maximum, is the inverse cube rule. This is because the pressure envelope that expands outward from the epicenter is three-dimensional, and the pressure of a gas is a function of its volume. The general equation is shown below.

(v) $\qquad P_r = K[I / r^3]$

where $\quad P_r \;\; = \;\;$ pressure at explosion front located distance r from epicenter,

$\qquad\qquad K \;\; = \;\;$ arbitrary constant for conversion of units and efficiency of explosion,

$\qquad\qquad I \;\; = \;\;$ explosion intensity, amount of explosive, or amount of energy release, and

$\qquad\qquad r \;\; = \;\;$ distance from explosion.

When the pressure at one point is known, it is possible to use equation (v) to calculate pressures at other locations.

(vi) $\quad P_1 = C$, a known amount at distance r_1.

$$P_1[r_1^3] = KI$$

$$P_2[r_2^3] = KI$$

$$P_2 = P_1[r_1^3 / r_2^3]$$

Damage "markers" can often help in the solution of equation (vi). For example, it is known that glass windows break out when the overpressure exceeds 0.5 to 1.0 psig (34.46 to 68.9 mb). Thus, when the farthest distance at which windows are known to have blown out is known, then an estimate of the pressure at various points along the pathway of the explosion front can be made.

Other markers which can be used to estimate the pressure of a deflagrating explosion at a specific point are:

- items which have been lifted whose weight is known or can be estimated, like roofs, ceilings, etc.

- items which have been hurled from the explosion area. In such cases it is possible to calculate the velocity parameters associated with their trajectory, and from that estimate the initial kinetic energy imparted to the item by the explosion. Since the change in kinetic energy is equal to the work done on the item, a measure of the pressure which caused the item to be hurled can be estimated by equating "P–V" work done on the item to its kinetic energy as shown below:

$$\text{Work} = [P_2V_2 - P_1V_1] / [1 - k] = \Delta KE = (\tfrac{1}{2})mv^2$$

- items which have been pushed a known distance or overturned such that the work needed to accomplish this can be determined and equated to "P–V" work.

In the detonation of explosive materials like ANFO or dynamite, the scatter of debris items can be roughly related to the explosive yield by the following relation:

(vii) $W_E = [r^3] / K$

where r =   distance from epicenter to farthest scatter of debris,
    WE =   amount of explosive yield in equivalent kilograms of TNT,
and K =   scaling factor, 91,000 m^3/kg.

It should be emphasized that the above relation is only to be used as a first cut estimate of the amount of explosive.

Explosive yield is a term used in association with detonations to indicate the amount of explosive effect produced. Usually, the explosion under consideration is compared to the equivalent amount of TNT which would cause the same level of damage or effect. TNT is often used as a standard against which other explosions are measured, because there are so many different types and variations of explosives.

A gram of TNT, by the way, produces about 4,680 joules of explosive energy. However, energy equivalence is not the whole story, and is only a rough indicator of explosive effect. Explosive effect equivalence must also take into account detonation velocity and fissile effects.

Thus, an explosion with a yield of 100 kilograms of TNT simply means that the explosion produced about the same explosive effect as 100 kilograms of TNT. For example, 100 kg of AMATOL is equivalent in effect to about 143 kg of TNT. ANFO, an inexpensive explosive often used for blasting surface rock, has 142% the explosive effect as TNT.

With respect to equivalent explosive yield, it is inappropriate to assign a deflagrating explosion a TNT equivalent explosive yield. It's simply an "apples and oranges" comparison. A review of the basic differences between detonations and deflagrations in the first part of this chapter will make this point clear.

Despite this, many investigators commonly spend a significant amount of time calculating an equivalent explosive yield in TNT kilograms for natural gas explosions, ammonia explosions, and so on. In one prominent case involving a boiler failure in the midwest, the explosion resulting from the flash expansion of hot pressurized boiler feed water from ruptured pipes was even equated to so many kilograms of TNT.

This equivalence calculation is usually done by simply equating the energy content of so many kilograms of TNT to the energy released by the deflagration of so many kilograms of natural gas, ammonia, etc. Of course, there obviously may be an energy equivalence on a joule-to-joule basis between the two, just as there can be a joule-to-joule equivalence of the electricity in a flashlight battery to some amount of gasoline. However, this certainly is not the basis for an equivalence of explosive effect.

Consider, for example, a cubic foot of air at 2,000 psia and 20°C. This has an energy content of 1.93×10^5 joules. A one-pound stick of dynamite has an energy content of about 2.09×10^5 joules. From just their energy content, it might be said that a cubic foot of air compressed to 2,000 psia is about equivalent to a stick of dynamite.

However, the sudden release of a cubic foot of compressed air in a blast hole will have little fissile effect on the surrounding rock. It will likely "whoosh" out the top of the hole harmlessly. On the other hand, the detonation of a stick of dynamite in the same hole can break apart solid rock, causing it to fracture into many pieces. Alternatively, it is nearly impossible to slow down the explosion of a stick of dynamite to power a gas turbine; a stick of dynamite shoved in a gas turbine will simply blow it apart. However, it is possible to slowly release the cubic foot of compressed air to make the gas turbine operate and extract work.

Thus, to examine the damage at an explosion site which has been caused by a deflagration and to equate it to so many sticks of dynamite or pounds of TNT is not a particularly valid comparison. Unfortunately, lawyers, reporters, public officials and investigators insist that this equivalence be done as a "wow" factor for the jury, newspaper readership, viewing audience, or whatever, despite its questionable scientific value.

The pressure wave or front which propagates from the explosion epicenter has a pressure distribution over time similar to that shown in Figure 6.2 below.

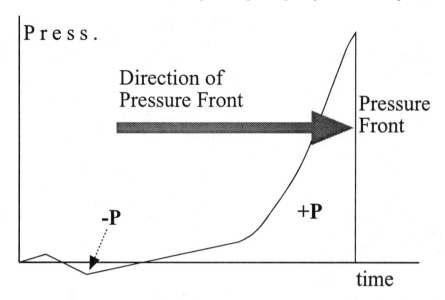

Figure 6.2 Profile of the pressure wave or front

As shown in the figure, the initial pressure front is a "wall" or "spike." The pressure on one side of the spike is the ambient pressure, and just at or slightly behind the spike, the pressure is maximum for that distance from the origin of the explosion.

As the front passes by a certain point, the pressure level drops. At some time after the front has passed, the pressure even drops below ambient and a slight low-pressure front occurs. In motion pictures showing the passage of pressure fronts in actual explosions, this "negative" pressure area sometimes looks like a slight reverse surge, especially after having observed the main pressure front initially push through with great destructive force. After the negative pressure subsides, the pressure stabilizes back to ambient.

This is why so much attention is paid to the determination of the maximum pressure. The destructive power of an explosion is basically contained in its pressure front. If a structure can survive that, it is likely that it will be able to survive the lower level pressure zone following it.

Of course, the above situation assumes that the explosion has taken place in the open. The presence of buildings, hills, valleys, and other features can complicate the profile of the pressure wave because of reflections, refractions, and shadowing. The pressure wave of an explosion can "bounce" off or be deflected by buildings and geographic features like waves in a pond bouncing off the side of a boat. There can even be destructive and constructive interference in certain situations.

"You can observe a lot by looking."

Attributed to Yogi Berra

*"Hey Boo-Boo.
Do you see what I see?"*

Attributed to Yogi Bear

*"One must learn to see things
with one's inner vision."*

Attributed to Yogi Maharishi

Chapter 7: Determining the Point of Ignition of an Explosion

A. General

The explosive limits of a gaseous fuel are useful in calculating the amount of fuel which may have been involved in an explosion. If the room or space in which the explosion occurred is known, its volume can be determined. If the type of gas which fueled the explosion is known or assumed, then the amount of fuel necessary to cause the explosion can be estimated from its lower explosive limits.

Consider the following example: suppose an explosion occurred in a small bedroom, 12 ft. × 10 ft. × 8 ft., which contained a natural-gas space heater. The explosion took place when a light switch located halfway down the 8-ft. high wall was turned on after the room had been closed up for two hours. Singeing was noted on the ceiling and walls down to the light switch, and faded below it. How much gas leaked, at what rate had it leaked, and what size leak was necessary to cause the explosion?

Since natural gas is lighter than air, much of the gas would initially collect on the ceiling and fill the ceiling space downward, like an inverted bowl. The explosion could only take place if the gas concentration at the light switch was at least 5% or more by volume. Assuming a "cloud" of 5% methane and air in the top portion of the room, then about 24 cubic feet of methane would have been needed. Since the room had been closed for two hours, the leak rate must have been about 0.2 cu.ft./min.

Because most household natural gas systems operate at a pressure of about 0.5 psig, application of the Bernoulli equation finds that the escape velocity of the natural gas from the gas lines or heater would be 2.32 ft/sec. To have a leak rate of 0.2 cu.ft./min, a leak cross sectional area of 0.21 sq.in. is needed. Thus, this estimate of leak size gives a hint as to what size hole or opening to look for in the gas lines and components around the space heater.

B. Diffusion and Fick's Law

It is commonly thought that when a light, buoyant gas is introduced into a room full of air, the gas floats to the top and forms a distinct layer. Initially, this is sometimes true; however, it is not true over time. Given enough time, the gas will diffuse through the room's air until the concentration at the top of the room is not significantly different from the bottom of the room.

If gases were to layer out according to their relative specific gravities, then the earth's atmosphere would be very different than it is now. Next to the ground would be the heaviest gases found in the air: argon and carbon dioxide, just above that would be a relatively thick layer of oxygen; on top of the oxygen, well above most people's heads and the tops of buildings, would be a layer of nitrogen. And finally, the topmost layer would be composed of water vapor, methane, and the lighter gases.

However, first-hand experience tells us that this is not the case: the lighter gases do not rise to the top, and the heavy gases do not sink to the bottom. Given time, the gases mingle until the composition is the same at the top as at the bottom. This is also true of liquid solutions when the solvent and solute are miscible with one another.

At a given temperature, the rates at which different gases diffuse are inversely proportional to the square root of their molecular weights. This observation is consistent with the *Kinetic Theory of Gases*, where the pressure, or concentration of a gas, is proportional to its average kinetic energy.

(i) $P = C[(1/2)mv^2_{ave}] = (3/2)CkT$

where C =   an arbitrary constant which also embeds the number of molecules per unit volume,
    v =   average velocity of gas molecule,
   m =   weight of gas molecule,
   k =   Boltzman's Constant, 1.38×10^{-23} joules/°K, and
   T =   absolute temperature, °K.

It follows that diffusion is a function of the average velocity of the gas as it wanders about, colliding with the various other gas molecules.

Gases with a high average velocity diffuse faster than gases with a low average velocity. Thus, algebraic manipulation of equation (i) finds that:

(ii) $m_1 / m_2 = v_2^2 / v_1^2$ or $v_2 / v_1 = [m_1 / m_2]^{1/2}$

For example, if one mole of hydrogen gas were released into a room full of air, what would be its diffusion rate as compared to a mole of methane released in the same fashion?

A mole of hydrogen has an molecular weight of 2. A mole of methane has a molecular weight of 16. Thus, the hydrogen would diffuse into the room full of air at a rate 2.83 times faster than the methane.

In the case of a solution of gases where the concentration is not uniform, the diffusion of the solute gas into the solvent gas from a region of high concentration to an area of lower concentration is modeled by *Fick's Law*, which is given below for the one-dimensional case.

(iii) $dm/dt = -DA[dc/dx]$

where
dm/dt = mass of solute gas diffusing per unit time,
−D = diffusion constant for the particular solvent gas at a given temperature,
A = cross sectional area of the diffusion flow, and
dc/dx = concentration gradient in the direction x perpendicular to the cross sectional area A.

By Fick's Law, the diffusion of material across the boundary stops when $dc/dx = 0$, that is, when the concentration of the solute gas in the solvent gas is the same everywhere in the space.

For example, consider a room that is 3 meters wide, 4 meters long and 3 meters high. At the bottom of the room is a layer of ethanol vapors. The layer is about 50 cm thick, the concentration being zero at the air/ethanol interface, and maximum nearest the floor. It is known that 92 grams of ethanol (2 moles) have evaporated to form the layer. What would be the diffusion rate of ethanol into the rest of the room when the temperature is 40°C?

In this case:

A = (300 cm)(400 cm) = 120,000 cm²
D = 0.137 cm²/sec @ 40°C
dc/dx = [(2 moles/(300 cm × 400 cm × 50 cm))]/[50 cm]
      = 6.67×10^{-9} mole/cm⁴
dm/dt = −DA[dc/dx]

$$= -[0.137 \text{ cm}^2/\text{sec}][120,000 \text{ cm}^2][6.67 \times 10^{-9} \text{ mole/cm}^4]$$

dm/dt = 0.0001 moles/sec or 0.0046 grams/sec.

An interesting point about this form of Fick's Law is that it is very similar to the one-dimensional equation for thermal conductivity. Note the comparisons below.

(iv) dm/dt = –DA[dc/dx] Fick's Law

dq/dt = –KA[dT/dx] thermal conductivity

The reasons for the similarity are rooted in the fundamental effects involved in both processes; both involve the exchange of kinetic energy from molecule to molecule, and both depend on a simple potential gradient to make the process go. In the case of the conduction law, the potential gradient is the change in temperature per distance along the material. In the case of Fick's Law, the potential gradient is the change in concentration per distance along the gas solvent.

Further, both processes involve very fundamental aspects of the property called *entropy*. While the concept of entropy has not been specifically addressed in this text, it is nonetheless interwoven throughout. It is left to the reader to research the connections between the conduction law and entropy, and between Fick's Law and entropy.

C. Flame Fronts and Fire Vectors

When an explosion occurs, especially a deflagrating explosion, it is often the case that some of the fuel will be pushed along with or ahead of the pressure front creating a fireball or flame-front effect. Fuel will often still be burning in the gaseous mixture while the explosion is in progress. The flame front will eventually quench itself when either the temperature drops below the ignition point or the fuel is exhausted.

As the pressure wave moves outward and expands, the burning gas will cool. Since pressure drops as the cube of the distance, the temperature of the flame front also drops quickly. Usually the flame front will die out well before the pressure front has harmlessly expended itself.

Thus, in many deflagrations there is a large general area of pressure damage, within which is a smaller area that contains singeing or fire damage.

As a fireball passes through an area, it will impinge on the side of an object perpendicular to its line of travel, but it will not impinge on the backside of the object. The effect is similar to that of a surface wave on pier supports. As the wave approaches the vertical support, the wave will crash on one side, but will only slightly affect the backside, or "shadow" side.

In the fire-affected area of an explosion there will be objects that suffer heat damage or singeing on one side, the side which directly faced the explosion. These objects act as directional vectors, and indicate from which direction the fireball came. Mapping of these various "vectors" and the intensity of burn or singeing associated with each one provides a ready map of the pressure front of the explosion, and of its temperature intensity. Taken together, these vectors will plot out the expansion of the pressure front, and will lead back to the point of ignition of the explosion.

Due to the very short time available for heat transfer from the flame front to the object, objects with higher thermal inertia will be less affected by the momentary flame front.

D. Pressure Vectors

When the pressure front moves through an area causing damage, a rough estimate of the pressure front at that location can be made from the type of damage or injury which occurred there. Table 1 lists some representative pressure values and their usual associated damages.

Table 1. Pressure Intensity versus Type of Damage or Injury

pressure level	type of damage or injury
0.5 – 1.0 psig	breakage of glass windows
> 1.0 psig	knock people down
1.0 > 2.0 psig	damage to corrugated panels or wood siding
2.0 – 3.0 psig	collapse of non-reinforced cinder block walls
5.0 – 6.0 psig	push over of wooden telephone poles
> 5.0 psig	rupture ear drums
> 15.0 psig	lung damage
> 35 psig	threshold for fatal injuries
> 50 psig	about 50% fatality rate
> 65 psig	about 99% fatality rate

Like a flame front, the pressure front will impinge most strongly on surfaces normal to its path of travel. Thus, the movement or shifting of items from their normal positions by the passage of the pressure wave can be used to trace the path of the pressure front back to its epicenter.

For example, if an explosion occurred in a certain room inside the house, it would be expected that the room might:

- have all four walls pushed outward, away from the room,
- the floor might be pushed downward, perhaps even collapsing into the basement,

- the ceiling might be pushed upwards, perhaps even lifting the roof or upper floor upwards,
- metal cabinets or ductwork might be dented inward on the side facing the epicenter.

On the other hand, if the explosion occurred in the basement, the following effects might be observed:

- if the basement walls are of block, the walls might have moved outward creating a gap between the wall and the surrounding dirt,
- the floor above the basement might have lifted upwards, and then collapsed inward,
- ductwork might be dented inward on the side facing the epicenter,
- free-standing shelves next to walls may have been pushed into the walls and rebounded, falling into the floor.

E. The Epicenter

When a gas leak occurs, the gas will initially form an irregularly shaped cloud of fuel that diffuses away from the leak. If the gas is methane and the air is more or less calm, the gas will slowly rise at first to the ceiling and accumulate in high areas. If the gas is propane, it will sink to the floor and accumulate in low areas.

As the fuel cloud diffuses and moves away from the point of leakage, the boundary of the fuel "cloud" may come into contact with an energy source capable of igniting the fuel, provided the fuel cloud is above the lower limit of flammability in air. At first contact, the fuel cloud likely will not have sufficient concentration for ignition, but given time and the right conditions, the concentration of the cloud near the energy source may increase sufficiently for ignition to take place.

In cases where the source of ignition is steady, like a pilot light, the fuel cloud will be ignited as soon as its concentration exceeds the lower limit of flammability. If the energy source is intermittent, like a relay or a switch, the cloud may ignite after surrounding the ignition source.

As noted in previous sections, the point of ignition can be determined from the fire and pressure damage vectors. The plot of these directional vectors on a fire scene sketch will collectively point to the epicenter of the explosion, the origin of the fireball and pressure fronts. This is the primary reason why the documentation of debris scatter after an explosion is important.

However, walls, hallways and other features within a building can direct and alter the path of the fireball and pressure fronts. Thus, the investigator must not assume that all the directional vectors will point radially inward towards an epicenter; some will indicate that the pressure front followed non-radial pathways from the epicenter, having been guided by strong walls or passageways. Thus, the damage vectors may form a trail. The backtracking of several trails which converge at the same location usually indicates that the epicenter has been successfully located.

F. Energy Considerations

The amount of energy contained in an explosion is a direct function of the type of fuel, the amount of space in which it is confined, and the concentration of the fuel. In general, the energy of an explosion is dissipated in the following forms:

1. Acoustical: the blast sound.

2. Kinetic: the displacement of objects away from the point of origin of the explosion.

3. Heat and expansion energy lost to the surroundings.

4. Fissile: the propagation of intense shock waves through nearby materials resulting in their fracturing.

Items 1–3 above usually apply to deflagrations, because little energy is dissipated in deflagrations in fissile effects. However, items 1–4 all apply to detonations with high explosives, where items 2 and 4 may constitute the primary means of energy dissipation.

A quick reconnoiter of the explosion scene near the epicenter can usually provide evidence of whether there were significant fissile effects. If there were, it is advisable to take samples of materials that the blast front would have impinged on near the epicenter, because high explosives will often embed small particles of explosive material into nearby surfaces, like small bullets. These particles can be detected by laboratory tests, and the explosive material clearly identified. In some cases, because of trace elements added to high explosives, the place of manufacture of the explosive can also be determined. This is usually a significant starting point in the tracking of the explosive material from initial producer to the last user.

Because a pressure wave dissipates as the cube of the distance from the explosion volume envelope, if the pressure needed to lift a ceiling, push over a wall, or break glass in a window across the street can be determined, then the pressure of the explosion at the envelope boundaries of the explosion can be calculated or estimated.

Knowing the room or space where the explosion originated, it may be possible to narrow the list of possible fuels. In short, it is possible to gauge the energy content of an explosion and deduce something about the nature of the fuel which caused the explosion.

For example, it might be deduced that an explosion which originated in a small bathroom had a pressure of about 4 psig when the ceiling of the bathroom lifted. The bathroom was noted to have a natural gas space heater, and an open bottle of nail polish remover (acetone) which had evaporated. The source of ignition energy for the explosion apparently came from a running electric wall clock (motor commutator ring). The gas lines to the space heater were pressure checked, and a small leak was found. Interviews with the home owner found that the 16-ounce bottle of nail polish remover was only half full when it was left open. How would a person tell which item caused the explosion?

First, from interviews it could be established how long the room had been left unattended. This would establish the amount of time available for either leaking or evaporation, since both items are smelly and would likely have been noticed. The evaporation and diffusion rates of acetone could be then checked to see if enough vapors would collect in that amount of time for an explosive mixture to have formed in the air. Similarly, the leak rate of the heating gas could be extrapolated to determine if enough fuel could be put into the room to cause an explosion.

If the heater leak caused the explosion, there might be a singe pattern that would be most intense around the heater. Similarly, if the nail polish remover were the culprit, the singe pattern might center about it. Acetone is not initially buoyant in air, while methane is. A singe pattern high in the ceiling may indicate the fuel "cloud" was mostly methane which had not fully diffused into the room. Alternatively, a singe pattern low in the room, from the floor upwards, might indicate the fuel "cloud" was heavier than air.

Of course, in our hypothetical example we should not overlook the possibility that both fuel sources contributed to the explosion.

The price one pays for pursuing any profession or calling is an intimate knowledge of its ugly side.

James Baldwin, from *Nobody Knows My Name*, 1961

Chapter 8:
Arson and Incendiary Fires

A. General

The legal definition of arson varies from state to state. However, a working definition of arson is: the malicious burning of homes, residences, buildings or other types of real property. *Malicious burning* in this context is intended to also include incendiary explosions as well as fire.

In the *Model Penal Code*, Section 220.1(1) the definition of arson includes the starting of a fire or explosion with the purpose of destroying a building or damaging property to collect insurance money. The building or property may belong to another, or to the person who commits the arson.

It is worth remembering that if a person burns down his own home or building, it is not necessarily arson. Barring local fire and public safety laws and ordinances, a person may usually do as he wishes with his own property, including burning it down. It is only when the building is burned down to fraudulently collect insurance, perhaps to deprive a bank or a divorced spouse of their property rights, or to avoid other types of obligations, that burning one's own property becomes an act of arson.

In some states, the crime of arson is divided into three degrees. *First-degree arson* is usually the burning of an inhabited house or building at night. *Second-degree arson* is the burning at night of an uninhabited building, where "uninhabited" means no humans are inside. *Third-degree arson* is the burning of any building or property with intent to defraud or injure a third party.

First and second degree arson is usually considered a felony. As such, it is necessary to prove that the person accused of the arson intentionally caused the fire or explosion. Some cases of third degree arson may be considered only misdemeanors if the fire was small, and are legally considered similar to malicious mischief or vandalism.

If a person dies as a result of arson, in some states the death is considered a murder. The death may have occurred during the fire because the victim was fatally burned, or the death may have occurred sometime after the fire due to grievous injuries resulting from the fire. This may include injuries directly caused by the fire such as burns and smoke inhalation, and also injuries indirectly resulting from the fire, such as might occur by people leaping from a building to escape being burned to death.

A fire set to conceal another crime is considered an arson in some jurisdictions. Sometimes criminals will set fires in the hopes that the fire will obliterate or at least obscure the evidence of a second crime, perhaps burglary or murder. Perhaps the criminal has shot a person and then set fire to that person's house hoping that the investigators will believe the victim died in the fire, rather than by shooting. Or perhaps a burglar will set fire to the house he has just robbed, hoping that the items taken will not be noticed missing from the fire debris.

In some jurisdictions, properly authorized city or state employed arson investigators have the same investigational and arresting authority and responsibilities as police officers or marshals; some may be allowed to carry weapons and police type equipment. This means that they have to follow the same rules that police officers and marshals follow, such as "Mirandizing" a suspect during interviews.

Of course, in nearly all jurisdictions it is unlawful for a citizen to disobey the lawful orders of a fire marshal or fire chief during the extinguishment of a fire, or similar fire safety activity. This is to protect public safety and to ensure orderly suppression of fires and fire hazards.

Incendiary fire is also a term used to describe a deliberately set fire. Alternatively, an incendiary fire may be defined as one that is not accidental, or that is not the result of natural processes. As opposed to the term "arson," the term "incendiary" also includes fires that may not qualify by legal definition as arson; these are fires where there may not be malicious intent, or an attempt to defraud for monetary gain. It is normally assumed, however, that the person responsible for an incendiary fire is aware that the fire should not have been set for legal, ethical, or safety related reasons.

The term *"suspicious fire"* typically designates a fire that has some of the characteristics of an arson or incendiary fire. Usually the term implies that findings are tentative or preliminary, and that further evidence gathering is required to properly confirm a finding of either arson or incendiary.

B. Arsonist Profile

The average person arrested for arson in the U.S. is male; women arsonists constitute only about 11 percent of the total arrests. Most arsonists are over 18 years old; of the men arrested for arson, only 42 percent are under 18. Of the women arrested for arson, only 30 percent are under 18.

On the average, there are about 18,000 arrests per year for arson. This is about 30 percent more than the arrests for embezzlement, and just slightly less than the number of arrests for murder and non-negligent manslaughter. As noted in the statistics cited in Chapter 1, Section C, arson appears to be a "growth" industry. Total momentary losses in the past decade in terms of constant dollars have increased.

It has been posited in other texts that there are seven motives for arson or incendiary fires. It is sometimes a parlor game when fire investigators get together to see who can remember all seven; sort of like trying to remember the names of all the Seven Dwarfs. Whether this seven-item list is truly exhaustive is perhaps open to question. I say this because there is always somebody in the crowd who feels challenged to imagine some trivial exception to an inclusive list. However, the list does appear to account for all the situations I can think of. So, without further ado, the list is as follows:

1) **Revenge.** To get even with someone for real or imagined slights. If the slight is very imaginary, see item 6 below.

2) **Personal gain.** This usually occurs when the arsonist needs money, and the property to be burned is expendable under the circumstances.

3) **Vandalism.** This is the "just plain orneriness" category. It is very popular among adolescents, gangs and transients. In some cities there is actually a tradition of vandalism on certain days of the year. Detroit, for example, is famous or rather infamous for the incendiary fires annually set to mark "Devil's Night" or "Witching Night;" this is the night before Halloween. The same event used to be called "Picket Night" in St. Louis, but the tradition there seems to have largely died out.

4) **To conceal another crime.** Burglaries and murders are often masked by fires. It is hoped that the missing items will be assumed to be burned up, or the shot person will be so badly burned that the bullet holes will be overlooked.

5) **Rioting.** Pillaging, looting, and setting fires have a long tradition in civil riots and unrest. "Burn, baby, burn" is not just a media-generated slogan. The recent riots associated with the Rodney King matter are a prime example. Other notable examples include the Watts Riots in 1968, the Civil War Draft Riots, and the French Revolution.

6) **Abnormal psychology.** The usual euphemism for being crazy. This includes firebugs, persons who want to be heroes at fires, people wishing to purify the world, self-appointed angels of justice, etc.

7) **To deny use of property by another person.** An example of this would be neighborhood vigilantes burning down a vacant house being used by undesirable drug dealers. The military use of fire, to deny the enemy the use of a building or structure, also fits into this category.

C. Basic Problems of Committing Arson for Profit

In order to be a successful arsonist, the person must burn enough of his house, property, or inventory for it to be considered a total loss. In that way, he will collect the policy limits for the fire, instead of having the insurance company rebuild or replace the property. When the latter occurs, he usually does not make enough money. After all, it was the policy limit that was the temptation in the first place, and not the allure of a redecorated bathroom.

Because of this, sometimes when a fire is promptly put out by the fire department, or the fire has simply not spread very well and damages are minor, a second fire will "mysteriously" break out in the same building a day or so later. Usually the second fire is bigger and better. Lessons about fire will have been learned from the first attempt; "practice makes perfect."

A rational person might think that after the first unsuccessful attempt, no one would be so foolish as to try again, especially in the same building. However, sometimes the motives that compelled a person to commit arson the first time are so powerful that normal prudence is abandoned; sometimes it is replaced with unrealistic rationales. Some arsonists are imbued with the notion that they are too smart to get caught. Others who have more desperate motives may believe that it doesn't matter. To them, jail may be less repugnant than not having the insurance money and having to face bankruptcy, foreclosure, or whatever.

Thus, the *fundamental problem facing the arsonist* is how to set a fire or explosion in such a way that it will have enough time to burn and consume the building or property before being spotted and put out by the fire department. The secondary problem is then how to do this deed without there being enough evidence found later to be blamed for it.

With regard to the problem of blame, usually one of two strategies is used: the first is to try to disguise the arson so that it looks like a natural fire. For example, the fire might be set up to appear as if it were accidentally caused by an overheated kerosene space heater which leaked fuel.

The second strategy is to make no real effort to disguise that the fire is arson, but to make sure that the person has an alibi or some other reason to not be specifically blamed. For example, the fire might be determined to be incendiary, but blamed on vandalism. Or, perhaps the arsonist is able to delay the start of the fire so that he can be at a social event to provide an "ironclad" alibi. Thus, while the fire might be determined to be arson, it can't be linked directly to the arsonist.

In cities where the response time of the fire department is just a few minutes, the arsonist will likely need an accelerant to speed the fire along. It also means that he will likely have to set fire in several places more or less simultaneously. He may also need to deliberately set fires in strategic areas which can enhance the fire spread. Such areas might include wooden stairways or storage areas for flammable materials.

Another problem confronting the arsonist is that he must set the fire and remain unseen by witnesses. And, of course, he must do so with as little danger to himself as possible. With respect to this last point, it is not uncommon for less than astute arsonists to burn or blast themselves to pieces as they attempt to ignite liquid gasoline on the floor of a room full of explosive gasoline vapors.

In some cases the arsonist is part of a team. The person who will actually collect the insurance money, usually the owner of the property, hires a second person to set the fire and assume the risk of being caught. The owner, of course, creates an alibi for himself by being in a public place when the fire occurs. Presumably, both will share in the insurance money.

D. The Prisoner's Dilemma

The obvious problem with the "team" arson strategy is that for the rest of their lives both persons will share a nefarious secret. In a pinch, will both partners keep silent, or will one betray the other for more favorable treatment?

Interestingly enough, this problem has been well studied by mathematicians who specialize in game theory, and is called the *"Prisoner's Dilemma."* The basic problem, as considered in terms of game theory, was first discussed by the Princeton mathematician Albert Tucker in 1950. Essentially, the problem is this: assuming that two persons are arrested for arson and that they are not allowed to communicate with one another during interrogation, the available options for the two arsonists are as follows:

1) They both keep mum in hopes of either beating a conviction, or receiving a lighter sentence due to a lack of corroborative evidence.

2) One arsonist rats on the other to obtain a lighter and perhaps commuted sentence, while the other one stays mum.

3) They both rat on each other, and both receive the maximum sentence.

If the object is to minimize the total prison time of both culprits, option 1 is likely the best choice. However, this requires that each prisoner trust the other's loyalty. While option 1 does minimize the total prison time of both culprits, it does not minimize the individual prison time of either prisoner.

If one person wants to get off as lightly as possible and has no a-biding loyalty to his partner, option 2 is the best option. He simply rats out his partner in return for the lightest possible sentence. This occurs, of course, while the second partner is keeping mum thinking that his co-conspirator has also kept loyalty.

However, there is the risk that if both prisoners think that option 2 is the best deal, then they may both end up getting option 3, which is the worst possible outcome.

Skillful questioning by investigators usually attempts to convince each suspect that option 2 is the best bet; that is why suspects are usually kept separated during questioning, so they cannot collude and reinforce each other's testimony. When an alibi story has been fabricated by the suspects to create a plausible lie, it is difficult for both parties to separately invent all the tiny but obvious details that a person who had actually been there would know and remember. The two testimonies are then compared for discrepancies, and these can then be used to confront the witnesses.

E. Typical Characteristics of an Arson or Incendiary Fire

As noted in Section C of this chapter, an arsonist has several problems to overcome in order to accomplish his goal. The ways in which an arsonist solves these problems are the same ways that provide identification of an arson or incendiary fire. The following is a short list of the more common characteristics of an incendiary fire.

1) Multiple origins of fire, especially several points of fire origin that are unconnected to each other. There are no fire pathways between the various points of origin to account for the simultaneous break out of fire in multiple locations.

2) The point of origin is in an area where there is no rational ignition potential. For example, a breakout of fire in the middle of a fireproof carpet with no obvious ignition source available.

3) Use of accelerants such as gasoline, kerosene, turpentine, etc. Often these agents are detectable by their lingering odor, the pour patterns they produce on floors when ignited, and by chemical analysis. Many times two points of fire origin will be connected by an accelerant pour pattern, called a trailer. Recently, specially trained dogs have been used to sniff out accelerants at fire scenes in the same way that they have been previously used to sniff out drugs.

This is a very timely technique. Also, dogs are smaller and more agile than humans and may pick up a scent in an area that is too difficult or dangerous for a human to get into.

4) The presence of *trailers;* these are fire or burn pathways that exhibit flammable liquid pour patterns and are used by the arsonist to accelerate the spread of fire to more areas of the building. This reduces the burn time of the building so that more of the building will have burned up by the time the fire department arrives.

5) The finding of deliberately arranged fire load. This is where everyday items typically found in the building are rearranged to enhance the fire. Examples include closets stuffed with crumpled newspapers, flammable clothing piled in heaps on floor around stoves and heaters, mattresses laid over space heaters, blankets laid over torpedo-type heaters, kerosene heaters placed under clothes hung on a clothesline, open gas cans placed near high-wattage light bulbs, etc. In essence, solid flammable materials are substituted for liquid type accelerants.

6) Buildings or residences which are missing personal items that normally would be present. This might include family photograph albums, special collections or instruments, trophies, prized dresses, tools, etc. These are items that the arsonist had a personal interest in.

7) Buildings or residences with extra items not normally present, or which are out of context. This is done by the arsonist to "beef up" the amount of contents lost in the fire. Useless junk items are carried into the building, which after the fire are claimed to be valuable furniture.

8) An unusually fast consuming fire for the time involved, and a very high burning temperature in areas where the fire load is to all respects very ordinary.

9) Tampering with fire protection and alarm systems. This is done to give the fire a longer time to burn.

10) Unnatural fire pattern. A fire pattern that does not follow the rules and has burned in an unusual or unnatural sequence. Natural fires always follow the physical laws of heat transfer and chemical combustion in a logical progression through the fire load. Human intervention usually subverts the normal logical progression of the fire, making the fire progression appear out of order.

11) The finding of "timers" and incendiary devices. Timers are devices used to delay the start of the fire so that the arsonist can get safely away, and perhaps have an alibi. A timer may be as simple as a candle placed so that the fire will not start until the candle has burned halfway down, or it may be as complicated as a device placed in the telephone which will cause ignition when the telephone rings. Hand in hand with a timer is usually an incendiary device. This is typically some kind of accelerant or highly flammable material that is set to catch on fire by the timer.

   For example, a tall taper is set in the floor of a closet surrounded by newspapers. On the other side of the closet is a rubber balloon filled with an accelerant. The taper takes an hour to burn down to the point where the flame can ignite the crumpled newspapers lying low on the floor. The ensuing newspaper fire spreads across the floor of the closet, and the flames leap up to the balloon, causing it to break open. The balloon then spills its load of accelerant into the newspaper fire. In this case, the taper is used as a timer, and the accelerant-laden balloon is the incendiary device.

12) Tampering with heating and air conditioning equipment to enhance fire spread. Moving air will help spread a fire through a building faster. Thus, many arsonists make sure that the blowers are turned on during a fire. In the winter time, this may mean that the thermostat is set as high as possible so that the furnace will run constantly. In the summer, it may mean that the air conditioning system is set as low as possible for the same reason. If the building is equipped with an attic blower,

the blower may have been operating under unusual circumstances, like in the dead of winter, or outside the time settings normally used on the timer for the blower's operation.

13) Tampering with utility systems. Sometimes the electrical wall outlets are rigged to short and catch fire. The arsonist hopes to create a "V" pattern emanating from the wall outlet, which the fire investigator will blame on electrical shorting in the building wiring. Unfortunately, because many fire investigators are unfamiliar with electrical equipment and codes, there is a tendency to label all fires associated with electrical equipment as being caused by shorting.

This tampering ploy seems to be more prevalent in rural areas where electrical codes are not strictly enforced and the quality of electrical workmanship is at the level of a handyman's special. In such cases it can be difficult to tell if the outlet or wiring was rigged by an expert or wired by an idiot.

Similarly, sometimes a gas pipe may be loosened so that during a fire, the leaking gas will cause the house to explode or cause the fire to burn more fiercely. Fresh tool marks on pipes that heretofore have not been leaking often allow easy spotting of this ploy.

F. Daisy Chains and Other Arson Precursors

A *daisy chain* occurs when a building is sold within a clique in order to jack up its value prior to an arson or incendiary fire crime being committed. It works like this: Joe buys a dilapidated warehouse building in an old section of town for $50,000. Joe sells the building two months later to his brother, Frank, for $60,000. In another four months or so, Frank sells the same building to his sister-in-law, Zelda, for $75,000. In another three months, Zelda sells the building to her cousin George for $100,000.

The purpose of the daisy chain is to artificially inflate the value of the building on paper. In each transaction, the building is insured against fire loss and the purchase price of the building is used to define the limits of the insurance policy.

At some point, the building burns down and the last owner collects the insurance money, which is based on the inflated purchase price of the last transaction. Often, no money actually changed hands during the various paper transactions, and the interim owners listed on the documents were simply fronts or straw men for the real owner. Some of them may not have even known that they were temporary owners of the property; their signatures may have been forged, or it was purchased on a power of attorney basis.

Thus, when obviously dilapidated buildings suddenly show an unusual number of buying and selling transactions, and the paper value of the buildings has significantly increased without any corresponding improvement in the property, this may indicate that a case of arson is in the making. Similarly, after a fire, if such a daisy chain can be traced, it helps establish that the fire was planned well in advance. Some cities have actually been able to predict fires in specific buildings by tracking real estate transaction activity in high fire areas.

There are also less sophisticated indications that an arson may be in the making. For example, some arsonists may call in a number of false alarms or set small fires in the neighborhood near where they will eventually commit the arson. They do this to measure how long it takes for a fire to be spotted by neighbors and how long it takes the local fire department to respond. In this way, the arsonist determines the approximate time in which he has to do his dirty work.

This technique is also sometimes used to set up a plausible reason for the fire at the main target of the arsonist. "There have been a lot of small fires in this area lately. I guess they set this one, too. Damn delinquents!" Of course, nearly any undesirable group pejorative can be used in the place of delinquents, such as kids, gangs, hoodlums, bums, winos, dopers, or the local minority group of your choice. I once heard a fire marshal use the pejorative, "rats with matches;" I sort of like that one.

The arsonist hopes that the main fire, the arson, will be classified as just one more of these vexing fires being set in the neighborhood by bad people for just plain orneriness. This ploy is actually somewhat interesting, because it is being conceded up front that the fire is incendiary. The fire can even be set in a very amateurish way, possibly giving further credence to the "damn delinquents" theory.

The conclusion that the fire was incendiary or a case of arson may be freely accepted by all parties; the rub is proving who committed it. Even if it is widely conceded by everyone involved that the fire in the building was arson, as long as the person or corporation that owns the building did not do the deed, the insurance company will still pay for the damages as per the provisions of the policy.

When the primary motive for an act of arson is to make a lot of money, following the "money trail" will often provide important insight. The insurance settlement from a fire will often take care of a lot of money problems for the arsonist that would otherwise not be resolvable without bankruptcy, foreclosure, or loss of control over property. Often a fire set for profit will be equivalent to winning the lottery; it gives instant financial relief. In accidental fires where there has been no arson, usually there is no unsolvable money problem prior to the fire.

The investigator should be well aware that "money trail" information has to be considered very, very carefully. Not all fires that occur to people in debt are incendiary, and occasionally perfectly honest folk may reap a needed windfall from an accidental fire. Thus, the mere fact that a fire has been propitious for a debt-ridden person is not evidence, *per se*, that there is something sinister going on. However, it doesn't hurt to look a little harder when this occurs to make sure.

The investigation of personal affairs, like financial information, is normally left up to law enforcement agencies and private investigators in the employ of the insurance companies. In general, forensic engineers are primarily concerned with the evaluation of physical evidence. However, sometimes such information is discovered in the course of an engineering evaluation of physical evidence, so it pays to keep one's eyes and ears open.

For example, in one case, a fire in a bungalow had been spotted early by a neighbor and the fire department was able to extinguish the fire before extensive damage had been done. An initial survey of the premises found many characteristic indicators of a set fire: smoke detectors tampered with, gas pipes loosened with fresh tool marks on the pipe, furnace set to 110°F, and a closet stuffed with newspapers. The point of origin of the fire was the closet.

However, the most tantalizing piece of evidence found at the scene was a sheet of legal pad paper on the kitchen counter next to a copy of the insurance policy. On that sheet of paper was a budget schedule, listing all the owner's debts! All of those debts were being subtracted from a single sum, which was equal to the maximum value of the insurance policy on the bungalow. Apparently, the owner of the place had worked out a budget of how the insurance money would be spent, and had absentmindedly left it on the kitchen counter, possibly thinking that the fire would consume it.

G. Arson Reporting Immunity Laws

Many states now have laws that provide immunity for the reporting of arson or incendiary fires by forensic engineers, adjusters, and other investigators. When evidence is discovered that a crime or arson has been committed, these laws allow the evidence to be confidentially disclosed to appropriate officials without the investigator or employer of the investigator (e.g., an insurance company) being subject to civil liability.

This is a valuable law: without it, an engineer or investigator could be sued for reporting an incendiary fire or arson, especially if criminal prosecution of the party was either unsuccessful or not pursued.

Some states require that evidence be properly disclosed when a crime is discovered. Some states indicate that disclosure is to be done when requested by proper authority. Still other states indicate that evidence may be disclosed to proper authorities. Since states vary in this matter, it is best to check which rule applies in your state.

Most states, however, have provisions in the immunity law that require that the information be obtained and released in good faith. If it can be shown that there was maliciousness, falsification, or bad faith in the reporting of the crime, the immunity can be withdrawn.

Also, there may be penalties for not adhering to the immunity law. For example, in a state that requires that disclosure be made, not disclosing evidence to the proper authorities may itself be a punishable offense. There may be certain procedures to be followed in making such a disclosure, and not following these procedures may be considered "bad faith" or be otherwise punishable.

H. Accelerant Pour Patterns

Gasoline, lighter fluid, barbecue fluid, kerosene, and other light distillate hydrocarbon compounds are the usual accelerants of choice, especially among the do-it-yourself incendiary crowd. They are easy to obtain, easy to conceal, cheap to buy, a person doesn't have to be 21 years old to have them, and a little bit goes a long way. The more common method for applying accelerant is what is shown on television crime shows and in the movies: just pour it over what you wish to burn, light it, and quickly run away.

An interesting aside to this involves gasoline and similar highly volatile hydrocarbon liquids. Since gasoline has a very low flashpoint, about $-32°F$, it quickly makes copious vapors even in cold weather. If an arsonist splashes gasoline in a closed area such as a house or building, and takes too long to do it, he may accidentally blow himself up when he strikes the match. This is because while he was busy spreading gasoline about the place, the gasoline already on the floor had time to form explosive vapors. It is not uncommon for the arsonist to sustain burns and related injuries as a result of the selfsame fire he set.

All the flammable liquids previously noted burn at high temperatures. Usually, they burn at much higher temperatures and release heat faster than the flammable material to which they have been applied, as in the case, for example, of gasoline on a wood floor. Because of this, the surface where the flammable material was applied will usually have a recognizably deeper and more severe char pattern than the rest of the surface which burned normally.

Also, for all practical purposes, the entire contiguous pool of accelerant ignites at the same time. Thus, instead of a point of origin, there is an *area* of fire origin: the continuous surface area wetted by the accelerant. The resulting fire will generally burn the accelerant quickly, sometimes exhausting it before the "normal" fire has had much of a chance to spread.

For these reasons, when accelerant is applied to surfaces and ignited, it often leaves what is called a *pour pattern.* The surface area on which the accelerant pool has lain, which is called the pour area, will often be clearly and distinctly outlined by the unusually deep or severe charring pattern resulting from intimate contact with the burning accelerant, while the area outside the pour pattern will usually be burned less severely. There will likely be indications that the fire spread more slowly there and burned cooler that it did within the pour area.

In the case of painted sheet metal, the painted areas which were in intimate contact with the burning accelerant will generally have lost their outer coating of paint, lost their undercoats of primer, and lost any layers of protective galvanization. (Zinc melts at 786°F and will simultaneously oxidize in that type of situation.) The high burning temperature of the accelerant will typically leave a very characteristic pattern on the metal. If a day or two has passed and the bare metal has rusted due to exposure, the pour pattern on steel sheeting will often appear as a bright rust pattern.

As long as the flooring or surface on which the accelerant was applied has not shifted position because of the fire, the pour pattern will generally follow the drainage gradient. Thus, an investigator could recreate a pour pattern by applying a liquid similar in terms of wetness to the same location and observing if it follows the same general spread pattern. The purpose of such a demonstration would be to show that the observed deep burn pattern was caused by a burning liquid following the natural gradient rather than some other effect. (Of course, it is assumed that the above experiment would not be done unless all sampling from the pour pattern were complete so that the area would not be inadvertently contaminated by the test.)

Unfortunately, given sufficient time the burning liquid will usually create shallow, concave depressions in a wood floor or other flammable material. In concrete or ceramic type materials, it will create spalls. Both types of damage tend to mask the original drainage pattern of the surface.

Pour patterns are not always certain indicators of incendiary intentions. During a fire, it is possible that containers holding flammable liquids may spill their contents, which are then ignited by the spreading fire. The resulting damage may be a pour pattern on the floor. Thus, sometimes pour patterns are simply the result of falldown effects during a fire.

Such secondary pour patterns can be distinguished from primary pour patterns in a similar way that secondary electrical shorting is distinguished from primary shorting. Thus, a primary pour pattern has the following general characteristics.

- It occurs at or is the point or area of origin of the fire. There are indications of fire spread away from the area, and the area often exhibits the severest burn damage.

- In consideration of the whole body of evidence, it is the area of burn which must have occurred first in the time line of the fire.

Similarly, a secondary pour pattern has the following general characteristics.

- It occurs in locations away from the point of origin of the fire. There are indications of fire spread to the area from other locations as opposed to the other way around.
- Little relative movement or travel of the fire from this area has occurred. The fire appears to have been active for only a short time as evident from the amount of fire load consumed, and may have been engulfed itself by simultaneous fire spread from other areas.
- There is nearby falldown which explains ignition and spread of the flammable liquid. The falldown was caused by the approach of an external fire front.
- In consideration of the whole body of evidence, it is an area which may have burned at any time during the course of the fire, and has had only little or modest effect upon the over-all destruction of the property.

Fire patterns that look like pour patterns can also occur when solid burning falldown materials make close contact with a floor area. Depending upon fire load, material burning temperature, and access to oxygen, some materials can fall on a floor and hug it closely while burning with a relatively hot flame. This can result in a burn pattern that somewhat resembles a pour pattern. However, it will generally be distinguishable from a pour pattern made by a flammable liquid because the burn and char damages will be uneven and more diffuse. Whereas a liquid spreads out evenly in a film along the gradient, solid materials fall in random, lumpy patterns that do not closely follow the drainage gradient.

However, there is one exception of note to the above: powders or granular materials. Under certain circumstances, spilled powders can spread out over a surface like a liquid. If the powder is flammable, the resulting burn pattern may very closely resemble a liquid pour pattern.

In sum, it is worth remembering that while most liquid accelerants will produce pour patterns, not all pour patterns indicate an incendiary fire.

I. Spalling

If an accelerant has been poured on a concrete floor and ignited, it sometimes causes spalling and other temperature-related damage to the concrete. Concrete is not a quick conductor of heat; it is however a good heat sink, which means it stores thermal energy well.

If the top surface of a concrete slab becomes relatively hot in a short amount of time, the heat does not quickly disperse into the slab; it stays concentrated near the surface. Thus, the topmost portion of the slab will expand as it heats up while the lower portion stays relatively cool and does not expand. This creates a shear stress between the expanding top layer and the lower layer. When the shear stress between the hot portion and the cold portion is sufficient, the top layer separates or spalls.

For example, high-strength concrete has a compressive strength of 4,000 p.s.i., and a tensile strength of 350 p.s.i. In direct shear, the same concrete has a shear stress strength of from 600 to 800 p.s.i. The coefficient of expansion for concrete is $4.5 \times 10^{-6}/°F$, and Young's modulus for concrete is about 29×10^{6} p.s.i.

Using the above information, consider the following simple model of a 6-inch thick concrete slab with burning accelerant on its top surface. It is assumed that the top ¼ inch of the concrete slab evenly warms up due to the burning effects of the liquid accelerant, but the lower 5¾ inches of the slab stays at 55°F, since it is in contact with the earth and is massive enough to absorb most of the heat conducted into it. This situation is shown below in Figure 8.1. The question is then how hot would the upper ¼ inch have to be to shear away from the lower portion?

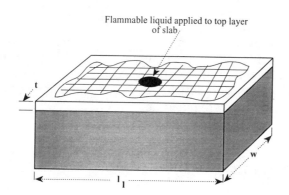

Flammable liquid applied to top layer of slab

Figure 8.1 Flammable liquid on concrete slab.

Equation (i) is the usual equation for expansion of a material due to heating.

(i) $\quad \Delta l = (l_1)(\alpha)(\Delta T)$

where l_1 = original length of section,

$\quad\quad \alpha$ = coefficient of expansion, and

ΔT = change in temperature.

If the upper ¼ inch is firmly constrained at both ends, the force generated at the ends of the ¼-inch thick layer of the slab by the expansion of the material is given by the following:

(ii) $F_1 = \sigma A_1 = \varepsilon(w)(t) = (\alpha)(\Delta T)E(w)(t \text{ in})$

where ρ =   equivalent stress required to resist thermal expansion of the upper section of slab,
  E =   Young's modulus,
  A_1 =   area of face at end, i.e., (t)(w),
  t =   thickness of top layer,
  w =   width of section of top layer, and
  ε = $(\Delta l)/(1_1)$ = strain induced by thermal expansion.

Now, instead of the upper ¼-inch thick layer being constrained at the ends by an unnamed force, consider that it is constrained by the shear between it and the lower, cooler layer of the slab. The force which then resists the expansion of the upper layer is provided by the shear force between the two layers. This shear force is given by the following:

(iii) $F_2 = \tau A_2 = \tau(w)(l_1)$

Thus, equations (ii) and (iii) can be used to calculate when the force due to expansion will overcome the shear force which the material can provide. By setting up an inequality and then solving for the temperature difference, the minimum temperature difference between the top and lower portions of the slab which will cause spalling can be calculated. This is done in the following inequality.

(iv) $F_1 > F_2$

$(\alpha)(\Delta T)E(w)(t) > \tau(w)(l_1)$

$(\Delta T) > \tau(w)(l_1) / (\alpha)E(w)(t)$

In this case assuming that l_1 is the length of a one-foot long section of slab, then:

$(\Delta T) > (800\text{lb/sq.in})(12 \text{ in})/(4.5 \times 10^{-6}/°F)(29 \times 106\text{lb/sq.in.})(¼ \text{ in})$
$(\Delta T) > [6.13] [l_1 / t]°F$
$(\Delta T) > 294°F.$

Thus, an increase of 294°F in a one-foot long section of concrete slab may cause the top ¼-inch layer to shear off or spall from the slab due to expansion.

It can also be seen in equation (iv) that the ratio of l_1 to t determines how great the temperature difference must be to spall a certain sized piece of material. In other words, large pieces can spall when the temperature difference is great, and small pieces can spall when the temperature difference is small. Thus, the size of the spall plate can be a crude indication of how hot the average temperature of the top layer of the concrete was during the fire.

It needs to be emphasized that the size of the spall plate is an indication of how hot the top layer of concrete became during the fire, not necessarily of how hot the burning material on top of the concrete was. Since heat transfer between the burning material on top of the floor and the floor slab itself depends on elapsed time, contact area, the interface temperature, and the total heat capacity of the slab section, that is, the amount of "heat sink" present, the size of the spall plate is not a direct indication of the temperature of the material which burned on top of the concrete.

In fact, if heat transfer between the burning flammable liquid and the concrete slab is poor, it is likely that no spalling will occur. A smooth concrete floor with a surface coating of paint or sealant may provide enough interface insulation to prevent sufficient heat transfer to the slab for spalling to occur. Thus, it is quite possible for a flammable accelerant to have been applied over a concrete slab floor and ignited, but no spalling to have taken place.

Spalling can also be caused by non-incendiary effects. For example, during a fire it is possible that bottles of flammable liquids may fall on the floor, break open, and then be ignited by fire already present in the area. Thus, like a pour pattern, it is important to determine if the spalling is primary or secondary.

Freeze thaw damages, deterioration by chemical attack such as salt, floor wear by wheeled vehicles, and other non-fire related effects which may have preceded the fire may also produce effects similar to a spall pattern. Exposure to fire and heat may then exacerbate these damages.

As noted above in the section on pour patterns, sometimes burning solid materials can fall down and "hug" a floor area. If the fall down materials have sufficient heat intensity, they also can cause spalling. However, as noted with pour patterns, the resulting spalling will often be more diffuse than had it been caused by a flammable liquid. This is due to the evenness of a liquid film as opposed to scattered solid materials of varying sizes and shapes.

Concrete that has not been properly cured is more sensitive to heat than well-cured concrete. Uncured concrete has a relatively high moisture content. Thus, if the temperature in the upper layer of the slab exceeds that which is necessary to create steam, the phase change of liquid moisture to steam in the concrete will cause a type of spalling. However, this type of spalling often causes the concrete to crack in small pieces, and the pieces are often crumbly. In the slab itself, it will resemble large-scale pitting.

Lastly, spalling can occasionally be caused by fire extinguishment operations themselves. If the fire has been long in duration, and the slab floor has been exposed to heat for a long time, it is possible for the whole slab to heat up. If cold water is then poured on the floor, the top surface will try to contract. The situation will be similar to that modeled in equations (i) through (iv). However, instead of expansion, the top layer will be subject to contraction; the direction of shear will be opposite, and the temperature difference will represent how much cooler the top portion of the slab is than the lower portion.

In sum, while spalling can result from the application and ignition of a flammable liquid on a concrete floor, its presence is not an automatic indicator that the fire was incendiary.

J. Detecting Accelerants After a Fire

Contrary to popular myth, accelerants do not completely burn up with the fire. Often, small amounts of the accelerant will be absorbed by the material on which it was applied. This includes wood, concrete, tiles, textiles, and other common construction materials that have some porosity. Sometimes, sufficient amounts will be absorbed in the material which then outgases after the fire. This sometimes creates a recognizable odor that is noticeable directly after the fire has been extinguished. Most fire fighters are instructed to be alert for such odors during overhaul after the fire.

Various types of portable electronic "sniffers," as was discussed in Chapter 3, can be used at the scene directly after a fire to detect residual vapors of light distillates. Some of these "sniffers" are very sensitive and are useful in the detection of accelerants.

Most recently, the B.A.T.F. and other federal agencies involved with fires and explosions have begun using trained dogs to sniff out accelerants at fire scenes. The dogs are trained like the dogs which are used to sniff out illegal drugs. When the dog smells an accelerant, it barks and alerts its trainer as to the location of the accelerant residue. The use of dogs for this type of work is very efficient, since the dog can sniff out a relatively large area in a short time.

In "pour pattern" areas, some of the accelerant may have soaked into the material, especially if the material has some porosity. Surprisingly, even fine-grained concrete has the ability to absorb enough accelerant to be detectable after a fire. With appropriate sampling and analysis, sometimes the accelerant can be identified by chemical analysis. However, to ensure that the evidence will stand up in court later, the sampling and analysis must be done properly.

Often the presence of a hydrocarbon-type accelerant in standing water will be signaled by the presence of light and dark banding, or rainbow colors on the surface of the water. An example of this can be observed by adding a small amount of gasoline or light oil to water. Light directed onto the surface and then reflected away from the surface will be diffracted as it passes through the hydrocarbon film on top. This produces the familiar rainbow effect.

Also, the light which reflects off the top surface of the hydrocarbon film may interfere with light that reflects off the top surface of the underlying water. This interference effect depends on the thickness of the film and the degree of absorption of the incident light by the film.

If the incident light which passes into the film is mostly absorbed, there is no significant second light beam to provide interference with the light beam bouncing off the top of the film. However, when absorptivity in the film layer is low, light passing through the film can bounce off the upper surface of the water and return through the film to emerge at the surface. This then provides a second beam of light which may produce interference with the first. The observer sees light and dark banding on the surface, especially at the edges of the film. It is possible for both the rainbow effect and light and dark banding to occur at the same time.

When standing water is thought to contain accelerant residues, samples can be collected simply by using a clean, uncontaminated eyedropper or syringe. If there is only a small amount of liquid, the liquid or moisture can be blotted up using sterile cotton balls, diatomaceous earth powder, common flour, or other moisture absorbing materials which will not react with or chemically mask the presence of the accelerant.

Of course, the container in which the sample is placed must be clean and free of contaminants. It must not react with the sample. It should be airtight. And, it should not mask the presence of the accelerant in subsequent chemical testing. For this reason, clean glass jars are often used, especially ones that do not have glued cap liners or seals. The glue often contains materials that may contaminate the sample. Some types of rigid plastic containers are also suitable.

One possible mistake in sampling solid materials for accelerants, for example, is the use of some types of plastic sandwich bags for the preservation and storage of samples. Such bags are commonly used by police and law enforcement agencies to store many types of evidence with no problem. They are also commonly used by fire investigators to preserve and store small items found at a fire scene for follow-up examination and inspection.

Thus, the common use of this type of bag to legitimately store other kinds of evidence might lead a person to assume that it is also all right to store samples possibly containing accelerants. It may also be rationalized that since the bags can be sealed air tight, they will help hold in any light distillate materials that might otherwise evaporate before chemical analysis could be done, which is certainly true.

Unfortunately, the problem with some types of plastic sandwich bags is that they themselves outgas light distillate hydrocarbon gases. Thus, the sample suspected of containing trace amounts of accelerant may absorb outgassed hydrocarbon vapors from the sandwich bag during storage and become contaminated by them. Problems occur if this outgassed vapor is then analyzed and identified as a possible accelerant in the sample.

While it is true that the outgassed hydrocarbon from the sandwich bag can be specifically identified and subtracted from the test results of the sample, this is an unwanted complication that may make the chemical analysis suspect during trial, possibly even inadmissible as evidence. The situation is even more serious if the hydrocarbon accelerant found by chemical analysis is very similar to the hydrocarbon material outgassed by the bag. In such situations, it is likely that the laboratory test results will be inadmissible as evidence.

However, in situations where timely collection is important, and there are no better alternatives, such plastic bags may be used as long as the suspected accelerant is clearly distinct from the type of vapors outgassed by the bags. It would also be a good idea to keep an empty, sealed bag from the same lot. This bag would then serve as the comparison sample. The analysis of vapor from the empty bag would provide the basis for identifying the contaminant vapors in the sample material, and subtracting or segregating them from the rest of the analysis.

Special plastic bags are available for the collecting evidence that may contain accelerants. These bags do not have the outgassing problem as occurs in some types of common sandwich bags. However, these bags must be specially ordered from law enforcement supply houses.

One good way to preserve and store solid material samples which may contain accelerants is to use clean metal cans with lids that can be hammered down to make an airtight seal, such as unused paint cans. These containers will also preserve any volatile vapors that may come off the sample during storage. By using head space analysis techniques, everything that was put into the can, even the vapors, can be checked for the presence of possible accelerants.

In the head space analysis method, the metal can itself is gently heated, and any accelerants are vaporized into the "head space" of the can. By their nature, accelerants are usually light distillates that vaporize easily at warm temperatures. A small hole is made in the can, and the gases in the can are run through a gas chromatograph, infrared spectrophotometer, or similar instrument for analysis.

A less desirable method of chemical analysis is the solvent method. In this method, the sample is first washed with a solvent, often an alcohol. The idea is that if an accelerant is present, the solvent will absorb some of it during the wash. The solvent is then analyzed in a gas chromatograph, infrared spectrophotometer, or similar instrument.

The problem with this method is that if the accelerant is chemically similar to the solvent, the accelerant may be confused with the solvent wash or the solvent wash may mask its presence. The analysis would then produce a false negative result, that is, it would fail to detect the presence of accelerant even though it was actually present.

The chemical analysis for accelerants should also be open to "creative" accelerants. While gasoline, kerosene, alcohol, lighter fluid, and other light distillates are popular, other items can also be used. For example, red or white phosphorus have been used, as well as finely milled aluminum powder. Even steel wool can be used as an accelerant. A forensic chemist who is directed to look only for one type of accelerant, e.g. gasoline or diesel fuel, may not notice that a metal or inorganic compound was the accelerant of choice.

Readers who have been Boy or Girl Scouts and have had to build a fire from scratch probably already understand the usefulness of a ball of fine steel wool. Many a Scout will have some securely tucked away for use on a rainy day when their regular tinder has absorbed the dampness. Steel wool will ignite from a flint spark very well, and will even burn when it has been damp. In fact, it is possible for very fine steel wool to spontaneously combust when exposed to moisture laden air.

It is important to obtain samples as soon as possible after a fire. Delays in obtaining samples greatly diminish the chances of detecting accelerant in the sample if it was present to begin with. After a week, it is doubtful that any of the typical light distillate hydrocarbon accelerants can be meaningfully detected by chemical analysis. Excessive hosing of an area during fire extinguishment or during overhaul may also diminish the chances of detecting accelerant.

There are standards in the literature which describe the proper way to secure and test samples for the presence of accelerants. A commonly cited standard is contained in ASTM E1387, *Standard Test Method for Flammable or Combustible Liquid Residue in Extracts from Samples of Fire Debris by Gas Chromatography.*

Will you love me when my carburetor's busted?
Will you love me when my windshield's broke in two?
Will you love me when my brakes can't be adjusted,
And my muffler, it goes zoop-poop-poopity-doo?
Will you love me when the radiator's leakin',
And my sparkplugs have lost their self-respect?
When the nuts and bolts are fallin',
And the junkyard is a-callin',
Will you love me when my flivver is a wreck?

Thomas R. Noon, refrain from "The Flivver Song," circa 1941

Chapter 9: Automotive Fires

A. General

Fires in automobiles, trucks, and vans fall into one of the following six categories of causes, which are listed roughly in order of importance or frequency:

1. **Fuel related fires.** The fire is caused by fuel leakage onto hot components, usually in the engine compartment, or along the exhaust system.

2. **Electrical related fires.** This includes short circuits, overheated wiring, and electrical malfunction of components such as fans, blowers, heaters, etc.

3. **Arson.**

4. **Garage fires, or similar.** This is where the garage in which the car is stored catches fire and burns the car or truck along with it. In some cases, the cause of the fire in the garage is wholly unrelated to the vehicle in any way. In other cases, there may be a causal link, e.g. gasoline fumes being ignited by a drop light lying on the floor.

5. **Dropped cigarettes and smoking materials.**

6. And of course, the ever popular, **"all other causes."** This includes fires in brake linings, fires due to hydraulic fluid leakage,

battery explosions, various types of mechanical failures, contact of the catalytic converter with combustibles, and so on.

Statistically, the first three categories represent the majority of all fires involving vehicles. Surprisingly, fires in vehicles due to collisions and impacts are low in number; car accidents than involve fire breaking out typically constitute less than 1% of such accidents. Despite the dramatic imagery created in movies and novels, few cars actually blow up and catch fire when they are wrecked.

B. Vehicle Arson and Incendiary Fires

As was noted in Chapter 1, there are nearly as many fires, cases of arson, and incendiary fires in personal vehicles as there are involving homes. The most common motives for incendiary fires in personal vehicles include:

1. **Cash flow problems.** The owner cannot afford the payments and is in danger of default.

2. **The value of the car is "upside down."** This is the situation when the remaining payments on the car total more than the present value of the car. For example, a car that has been poorly cared for and abused may be shot after just two years. However, if the owner financed the car for four or even five years, he may still have thousands of dollars left to pay on a piece of junk.

3. **A lemon.** The car has simply been nothing but trouble for the owner since it was purchased. Burning the car removes the millstone from the owner's neck, and allows the owner to get a new one that does not spend all its time in the shop.

4. **Theft.** It is common practice for some car jackers and joy riders to set fire to a vehicle in a remote area after they have finished with it. The car was likely not stolen by professionals, but by gang members or adolescents who simply used it for a good time, or perhaps even a gang initiation rite.

Of course, the above list is not complete; it just represents the most common motives.

Verification of either of the first two motives is relatively easy by routine background credit checks by an adjuster, private investigator, or law enforcement authority. In the case of the lemon motive, maintenance records at the dealership or local garage used by the suspect are generally readily available.

Be careful of the fourth category, theft. Sometimes people who wish to rid themselves of a car will fake a theft. While it is best to leave the investigative work in determining whether a theft has been committed to the proper law enforcement authorities, the investigator should be aware that faked thefts do occur.

Incendiary automobile fires whose primary motive is revenge or jealousy do happen, but are rare compared to the other causes.

One common element in incendiary vehicle fires is that there are often either no witnesses, or just one witness, the owner. When there is no witness, the fire will often occur in a remote area, or in a hidden area like a secluded garage, where passers-by cannot observe the initiation of the fire. In a "no witness" incendiary car fire, the owner will often have no idea how the fire started, and will often say that he had not used the car for some time prior to the fire. This is to give the car enough time to burn completely.

When there is just one witness, the owner, often he will state that the fire started while he was driving the vehicle and that he had to abandon the vehicle and walk "x" amount of distance to get to a telephone while the vehicle was burning. This action also provides the time for the vehicle to be fully consumed by the fire. It would do an arsonist no good if the fire was seen, reported, and put out promptly, leaving the car repairable.

One of the more common dead giveaways of arson is when the point of origin of the fire is in the seats, floor or upholstery of the car's interior. In late-model cars, most of the interior materials are made of fire-resistant or fire-treated materials to prevent fire from quickly propagating through an occupied car. Most of the materials now used will not sustain flames on their own, and require an outside source of heat. However, this was not true in the past. In older cars, the cloth and coverings, seat stuffing, and carpets could support combustion, and sometimes would burn fiercely.

When a cigarette is dropped on the seat of a late model car, the cigarette will generally burn a hole in the shape of an inverted cone in the seat, and then go out when the cigarette is exhausted. Cigarette type fires often have points of origin under the seat, where an errant cigarette has rolled, in the crack of the seat, or in the ashtray itself. Car ashtrays loaded with old butts can make a nice fire in the middle of the dashboard.

A common method of incendiary fire making the rounds is to squirt lighter fluid into the vent openings of the dashboard of the car. This is an attempt to make the fire appear to be a short in the wiring under the dashboard. (Check the fuses. Sometimes they aren't even blown because the circuits in the particular area were not operating at the time of the fire.) The arsonist then lights the accelerant and closes the door, or lights it with the door window left open an inch or two to provide air. If the car can be examined right after the fire, residual lighter fluid can usually be easily found in the carpet below the fire area where it has dripped down.

Another common technique is to squirt gas in the engine compartment and light it, closing the hood in quick order. This is also easy to detect because the fire origin will be nonspecific, the severest burn damage will cover a broad pattern, and no particular fuel-related parts will be more severely burned than others.

Figure 9.1 Short section of rubber hose fuel line which leaked, causing fuel fire in engine.

C. Fuel Related Fires

By far the largest category of automotive fire usually involves fuel leaking onto a hot portion of the engine. The engine block, and especially the exhaust manifold and exhaust, is a ready source of ignition energy after the engine has run for a time. Fuel can leak onto the engine from many locations. In modern engines, there is not only the main fuel line from the fuel tank to the engine, but there are also fuel return lines associated with the vapor control system, the emissions system, and the separate fuel lines from the injectors to the cylinders.

In newer vehicles, one of the more common places for leaks to occur is at line connections. If the various connections of the fuel lines are not properly fastened, fuel can leak from the connection. Many manufacturers' fuel system recalls are related to the failure of clips or fasteners to properly secure the fuel line and prevent it from leaking. In older cars, especially ones with rubber or elastomer type fuel lines, the fuel lines may crack at bends and corners, and fuel can leak from these cracks.

Some vehicles use metal fuel lines. Metal lines, especially steel lines, seem to be superior to other types because burning gasoline does not melt steel. Rubberized lines will be burned with the fuel, and will act a little like a fusee when fuel has caught fire. The fire will follow the leak back to the point of leakage, fire will engulf the rubber line, and the line will eventually break open the rubber line and allow the fire to burn the remaining fuel inside the line, following it down the hose. Aluminum lines easily melt during a fuel fire. Copper lines can melt when there is direct contact between the copper and the burning fuel, which is common.

To minimize the transfer of vibrations from the engine to the car body, some manufacturers use a short piece of rubber hose between the connection at the engine and the metal line. These short pieces of rubber hose are where fuel leaks often occur, because they are often disconnected and reconnected during mechanical work, and hence there is an opportunity for error in reconnecting them. Also, the rubberized portions of the line are subject to more fatigue after long periods of service, or when the engine has had a high amount of vibrations.

Since a drip can often follow a line for several inches before dropping onto the engine or manifold, the point of leakage is not always the same as the point of ignition of the fuel. It is usual for the fire to follow the leakage back to the source. Thus, there may be a fire trail from the point of ignition back to the point of leakage.

When fuel fires occur in the engine compartment, as most do, the fire damage pattern on the hood can be very helpful. Since many fuel fires occur in the upper portions of the engine compartment, the flames will often directly impinge on the underside of the hood. The hood will often be a sort of plan view of the fire and fire-spread in the engine compartment. The hottest areas of fire will be marked by complete loss of paint, primer, and any galvanic coatings. Cooler areas will have correspondingly less severe damage to the finish.

In a carburetted engine, if a fire begins at a connection alongside the carburetor due to leakage, the carburetor will be melted away on that side. Most carburetors are now made of aluminum, and thus melt easily when in contact with burning fuel. If the fire began inside the carburetor due to a backfire/flooded condition, the carburetor will have collapsed away from its center, like the way the sides of a large wax candle collapse away from the hot wick. If the fire is simply hot, and has begun elsewhere, the carburetor will whiten or oxidize on the side from which the heat originates. If the heat is severe, the carburetor may melt or collapse on the side towards the heat.

If the air filter canister to the carburetor is made of steel, the air filter canister can also be used to discriminate between a fire originating at a connection to the carburetor, or from within the throat of the carburetor. Fire in the carburetor throat will shoot up into the air filter canister and perhaps directly burn the filter. Fire alongside the carburetor will burn away on the underside of the canister, leave the center of the canister more or less intact, and "cook" or char the filter.

In some cases, the part that actually leaked fuel will be the missing part. Many parts within the fuel system in a modern engine are made of aluminum, plastic, or rubber elastomer. Direct contact with burning gasoline will usually destroy those parts, turning them into melted blobs, char, or debris.

In a modern vehicle, the engine firewall does not keep fire from entering the passenger areas from the engine compartment as well as in older cars. In recognition of this fact, some car companies no longer use the term *firewall*, and instead call it a *bulkhead*. This is because there are so many openings in the bulkhead for ventilation, hoses, wiring, and the like. Most of these openings are for plastic ventilation ducts, rubberized hoses, and plastic insulated wiring. When fire reaches these parts, they quickly collapse or slough away, leaving the hole open for fire to pass into the passenger space. Thus, when an engine fire is severe, it is usual for the fire to pass through the bulkhead into the interior space in the vehicle.

Figure 9.2 Very severe engine fire. Vapors from fuel leak at engine were ignited by nearby hot water tank pilot light in garage.

In vehicles where the fuel pumps are run electrically off the battery, it is possible for the fuel pumps to continue to operate for a time while the fire is burning, even if the engine has stopped. This usually occurs if the fire begins while the car is being driven, and the driver gets out but does not shut off the engine. Often, the driver does this to investigate the source of smoke observed coming through the floor boards in the vehicle interior.

When a car engine has been run for a while and then turned off, it is usual for the engine block and manifold to actually rise in temperature right after the engine has been turned off. This is because when the engine is turned off, the oil stops circulating, the coolant stops circulating, the radiator fan may be turned off, and the car is no longer moving. The last two items supply forced convection cooling to the radiator. Thus, the heat from the last engine firings is trapped in the engine, and is not carried away.

Figure 9.3 Carburetor melt-down in V-8 motor home engine. Fire begin at fuel leak at fuel line connection to carburetor.

To alleviate this temperature rise, which shortens the life of an engine, many modern cars have a thermostat that causes the radiator fan to operate even though the engine has been turned off. This does not completely get rid of the temperature rise, but it can significantly reduce it.

This temperature rise effect is important to understand because many car fires begin when the car is stopped, even though the leak may have been occurring while the car was being driven. While the car is being driven, the engine runs cooler, and the leaked fuel may be simply blown away from the engine by the moving air. Most cars and trucks are designed so that the moving air will pass through the radiator and wash over the engine to carry away heat.

When a car is stopped, the engine block and manifold temperature rise, and the leak is no longer blown away by moving air. It can drip intact upon the hot engine block, manifold, or exhaust, and ignite. Most importantly, with no moving air, the fire can backtrack and follow the leakage path back to its source to get things really going. For this reason vehicle fires often break out just after the engine has been turned off, or the driver has just stopped the vehicle.

In some cases, if the leak is in the main fuel line, the leak may cause a small pressure drop in the fuel line pressure, and this drop in pressure may be sufficient to cause the engine to sputter or stall when climbing a hill, passing, or otherwise operating at a higher load. If the driver recalls when this occurred, it may give a useful clue as to when the engine first was known to leak fuel.

D. Other Fire Loads under the Hood

While fuel-related fires easily outnumber the rest, fires under the hood can also be caused by other flammable liquids leaking onto hot surfaces. This includes:

- brake fluid squirting from a bad seal or line connection,
- hydraulic fluid leaking from a seal in the power assist systems,
- engine oil from a leaky valve cover,
- transmission oil boiling out of the dip stick opening in overheating automatic transmissions,
- air conditioner compressor oil from a leak in the high pressure side of the refrigerant loop, and
- some types of engine coolants leaking from a radiator hose can also burn.

For example, ethylene glycol, one of the common coolants used in radiators, has a flash point of 241°F and ignites at 775°F. While it is not nearly as hazardous with respect to fire as gasoline, it still can burn and take out a car under the right circumstances. Some types of rubberized hoses may even catch fire if they are displaced and contact the manifold or other hot portions of the engine block.

E. Electrical Fires

A majority of electrical fires in a vehicle are caused by the following:

- wires which have been cut by abrasion and have grounded out,
- wires which have become displaced and have contacted the manifold or hot portions of the engine block and grounded out,
- wires which have simply overheated due to overload where the fuses have been bypassed (usually done in home-installed after-market equipment), and
- appliances which have failed and have inadequate fusing to catch the fault (also popular in home-installed after-market equipment like CB's, radios, and tape decks).

Often, the damages associated with an electrical fire are located on either side of the bulkhead or fire wall. This is, of course, because most of the wiring harnesses are located here. Because of the way equipment in the engine compartment is packed together, it is possible for an electrically caused fire to turn into a fuel system fed fire. If the fuel system fed fire is severe enough, it may hide or obscure the electrical origins of the fire.

Figure 9.4 After-market radio wire laid over seat wire, which cut into wire and shorted.

An electrical fire under the dashboard will usually create inside-out type damages, that is, damages that are most severe on the interior, and whose severity diminishes towards the exterior or perimeter of the area. Because the wiring is usually run just under the dashboard, the area will have a "hollowed out" appearance.

Most of the plastic materials used in modern automobile dashboards do not readily support a flame or fire. However, they will melt, char, and emit copious dense smoke, and may support flames and fire as long as the electrical fault supplies heat energy.

An examination of the fuses will often yield information as to which grouping of equipment was involved in the fault. Then the point of origin has to be tracked down like any other electrical fault. However, in an automobile, a ground fault can occur at any time the bare wiring can make contact with the metal frame or parts of a car, since the metal frame is the return wire for most circuits. The negative sides of all the circuits in the vehicle are run through the metal frame as a common ground return. Thus, once heat reaches a group of wires in a harness that is positioned on a metal fender or the bulkhead and the protective insulation melts away, it is possible for nearly all the wires in the harness to ground fault at more or less the same time at the same place.

The home installation of after-market equipment often causes electrical fires in vehicles. The handyman is often unfamiliar with the circuits, and will simply tap into the most convenient wire he can find. Usually, the fuse block is by-passed, so the new item does not have the benefit of overcurrent protection. Further, the wire to the new item will be loose, and often is simply tucked loosely under the carpet (where it can be stepped on repeatedly), or laid over metal pieces that may eventually abrade and cut into the insulation.

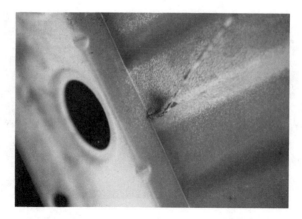

Figure 9.5 Wire which was run between bed of van and frame. Frame-to-bed movements cut through insulation, causing wire to short.

Because a car constantly vibrates when rolling along, loose wiring has a much higher probability being abraded on nearby edges or rough surfaces. This is one reason why the manufacturer groups the wiring in harnesses. Sometimes, when repair work is done on an electrical circuit, it is considered too much trouble for the mechanic to put a wire back into the bundle or harness as before. He may simply tuck it in at a convenient spot, or tape it to something nearby to hold it down.

Of course, loose wiring in the engine compartment may also eventually come to rest on either the manifold or the engine block. Since much of the wiring is sheathed in relatively low-temperature plastic insulation, just getting close to the hot items may be enough to damage the insulation and allow the circuit to ground fault.

F. Mechanical and Other Causes

Fires in cars are also, but less frequently, caused by mechanical failure. Wheel bearings, brakes and exhaust components are the most common culprits.

When brakes are involved, usually the individual wheel brake cylinders have lost their seals and brake fluid has leaked into the drum or disk where the high temperatures generated by braking friction ignite the fuel. The point of origin at the wheel is usually easy to spot.

Most axles and wheels use a heavy oil or grease for lubrication. The loss of wheel bearings can allow these lubricants to leak or flow into the brakes, or the failure of the bearing itself may generate sufficient heat for ignition to occur.

Some fires are blamed on the catalytic converter. Most are in one of two groups:

*Figure 9.6 Burn pattern on garage floor from car fire.
Bottom of photo is the engine area.*

1. Where the fire is caused by the catalytic converter contacting weeds or dry grass when hot, and igniting materials exterior to the car. In the process, the vehicle is burned up by the grass or flammables underneath it.

2. The fuel mixture of the engine is too rich, and clogs up the catalytic converter so that it operates very hot. A fire can then start within the converter itself.

Of course, a catalytic converter is a place where fire is already occurring. The converter actually "slow burns" unburned fuel in the exhaust stream so that fewer unburned carbon compounds leave the exhaust pipe. This slow burn is accomplished by the use of a surface catalyst, usually a platinum compound, which causes the fuel to oxidize at temperatures and conditions lower than it would otherwise.

Because of this, catalytic converters are coolest when the vehicle is driving along with the engine efficiency high; this normally occurs when the vehicle is traveling on the highway. The moving air under the vehicle also helps keep it cool.

Catalytic converters operate hottest when the car is sitting still. The engine is operating under very poor thermodynamic efficiency then, and there is no moving air for forced convection. If the vehicle is then parked and left running in a dense, dry, and tall growth of weeds or foliage, the vegetative material may not only insulate the bottom of the vehicle, prevent air flow on the underside of the vehicle and further worsen convection, but may also directly contact the hot metal skin of the converter. The combination of these factors may lead to the ignition of the combustible vegetation under the vehicle.

A cause of fire that occasionally occurs is right after refueling. Sloppy fueling of the vehicle can often leave a small amount of gasoline trapped in the refueling port. This can then drop down onto the exhaust pipe and ignite, especially if the car has been left running and the pipe is hot. The flames then engulf the fuel-wetted areas, which are usually around the refueling port or door. This is why gas stations always post the sign, "Turn off engine when refueling" or something similar. This type of fire is perhaps a little more prevalent now than in years past because of the proliferation of self-service gas stations. Many drivers are not particularly careful in the handling of gasoline around the pumps. Seeing drivers smoke while refueling also gives me the heebie-jeebies.

Because I could not stop for Death,
He kindly stopped for me;
The carriage held but just ourselves
And Immortality.

Emily Dickinson, from *Poems, Third Series,* 1896

Chapter 10:
Fire and Explosion Case Study

A. General

The following is a case study of a fire and two resulting explosions which occurred on November 29, 1988, in Kansas City, Missouri. In that event, six gallant Kansas City firemen were tragically killed by two large explosions at a construction site. When the explosions occurred, the firemen were trying to put out a fire which apparently had been set by vandals in two semi-trailers. The two semi-trailers were loaded with 25 tons of construction type explosives.

The original purpose of the engineering analysis of this case was to determine the overpressure and ground vibration levels associated with the resulting explosions. This information was needed to estimate the probable damage to structures in the surrounding area of the explosions. However, in order to determine these things, it was first necessary to reconstruct the event and solve many of the questions related to the accident.

This particular case was chosen to close the main part of the text for several reasons. First, it demonstrates with a real-life example some of the principles already discussed elsewhere in the book, especially in the explosion chapters. Secondly, it introduces a few topics about explosions not mentioned previously. Thirdly, it demonstrates to a small degree the problem solving process. Lastly, and perhaps most importantly, however, it demonstrates the sobering, human side of this type of work.

Fire and explosion reconstruction is not just an academic pursuit. When a forensic engineer undertakes an assignment, the subsequent investigation and analysis may uncover information which can affect people's reputations, their pride, their fortunes, and their well-being in ways not anticipated at the start.

In some cases, people just like you and me have been killed, maimed, or have lost loved ones. They may have lost all of their belongings, which was perhaps the sum total of their whole lives. Sometimes they may have lost a personal treasure that not only breaks their hearts, but is an item whose age or scarcity makes it irreplaceable. The answer to "what happened" is more important to them than just the answer to an engineering problem; it is an explanation of what has happened to their lives. This goes beyond the simple solution to an equation.

When serious accidents occur, civil or criminal litigation often follows. In such cases, no matter what the engineer finds or concludes, or how well and professionally he does his work, it is likely that someone on one side or another, or both, will attempt to discredit the engineer's findings or even the engineer personally to blunt the effects of his findings. This is to be expected; the adversarial nature of the U.S. court system practically demands it.

Thus, when the stakes are serious, it ceases to be a scholar's game. Like carrion in the ocean, big money attracts big sharks with big teeth. You can be sure that if enough money is at stake, the attorney for the side that disagrees with a particular engineer's report will hire whomever and whatever is necessary to discredit, cast doubt on, or obfuscate its findings. That is the attorney's job; that is what he is supposed to do. Forensic engineers should be aware of this fact of life, and prepare their reports accordingly.

In this particular case, investigations were done by the local police and fire departments, the Bureau of Alcohol, Tobacco, and Firearms, the National Fire Protection Association, a number of federal and state regulatory entities, and several private entities including insurers and insurance claimants.

Following these investigations there was civil litigation related to the deaths of the six firemen, civil litigation related to the damages allegedly sustained to nearby structures around the explosion site, criminal prosecution of the alleged vandals, and various changes were made in the city regulations concerning explosives stored at construction sites, especially with regards to amounts and notification requirements. Changes in some state and federal regulations were also under study.

Some of the initial civil litigation was settled privately before the cases reached trial, which often happens when both sides are able to accurately assess the "worth" of a case. As is typical of civil matters in this area of the U.S., all this took about three years. The criminal investigation and prosecution proceedings went normally and also took about the same amount of time.

It is sobering to realize how many lives were affected, and how much time and money was spent because of that one act of vandalism on November 29, 1988, in Kansas City.

B. Brief Chronology and Materials Involved

As noted, the accident event occurred on November 29, 1988 at a highway construction site located about 650 feet northeast of the present-day intersection of 87th Street and U.S. 71 in Kansas City, Missouri. The immediate area surrounding the blast was undeveloped at the time and was populated with trees and scrub brush.

The sequence of events leading up to the explosions began with the discovery of prowlers by construction site security guards shortly after 3 a.m. on November 29, 1988. The two guards went to investigate the prowlers. While doing this, the guards observed that a vandalism-type fire had been set in the pickup truck of one of the guards on the other side of the construction site. Both guards then rushed over to the pickup truck. The pickup truck fire was reported to the Kansas City Fire Department at 3:40 a.m.

A second fire was then noted by the guards in the area of two construction company semi-trailers parked at the site; both were located a short distance from the pickup truck. Both semi-trailers contained ammonium nitrate fuel oil (ANFO) type construction explosives. The second fire occurring at the two semi-trailers was also reported to the fire department by the guards.

A pumper truck was dispatched to the site and put out the fire in the pickup truck by about 4 a.m. When this was done, the pumper truck went over to assist a second pump truck which had already been dispatched to put out the fire at the location of the two semi-trailers.

The first explosion occurred about 4:06 a.m. in the area of the semi-trailers. Reportedly, the blast overpressure near the scene was sufficient to move parked vehicles several feet. A bright, white fire continued to burn at the scene after the explosion. At 4:48 a.m., the second explosion occurred. A similar bright fire also continued to burn at the site after the second explosion.

Investigative authorities entered the explosion site area sometime after the second explosion, about 6 a.m., when it was deemed safe to do so. All the firemen who had manned the two pumpers were dead, and the two pumpers were wholly destroyed. Because of the closeness to the explosions, there were few remains of the firemen to be found.

The first semi-trailer parked at the construction site was known to contain 17,000 pounds of aluminized ammonium nitrate fuel oil (ANFO) in 5 and 6 inch diameter blasting socks. The first semi-trailer also contained 3,500 pounds of non-aluminized ANFO in 50-pound bags.

The second semi-trailer, which was parked near and roughly parallel to the first semi-trailer, contained 30,000 pounds of aluminized ANFO in 30-pound socks. Thus there had been 50,500 pounds, or just over 25 tons of ANFO stored at the site divided between the two semi-trailers. The construction of both of the semi-trailers was such that it was assumed in the following analysis that their structures offered no significant containment of the explosions.

When the explosion site was examined after the blasts, three distinctive craters were found. Two fully separate craters, one 38 feet across and 6 feet deep, and another 20 feet across and 4.5 feet deep were where the first semi-trailer had been. A third crater which was measured to be 49 feet across and 6.5 to 7.0 feet deep was located where the second semi-trailer had been. This third crater was not regular in shape, but had a smaller overlapping crater, or a crater extension of 20 feet at one end.

Thus, where both semi-trailers had set, there was a pattern of a large crater next to a smaller one corresponding to each semi-trailer. In the first semi-trailer, the large and small craters were fully separate from one another. In the second semi-trailer, they overlapped. The overlapping was due to the significantly larger amount of explosive material in the second semi-trailer. The explosions in that semi-trailer were large enough to cause the resulting craters to overlap.

C. Consumption of Some of the Explosives by Fire

Not all of the explosives contained in the two semi-trailers were involved in the explosions at the site. Eyewitness accounts indicated that fires preceded both of the two explosions, and that the fires appeared unusually bright and white. These are the usual color characteristics of burning ANFO which has been mixed with aluminum. Eyewitness accounts also indicated that a similar bright and white fire was observed after the second explosion. There was no significant fireload elsewhere in the area of the two semi-trailers which could account for the fire, or the coloring and distinctive brightness of the fire.

It is known that the fire preceding the first main explosion burned for about 30 minutes. The fire preceding the second main explosion burned for about 42 minutes. The fire after the second main explosion burned for perhaps another 30 minutes or more. Thus there was over one hour and forty-two minutes where burning was observed by eyewitnesses in the area of the trailers.

From this, it was concluded that the amount of explosive material actually involved in the two main explosions was significantly less than the total amount of explosive materials known to have been present at the site. In other words, a significant amount of the ANFO burned up instead of exploding.

One of the issues related to how much of the ANFO was consumed by the fire is that until this event occurred, ANFO was considered more or less safe around fires. In fact, the recommended procedure for disposing of ANFO was, and still is, burning. It was believed that when ANFO caught fire, the ANFO would burn up but would not detonate.

Because of this, one procedure for dealing with fires in ANFO storage areas was simply to wet down the surrounding area to prevent further spread of the fire, and to remain at a safe distance from the storage area until the fire burned out. The "safe distance" admonishment was in case there were other items around the ANFO which could detonate in a fire.

In checking the references on which the "safe around fires" conclusion had been made, it was found that the experiments had involved relatively small amounts of ANFO, much less than the amounts involved in this case. In those experiments, various amounts of ANFO were burned, and in no case did the ANFO detonate. From that data, it was concluded that ANFO was safe in a fire. However, this accident showed that there is a size effect to consider; in amounts above a certain threshold, burning ANFO can obviously detonate.

D. Significance of the Crater Patterns

It is well documented by witnesses that the two major explosions which were heard were separated in time by 42 minutes. However, the pattern of two craters, one large and one small, at each semi-trailer location also indicates that each major explosion actually consisted of a large and a small explosion in quick succession. Thus, actually there had been four separate explosions. In each semi-trailer, a large explosion occurred first, followed by a smaller one which was sympathetically triggered by the blast effects of the first.

In conventional blasting, when two sequential blasts are placed close together and are detonated 20 to 25 milliseconds apart, it is difficult for a person located some distance away to discern that there have been two separate blasts; only one distinct explosion sound is heard. Likewise, while only one blast per semi-trailer was heard by witnesses some distance away, the evidence indicates that each semi-trailer had two explosions: one large and one small. The sound simply combined into a single roar, in a similar way that multiple lightning strikes are usually heard as a single roll of thunder.

While the separation in time between the two explosions per semi-trailer is not sufficient to allow them to be audibly discerned, the slight delay between explosions ensures that the resulting ground vibrations and air overpressure levels are no more intense than the largest individual explosion. In other words, the highest intensity of the resulting ground vibrations and air overpressure levels is not related to the sum total of the explosive materials, but is related only to the single largest individual amount of explosive material that detonated.

All the other explosions, since they result from smaller amounts of explosive materials, result in lesser ground vibrations and air overpressure levels. In this sense then, to determine the highest amount of ground vibrations and air overpressure levels that would have affected nearby houses and structures, it is only necessary to consider the effects of the single largest explosion of the four which occurred. In short, only the biggest crater counts.

The principle of delay type blasting, where individual blasts are separated by short periods of time in order to minimize ground vibrations and air overpressure levels, is well understood. This technique has been used for years by "powder monkeys" to maximize blasting of rock while minimizing the risk of damage to nearby structures.

In the case of the first semi-trailer, the center of the large crater was separated from the center of the smaller carter by 32 feet. Mach 1, the speed of sound, is about 1,080 ft/sec, and is also the minimum speed of explosion pressure wave expansion for a detonation type explosion. Generally, detonation wave fronts near the point of detonation have a front velocity of between Mach 1 and Mach 2. In this regard, ANFO is considered to be a relatively slow explosive.

Thus, at an average speed of Mach 1, a pressure front generated by a large explosion at the center of the large crater would take about 30 milliseconds to reach the center of the second, smaller crater. Similarly, at an average speed of Mach 2, the estimated delay time from large explosion to small explosion in the first semi-trailer would have been 15 milliseconds. Of course, some additional delay would occur due to the time it took the second cache of explosives to detonate.

The point of checking the time between the large and small explosions is to ensure that there is sufficient time delay for the explosions to be considered separate. Delays of over about 10 milliseconds ensure that. The numbers, therefore, indicate that this was the case.

The same reasoning applies to the second semi-trailer, except that it is 34 feet from the center of the large crater to the center of the smaller crater. Thus, the delay time is slightly higher for the second semi-trailer.

E. Observations Concerning the Semi-Trailers

It is known that the first semi-trailer was about 35 feet long, and the second semi-trailer was about 38 feet long. The separation of the crater centers of the first semi-trailer was 32 feet, and the second 34 feet. Both semi-trailers had dual axles.

Loading space limitations dictate that the load of explosive materials in each semi-trailer be split between the two ends. The excellent correlation between lengths of the semi-trailers and the spacing between their respective crater centers also corroborates this.

Thus, from the observations, it is concluded that there were two areas of stored explosives in each semi-trailer, one large and one small, over each axle. Also, the blast from one of the explosive caches within a semi-trailer detonated the cache at the opposite end. This resulted in a delay timing effect similar to that used in conventional construction blasting work which minimized the effects of ground vibrations and air overpressure fronts.

Because of the short but significant time delay between detonations in each semi-trailer, the maximum ground vibrations and air overpressure front effects would be associated with the formation of the largest crater, that is, the largest of the four explosions. Ground vibrations and air pressure front resulting from the other three lesser explosions would be of lesser magnitude. The largest crater was 49 feet across and 6.5 to 7.0 feet deep.

F. Amount of Charge Needed to Form Craters

A formula for estimating the amount of charge required to produce a certain size crater from a surface explosion is provided in the text, *Explosive Shocks in Air*, by Kinney and Graham (see bibliography). The formula is as follows:

(i) $\quad d = 0.8(W)^{1/3}$

where d = crater diameter in meters, and
$\quad\quad$ W = explosion yield in equivalent kilograms of TNT.

The above formula was based upon a statistical study of 200 accidental large explosions.

In this case, d equals 15 meters. Solving the equation finds that W is then equal to 6,600 kg or 14,500 pounds of TNT. Because ANFO has a TNT explosive strength equivalence of 142%, then the crater calculation indicates that about 10,211 pounds of ANFO were detonated to cause the largest crater of the second semi-trailer.

The smaller crater of the second semi-trailer had a diameter of 20 feet, or about 6 meters. Using the same procedure, the amount of ANFO which caused the smaller crater is estimated to be 686 pounds. The total amount of ANFO which exploded in the second trailer is then estimated to be 10,897 pounds. Since there was known to be about 30,000 pounds of ANFO in the second semi-trailer, then 19,103 pounds of ANFO must have been consumed by the fire or was otherwise not detonated.

Similarly, the two craters of the first semi-trailer indicate that the amount of ANFO involved in the explosion was 4,705 pounds for the 38-foot diameter crater, and 686 pounds for the 20-foot diameter crater. This is a total of 5,391 pounds of ANFO which was involved in the explosion of the first semi-trailer. Since it is known that the first semi-trailer had 20,500 pounds of ANFO on board, then 15,109 pounds of the ANFO was consumed by fire or otherwise did not explode.

The above findings agree reasonably with the eyewitness reports. It is known that there was fire at the first trailer for about 30 minutes prior to the first major explosion, and there was fire at the second semi-trailer prior to the second major explosion for 40 minutes. It would be expected, then, that the second semi-trailer would have lost more ANFO to fire than the first.

In sum, analysis of the largest crater finds that the largest blast involved 10,211 pounds of ANFO, or a TNT equivalent of 14,500 pounds.

G. Blast Overpressure

The blast overpressure can be calculated for any unobstructed distance from the center of the blast by the use of scaled distance factor. Equation (ii) below shows the general functional relationship of regular atmospheric pressure, overpressure, and the scaled distance factor.

(ii) $(P_y - P_x) / P_x = f(Z)$

where P_x = atmospheric pressure,
$\quad\quad P_y$ = pressure of explosion front,
$\quad\quad f$ = symbol for "function of",
$\quad\quad Z$ = scaled distance factor in meters/kg$^{1/3}$
$\quad\quad\quad\quad$ where the distance is in meters, and the amount of charge
$\quad\quad\quad\quad$ is in kilograms of equivalent TNT.

Using either Figure 6-4 or Table XI in *Explosive Shocks in Air* by Kinney and Graham to obtain a scaling factor Z, it is found that a 1-kilogram charge of TNT will produce an overpressure factor of 0.097 at 10 meters.

Because the explosion's pressure front diminishes with the cube of the distance, a second scaling equation can be used to relate distances and charge size to the Z value noted above.

(iii) $d1 / W_1^{1/3} = d_2 / W_2^{1/3} = Z$

$\quad\quad d_2 = Z W_2^{1/3} = d_1 (W_2^{1/3} / W_1^{1/3})$

Using the Z value of 10 m /(1 kg TNT)$^{1/3}$ as previously obtained from the reference text, it is found that with a charge of 6,600 kilograms of TNT, an overpressure factor of 0.097 times the atmospheric pressure will occur at a distance of 188 meters or 615 feet.

$\quad\quad d_2 = Z W_2^{1/3} = (10 \text{ m/kg}^{1/3})(6{,}600 \text{ kg})^{1/3} = 188 \text{ m} = 615 \text{ ft.}$

The following table is then developed in the same manner.

Table 1. Overpressure Factors versus Distance from Center of Blast

distance	overpressure factor
83 ft	5.04 (74.1 psig)
123 ft	2.025 (29.8 psig)
615 ft	0.097 (1.43 psig)
1,107 ft	0.048 (0.71 psig)
1,691 ft	0.030 (0.44 psig)
3,075 ft	0.016 (0.24 psig)
9,225 ft	0.005 (0.07 psig)

According to *Structure Response and Damage Produced by Airblast from Surface Mining* by Siskind, Stachura, Stagg and Kopp (Bureau of Mines Report of Investigations, 1980, #845, page 95), glass windows are known to break when overpressures exceed 0.88 to 1.1 psig. No damages were observed to occur when overpressures were at a range of 0.62 psig to 0.72 psig. Based upon these figures then, a safe threshold of 0.75 psig for airblast overpressures was defined for properly mounted glass.

According to *Blasting Vibrations and Their Effects on Structures*, U.S. Department of the Interior, Bureau of Mines Bulletin 656 (1971), a safe blasting limit of 0.5 psig of overpressure is recommended to ensure no breakage of glass in structures. Based on this criterion and on data contained in Table 1, it would be expected that no glass breakage from the overpressure would occur at distances over about 1,600 feet from the center of the blast. However, window rattling would be noticed at a distance of about two miles or more from the blast site.

H. Sound Levels

As given in *Structural Response and Damage Produced by Airblast from Surface Mining*, page 8, the relationship between overpressure levels to sound pressure levels is given by the following formula:

(iv) $L = 20 \log_{10} P/P_r$

where L = sound pressure level in decibels,
   P = overpressure level, and
   P_r = reference sound pressure level for 0 decibels = 2.9×10^{-9} psig.

Using the relationship in equation (iv), the following table is constructed using data from Table 1.

Table 2. Sound Pressure Levels versus Distance from Explosion

distance	overpressure factor	sound level
83 ft	5.04 (74.1 psig)	208 db
123 ft	2.025 (29.8 psig)	200 db
615 ft	0.097 (1.43 psig)	174 db
1,107 ft	0.048 (0.71 psig)	168 db
1,691 ft	0.030 (0.44 psig)	163 db
3,075 ft	0.016 (0.24 psig)	158 db
9,225 ft	0.005 (0.07 psig)	148 db

As the above table indicates, the sound levels up to 9,225 feet away from the explosion would have been quite loud and startling, and sound pressure levels above 130 decibels (db) can cause discomfort or pain. Values above 160 db can cause damage to the eardrum. Table 2 also indicates that at about 1,700 feet from the explosion, the distance within which glass damage would be expected, the sound pressure levels are 160 db or higher.

It is estimated that at a distance of 10 miles, the overpressure would have dropped to 0.00087 psig, which corresponds to a sound pressure level of 109 decibels. This estimate lends credence to the statements noted by persons who claimed to have heard the blast about 10 miles away.

However, due to the refractive effects of the lower atmosphere, most loud noises, like thunder, are not heard further than about 16 miles away from the source unless there are intervening inversion layers in the atmosphere which can "bend" the sound back to earth. (from: Fleagle, *The Audibility of Thunder*, Journal of Acoustical Society of America, 1949, vol. 21, pages 411–412). For this reason, witness reports of the sound being heard farther away than 16 miles were considered with some reservation.

I. Ground Vibrations from the Blast

Ground vibrations can be measured in several ways: peak to peak displacement, peak to peak velocity, and peak to peak acceleration. It has been found experimentally that the best parameter to use to predict damage to a structure is peak to peak velocity.

The standard for "safe" ground vibration levels from blasting, as per *Bulletin 656* of the Department of Mines, is 2.0 in/sec, peak to peak ground particle velocity. At this level of ground vibration velocity, no structural damage is expected to occur. At a level of 5.4 in/sec, peak to peak ground particle velocity (PPV), minor damage might occur to a structure. At a level of 7.6 in/sec PPV, major damage would be expected in a structure.

The standard equation for the determination of the distance at which a certain ground vibration level, measured in peak-to-peak velocity units, occurs in response to a known amount of explosive material is given as follows:

(v) $d = (K)(W)^{1/2}$

where d = distance from blast in feet,
    W = weight per delay in pounds of dynamite, and
    K = blasting scaling factor for PPV.

Because the above equation is usually applied to construction blasting work, and dynamite is a traditional blasting material, the W in equation (v) is typically given in equivalent pounds of dynamite. Generally, dynamite is rated as having 82% the explosive power of TNT. Thus, 14,500 lbs. of TNT, the equivalent explosive power of 10,211 pounds of ANFO, is equivalent to about 17,680 pounds of dynamite.

In order to apply equation (v), a value for the blasting scaling factor K must be known. In *Bulletin 656*, a blasting scaling factor of 50 ft/lb$^{1/2}$ is recommended for a PPV of 2.0 in/sec whenever a specific blasting scaling factor has not been determined experimentally by seismographic monitoring.

The above "safe" blasting scaling factor value was chosen by the U.S. Department of Mines to provide a wide margin of safety in determining a "safe blasting distance" where the distance to the blast is sufficient for ground vibrations to attenuate to no more than 2.0 in/sec PPV. When this value for K is used, the formula is sometimes known as the "safe blasting formula" as given below.

(vi) $d = (50 \text{ ft/lb}^{1/2})(W^{1/2})$ at a PPV of 2.0 in/sec,

where d = safe distance in feet from blast where vibrations will not exceed 2.0 in/sec PPV,
    W = equivalent pounds of dynamite.

However, the use of the "safe blasting formula" to predict the distance at which the ground vibrations are equal to 2.0 in/sec PPV is inappropriate; it often errs by as much as 50% when compared to actual seismograph measurements, because a high factor of safety has been built into the value. This is why it is recommended that the "safe blasting formula" be used only when experimental data is not available.

Despite its inherent limitations, if the safe blasting formula were applied to the largest explosion which occurred in this case as determined from the largest crater size, then the safe distance predicted by the formula is as follows:

$$d = (50 \text{ ft/lb}^{1/2})(17{,}680 \text{ lbs dynamite equivalent})^{1/2} = 6{,}648 \text{ ft.}$$

Thus, buildings and structures more than 6,648 feet away from the blast crater would not have been damaged by ground vibrations from the blast. Using the safe blasting formula then provides a quick and dirty first cut in determining the outermost boundary radius within which damage might have occurred. However, it is also inherent in the large factor of safety built into the blasting scaling factor that the actual boundary radius within which damages might have occurred will be smaller than that predicted by the safe blasting formula.

In this regard, since some construction blasting had already been done in the area, it was a simple matter to check the contractor's blasting logs, which must be kept to be in compliance with federal law, to determine the actual K value for the specific area.

From about a dozen shots in the area completed just a few days before the accident, it was determined that the actual K value for the area was 17.9 ft/lb$^{1/2}$ with a standard deviation of 4.5 ft/lb$^{1/2}$ and a small sample deviation of 4.7 ft/lb$^{1/2}$.

Because the sampling size is considered small, n = 12, the small sample standard error of the mean in this case is calculated to be 1.36 ft/lb$^{1/2}$. With 11 degrees of freedom, the "t" significance for a 5% confidence is 2.18 ft/lb$^{1/2}$. Thus, for a 95% confidence level, the scaling factor for this specific site is as follows:

$$K = 17.9 \pm 3.0 \text{ ft/lb}^{1/2}.$$

Thus, the site specific formula for determining the farthest distance from the blast where ground vibrations would be 2.0 in/sec PPV at a confidence level of 95% is given as follows:

$$d = (20.9 \text{ ft/lb}^{1/2})(W^{1/2})$$

In this case, since W is equivalent to about 17,680 pounds of dynamite, then the distance at which ground vibrations are at 2.0 in/sec PPV is 2,779 feet away from the blast. Thus, the ground vibrations will be no more than 2.0 in/sec at distances at or more than 2,779 feet away from the blast crater.

Because the ground vibration formula is based on an inverse square relationship, it is possible to also calculate the ground vibration levels for other distances. For example at a vibration level of 5.4 in/sec PPV, the level at which minor damages occur to a structure, the distance is 1,691 feet. For a vibration level of 7.6 in/sec PPV, the level at which major damages to a structure occur, the distance is 1,426 feet.

J. Check of Figures

As a check of the foregoing analysis, a copy of a computer program used by the military to assess surface bomb damages to structures was obtained. The military program, however, only assessed air blast overpressures and did not assess ground vibrations. I suppose this is because simple cracks in a building created by ground vibrations are not sufficient to render it useless to the enemy.

However, the air blast figures provided by the computer program confirmed the figures already noted, and precision of the two was to two-place accuracy. The military computer program did allow for the inclusion of geographic features, and could have been used to predict general "shadowing" effects, where one building shields another from air blast effects. However, since destructive level ground vibrations reach out farther than destructive level air blast overpressure, this is a moot point.

K. Summary

The analysis of the data related to the November 29, 1988, accident then indicates that the air overpressure would not have exceeded 0.5 psig, the minimum level at which glass breakage occurs in a building, at distances more than 1,600 feet from the large blast crater.

With respect to building damages, some damages would be expected to begin within a circle radius extending 2,779 feet from the blast. Some minor damages would be expected within a radius of 1,691 feet, and serious damages would be expected within a radius of about 1,426 feet.

It is interesting to note that because air blast overpressures diminish as the cube of the distance, and ground vibration levels diminish as the square of the distance, the air blast effects drop off to "safe" levels well before ground vibrations drop to "safe" levels. Thus, while there may be window glass breakage at distances of more than 1,600 feet from the blast, that breakage is caused by building motion and not by air overpressure effects. Since glass breakage from ground motion effects occurs farther from the blast site than air overpressure effects, most of the time air overpressure effects are ignored in this type of analysis.

Chapter 11: Study Problems

A. General

The following study problems have been set aside in a separate chapter at the end of the book so that they can be either used or ignored without being in the way of the regular text. For convenience, each chapter in the book has an associated group of study problems.

The study problems serve several purposes:

1. To give the reader some idea of what the material in the book is good for.
2. To serve as a point of discussion for principles and ideas discussed in the text.
3. Just as exercises strengthen an athlete and develop agility, solving good problems strengthens the skills of an engineer and develops mental agility.
4. In working out solutions for these problems, the reader will become acquainted with additional materials pertinent to this field of study.

The reader should be aware that not all of the information needed to solve the problems is contained in this book; in some instances, the reader will have to do some library research, or even some small-scale experiments to find the information necessary to solve them. But then again, that is what professional forensic engineers do all the time.

If the reader finds that it is necessary to do some laboratory work to solve some of the study problems, please observe good laboratory safety rules. If the reader is inexperienced in laboratory work, I strongly recommend that any experimentation be done under the supervision of a qualified laboratory instructor or technician. If the reader cannot do the experiments safely, do not do them at all.

Answers to the various study problems are not provided for a reason: professional forensic engineers don't find the answers to their assignments at the back of a book. The reader will find that "working without a net" sharpens research and thinking skills, and provides a taste of the real world working environment. Just how sure of your solution are you?

B. Chapter One: Introduction

1. What is the difference between a Lucifer, a phosphor, and a match?

2. Explain the difference between "strike anywhere" matches and "safety" matches. How is this difference accomplished?

3. Explain the various grades of fire extinguishers.

4. What is the difference between a dry sprinkler system and a wet sprinkler system? How does each work?

5. What is Woods metal, and what is it used for?

6. How does a dry chemical extinguisher system, like the kind used in fast food kitchens, work?

7. What are the maintenance requirements for fire extinguishers? Where are these specifications found?

8. What are the requirements in your state for the following:

    - Fire marshal?
    - Fire investigator at a local fire department?
    - Private detective?
    - Professional licensed engineer?
    - Insurance adjuster?

    Which of these are required to pass coursework in chemistry and thermodynamics? How do you think these facts may relate to cross examination in a court room?

9. What is the "Frye" rule with respect to expert testimony?

10. The number of people who smoke has begun to decline. Compare the number of smokers in the past five years with the number of fires attributed to careless use of smoking materials. Have the fires caused by smoking materials dropped also?

11. A lawyer can work on a contingency fee basis. Can a registered professional engineer do the same when he or she is hired to do fire

investigative work that may require court testimony? Why or why not?

12. Western pioneers sometimes used their muskets to get a campfire started. How did they do this?

13. Explain at least three methods of building a fire that do not require matches or lighters.

14. In the late 19th century, horse-drawn fire engines had a boiler. What was it for?

15. On a small book of paper matches, it usually says "Close cover before striking." Why?

16. How does the *"Fire Safety Code"* relate to the *"Unified Building Code,"* and how do the *"National Fire Protection Association"* regulations and specifications relate to the *"Occupational Safety and Health Administration"* regulations and specifications?

17. What are the conversion formulae for the following:

   - degrees Celsius into degrees Fahrenheit?
   - degrees Celsius into degrees Kelvin?
   - degrees Fahrenheit into degrees Rankine?
   - pressure in psi into kilopascals?
   - newtons into pounds force?
   - slugs into kilograms?
   - meters into inches?

18. Explain subrogation.

C. Chapter 2: Some Combustion Chemistry

1. What is the chemical equation for the combustion of gasoline? How much energy must be absorbed by 3 kilograms of gasoline for it to wholly vaporize? At what temperature will this occur?

2. What is producer gas, and how is it made? How might it be made in a fire situation?

3. Using the Ideal Gas Law, determine the temperature at which absolute zero occurs.

4. A room is 3 meters long, 4 meters wide, and 2.5 meters high. Inside the room there is a cord of well-seasoned wood. The room is full of air, but is sealed tight. If the wood is set on fire, will all of it burn? Assuming that no heat is lost to the environment, and that the room is tightly sealed, what will the pressure be inside the room when the fire goes out?

5. Explain how Charles' Law and Boyle's Law can be combined to derive the Ideal Gas Law.

6. How many molecules are there in 22.4 liters of a gas at standard conditions?

7. Can wood burn on Mars?

8. A pipe is full of water which is at 250°F and 200 psia. The pipe has an internal diameter of 2 inches, and is 15 feet long. If the pipe ruptures, what will happen to the water?

9. At what temperature does thermosetting plastic lose most of its strength?

10. A 5"× 3" American Standard I-beam that extends across a basement to support the upper floor is 24 feet long. During a fire, the I-beam is heated to an average temperature of 400°F. How much longer was it during the fire than previously?

11. A one-inch-square ice cube is dropped into a 10-ounce glass of water that is at room temperature. How much colder will the water in the glass be after the ice cube has completely melted?

12. A fuel technician forgets to put deicer into some jet fuel. So, he hand pumps 4 gallons from a drum into a plastic bucket. He then climbs up to the hatch of the tank truck, and pours the bucket of deicer into the tank which is filled with 10,000 gallons of jet fuel. Will he live through this experience? Explain what is happening. How could this be avoided? What are the safety regulations that cover this situation?

13. In some factories and process plants, the piping is equipped with safety diaphragms in case of an explosion. Explain what they are for, and how they work.

14. Calculate the adiabatic flame temperature of acetylene in air. What common metals could a person melt with an acetylene/air flame?

15. In order to quench the combustion of propane in a closed chamber, how much nitrogen would have to be added to the air so that the flame temperature would be below the ignition point?

16. Most public buildings now have colored signs posted on the outside that indicate the type of fire hazard located inside. Explain what the various designations mean. Where are the regulations found that specify these signs?

17. How is carbon black made commercially? What is the chemical formula for the reaction? How might the lessons learned from the commercial production of carbon black be related to finding a thick layer of soot in the flue pipe of a gas furnace?

18. Can ozone burn? Explain your answer.

19. There is one kilogram of cotton with no significant moisture content. How wet would the cotton have to be so that it would just barely not support combustion?

20. A truck carrying 5,000 gallons of ethanol wrecks and spills. What is the minimum amount of water that has to be mixed with the spilled ethanol so that it will not catch fire and burn?

21. Concrete is a complex hydrate. Explain how you could tell how hot a sample of concrete had become during a fire by weighing it and determining its specific gravity.

22. What does the "proof" mean with respect to whiskey? Will 86 proof whiskey burn by itself?

23. Put a piece of cotton fabric in a small pool of 86-proof whiskey so that the fabric acts as a wick for the whiskey. Will the 86-proof whiskey now burn and sustain flame? Why or why not?

24. Can aluminum burn with a flame? Explain your answer.

25. Baking soda is often used as the primary extinguishing chemical in dry chemical extinguishers. Why does it work?

26. A one-gram sample of an unknown liquid is found. The liquid is put into a closed flask and gently heated until all of it vaporizes. The boiling point is noted to be 56.2°C. The vapors are collected over mercury. At 60°C and atmospheric pressure, 0.47 liters of vapors are given off. The material was found to burn, and would mix with

water. When the one-gram sample is burned in air, 0.93 grams of water are formed. What is the substance?

D. Chapter 3: Odorants and Leak Detection

1. What is the combustion equation for ethyl mercaptan? Determine the heat of formation of ethyl mercaptan from its heat of combustion and the application of Hess' Law.

2. When ethyl mercaptan is fully combusted, do the products of combustion also smell bad? What do they smell like? Do you think a person can distinguish between unburned natural gas that is odorized, and the products of combustion of natural gas?

3. How do the gas detectors work; which appear similar to smoke detectors; which are designed to alert a person when methane or propane is present in the air?

4. How does a "sniffer" work?

5. A pipe is ¼ inch in diameter. If the gas pressure inside a house is 13" WC, how long will it take for the natural gas to fill the room to a 6% concentration if the room is 20 feet long, 15 feet wide, and 8 feet high?

6. If gas is leaking from a buried pipe, the grass above it will often die or appear stunted. Why?

7. Why is it a bad idea to use natural gas metal pipes for the grounding of the electrical system of a house? What regulations prohibit this?

8. An old-fashioned kitchen range has a pilot light whose flame is blown out by a gust of wind. Classify this "leak" hazard.

9. Explain the difference between methyl mercaptan and ethyl mercaptan. What are the properties of ethyl mercaptan that make it more desirable for use in propane?

10. A piece of pipe is found in the debris. From looking, it is not readily apparent whether the pipe was used for water or gas. Explain two ways how a person can tell if the pipe was used in the gas system.

11. It is claimed that an explosion whose epicenter was in the attic was caused by sewer gas. The sewer gas reportedly originated in the sewer system and entered the basement through a drain because the

trap dried out, and then diffused up through an exterior wall cavity and into the attic. The wall cavity is filled with spun fiberglass insulation, and there was rock wool in the attic. How might the sewer gas theory be proved or disproved?

E. Chapter 4: Determining the Point of Origin of a Fire

1. The point of origin of a fire appears to be a clothes dryer. Its inside is examined and the clothes, while singed, do not appear to have been the cause. Furthermore, there are indications of singeing all around the dryer basket, and a singe pattern that leads to the dryer exhaust. What might be the cause of the fire? How could you confirm this?

2. A "V" pattern is measured to be 52 degrees at the notch. What is the ratio of lateral fire spread velocity to upward fire velocity on the wall? Is this a top down, or bottom up fire?

3. Suppose a fire has the following burn velocities:

    • upwards on a vertical wall: 10 cm/sec
    • lateral on the underside of a ceiling: 2.5 cm/sec
    • downward on a vertical wall: 0.5 cm/sec.

    The fire begins at a wall outlet located 24 inches above the floor level, in the middle of the long wall of the room, which is 15 ft. × 10 ft. × 7.5 ft. How long will it take for all of the ceiling to be engulfed in flames? What will the "V" pattern angle look like? Will the fire reach the floor from the wall outlet?

4. A light bulb is located in the middle of a square ceiling that is 24 ft. × 24 ft. The light bulb divides the ceiling into two halves. Covering one half are several layers of wallpaper, which has a lateral burn velocity of 15 cm/sec (on the underside, of course). Covering the other half is a lacquer-based paint with a lateral burn rate of 25 cm/sec. What will the burn pattern look like if the fire is extinguished after 18 minutes?

5. How fast is the horizontal burn rate of a piece of material tested in the Steiner Tunnel Test that has a rating of 200?

6. A piece of ceiling tile is suspected of not being fire resistant. How could you do a quick field test to determine whether it is?

7. It is proper to use ½-inch thick plywood for fire stops in the attic space of an apartment house?

8. How do fire retardant chemicals work? What is the chemistry involved?

9. A 12"× 5" steel I-beam is used as a support column in a one-story building, and extends from the basement and up through the first floor. Wooden roof trusses rest on the top of the column, and the column is wrapped in gypsum board. An intense fire breaks out in the basement. From examination of the debris it is known that temperatures in the basement were hot enough to melt the window glass in the basement windows. Could the column cause the trusses that rest on it to catch on fire by conduction, or would the column buckle and collapse first?

10. An electric heater is used to heat a tub of liquid used in a plating process. For the most part, the liquid can be considered to be identical with water except that its boiling point is 220°F at atmospheric pressure. There are 300 gallons of liquid in the tank. When everything is working well, the tank stays warm at about 114°F when the room temperature is 72°F. The electric heater uses 3,000 watts, and is made of an alloy that for all practical purposes can be considered to be nickel. The heater element weights 3 pounds, and is usually wholly covered by the liquid. If the liquid is lost, what is the shortest time in which the heating element would melt down?

11. At what temperature will the zinc coating on galvanized steel turn white?

12. A fire investigator claims that a stack of storm windows focused the sunlight on an open bucket of tar and caused it to catch on fire. Can this be true?

13. What is a Hadley cell?

14. What is the purpose of hosing water on propane tanks during a fire?

15. Some fire investigators will say that the point of origin of a fire is where there isn't anything left to look at. What is meant by this?

16. A small propane tank, the kind used for outdoor barbecue grills, popped off its safety valve and shot flames upward, catching a canopy on fire. One investigator claims the tank was overfilled, its

valve burst, and caused the fire. Another investigator claims the tank was heated up by nearby flames and popped off as designed. Explain how the heat patterns on the tank itself could be used to determine which of these possibilities is true.

F. Chapter 5: Electrical Shorting

1. Why is it a bad idea to lay paper-backed insulation or ceiling tiles over fluorescent light fixtures? What does the *National Electrical Code* say about this?

2. Is water an insulator or a conductor? What is the resistance of deionized, distilled water as compared to water from the tap?

3. What is the electrical resistance of a human?

4. Are there any materials that, when they get hot, their resistance decreases?

5. When a three-phase motor loses one of its electrical leads, the motor will experience *single-phasing.* What is this, and why is it a fire problem?

6. Some small box fan motors have a bimetallic thermoswitch embedded in the windings. For what temperature should the thermoswitch be set?

7. An old-fashioned fuse box has screw-type fuses. After a fire, it was found that there were 30-ampere fuses screwed into the fuse box. How could you determine by an on-site inspection whether this was the correct fuse rating for the sockets?

8. Why is it improper to directly connect copper conductors to aluminum conductors?

9. What is the proper size of copper wire to carry 35 amperes? What is the proper size aluminum wire to carry 35 amperes? What if the wires are to be run underground?

10. Do fuses protect against fires?

11. Why is it that lightning surges often do not cause fuses or breakers to blow out?

12. Explain what is meant by an "inside-out" fire as opposed to an "outside-in" fire with respect to fire originating in an electrical appliance.

13. How can the local electrical utility company sometimes be helpful in determining when a fire occurred? This is especially true in rural areas, where a house can burn down and no one notices.

14. An extension cord is found, and the copper strands are brittle enough in one area that they are easily broken by handling. How hot did they get? In another area, the copper is a blue-green color. How hot did that portion get?

15. A 20-foot length of #00 size aluminum cable is suspended horizontally by a clamp at the top and hangs down. How much current would the cable have to be carrying to cause the electrical insulation to slough off? Would the cable fall down by its own weight and loss of strength of the aluminum? What if the cable were clamped at both ends and the cable were held in a horizontal position?

16. In some cases, a fire caused by shorting in interior wiring can appear to have multiple points of origin. Explain how this is possible. How can an investigator tell the difference between this effect and an incendiary fire?

Figure 11.1 Transformer failure which sometimes sounds like an explosion.

G. Chapter 6: Explosions

1. A lady has a dresser with an old fashioned make-up mirror, with light bulbs arranged in a circle around the mirror. The light bulbs are 75 watt. If the lady leaves a bottle of rubbing alcohol open, can the fumes catch fire from one of the bulbs?

2. A deflagrating explosion occurs in a closed room with a large window. The glass in the window will break out when the overpressure is about 1.0 psig. At what velocity will the air rush out when the window breaks out?

3. An explosion occurs in a parking garage. A car that weighs 2,300 pounds is parked close to the epicenter, and is moved sideways 3 feet by the explosion. The coefficient of friction between a tire and a concrete floor is 0.70. What was the pressure of the explosion on the side of the car facing the explosion?

4. What is mercury fulminate, and what is it used for?

5. The roof of a closed garage is constructed of 2 × 4 triangular trusses placed on 24-inch centers. The trusses have a king post under the ridge. The area of the rectangular house is 40 ft. × 20 ft. The roof decking is ⅜-inch plywood. The roof has an angle of 22 degrees, with a ridge in the center running along the long axis. The asphalt shingles weigh 2 pounds per square foot of roof area. The roof is lifted up by a gasoline explosion in the garage. What was the pressure that lifted the roof? Assuming the walls are 8 feet high, how much gasoline would have to have been spilled on the floor to do this?

6. What is atomization? Why would this cause flammable liquids with a high flash point to be an explosion hazard? What would be the relationship of hazard to particle size?

7. Air conditioners contain a lightweight mineral oil that has a flash-point of about 350°F. Assume that the oil from an air conditioner leaks from a hole 0.5 mm in diameter on the high-pressure side of an air conditioner compressor, where the temperature is about 290°F. The atomized oil passes over an electrical relay that handles 120 volts a.c. at 12 amperes between the relay contacts. Will the atomized oil ignite?

8. Why is it that the flue pipes from furnaces should not have horizontal runs? What is the rule on this?

9.   The overpressure wave of an explosion was measured to be 10 psig at point "1," and the wave came from the due north direction. At point "2," the overpressure was measured to be 15 psig and came from the due east direction. Point "2" is located 50 feet west and 10 feet north of point "1." Where is the epicenter of the explosion located? What would the pressure of the explosion be at a location 50 feet from the epicenter?

10. An explosion occurs in a small brick building with a concrete slab floor. At the epicenter, the concrete floor has been broken into small pieces, and there is a small crater. Bricks were found to be scattered about 15 meters from the epicenter. Estimate the amount of explosive material. If the explosive was determined to be AMATOL, how much was used?

11. OSHA and NFPA regulations provide classifications for the type of explosion hazard with respect to natural-gas stations and processing plants. Explain the differences between Class I, II, and III explosion hazard areas. What are the subclassifications?

12. Explain the relationship between aerosol bug extermination bombs, pilot lights, and law suits.

H. Chapter 7:
Determining the Point of Ignition of An Explosion

1.   Two sealed rooms are side by side, with a 1-m^2 opening between them located along the floor. One room has air in it and is 10 m × 7 m × 2.5 m. The other room is 15 m × 7 m × 2.5 m, and is filled with propane at a concentration of 20% in air. In the large room, opposite the window, there is a hot light bulb at the top of the ceiling. Will the rooms explode? If so, when?

2.   A hallway that is 6 ft wide and 8 feet high has a concentration of methane at one end of 30%, and 50 feet along the hallway the concentration drops to 5%. What is the rate of methane diffusion in the hallway?

3.   If the "C" term in equation (i) of Chapter 7 is equal to [2/3][N/V] where N is the number of molecules and V is the volume, then at atmospheric pressure, what temperature would be required for the air molecules to have an average speed of 11 ft/sec? At what tempera-

ture would the gas have to be for the molecules to exceed the escape velocity of the earth? At what temperature will average motion stop?

4. The temperature of the air in the earth's troposphere generally diminishes with inreasing altitude. Explain why this limits the distance a person can hear an explosion. Can you imagine a weather scenario where the sound "skips" over an area, but is heard beyond that?

5. A car with a mass of 1,000 kg rolls down a hill that has a change in elevation of 30 m. At the bottom of the hill, the car brakes to a stop. How much energy in grams of TNT was dissipated by the braking action of the car?

I. Chapter 8: Arson and Incendiary Fires

1. Explain the difference between mass spectroscopy, infrared spectroscopy, and gas chromatography.

2. Invent five ways, that is, five timers, that would delay the initiation of a fire for 30 minutes, at least one of which involves electricity.

3. A fire occurred in a tropical greenhouse where the temperature is maintained above 90°F. The point of origin was in the office on the floor. Around the point of origin were arranged stacks of office papers and some old wooden office furniture. In the approximate center of the point of origin was found a partially melted coffee can. A small nail hole was noted in the remaining portion of the bottom of the can. In the area of the coffee can was found phosphoric anhydride (P_2O_5). The concrete under the can was noted to be spalled in a circular pattern, matching the outline of the can. It appeared that the can had been set under wooden desk. How was the timer set up?

4. Sometimes after a fire, the local police will ask the owner to inventory the facility to determine if anything is missing. Why is this done?

5. Is diesel fuel a poor choice of accelerant for an arsonist?

6. Some materials degrade during a fire, undergoing partial pyrolysis. In doing this, they often produce organic compounds that resemble various accelerants. How would you differentiate between compounds made by pyrolysis, and accelerants used by an arsonist?

J. Chapter 9: Automotive Fires

1. How much water has to be mixed with ethylene glycol so that it won't burn?

2. What is the flash point of motor oil, and at what temperature will it catch fire?

3. What is the percentage of fires in cars older than 4 years (mostly paid-off cars), versus fires in cars less than four years old?

4. What are the flash points of gasoline and diesel fuel? Does a lighted cigarette have the necessary MIE to ignite both or either?

5. What is the adiabatic flame temperature of motor oil?

6. What is the combustion equation for brake fluid?

7. At what temperature does a tire ignite?

8. Can a tire catch fire from heavy skidding? How about when the car is stuck on ice, and the driver guns the wheels trying to get out? Why is this?

9. What is color of smoke from gasoline, motor oil, brake fluid, and transmission fluid?

10. In some cars, the automatic transmission is located alongside the catalytic converter. Is there a risk that if a seal fails on the transmission, the fluid might impinge on the converter and ignite?

11. Many motor homes use rubber fuel lines to get fuel from the fuel tanks under the rear up to the engine in front. Also, most have at least one electrically powered fuel pump located in the rear tank, with a second located at or near the engine. Why does this increase the severity of fires in motor homes, or does it?

12. What are the rules that govern the design and safety of motor homes? Are they different from passenger cars? At what points do they diverge? Explain how this affects fire safety.

13. Explain the differences between rules for trucks and the rules for passenger cars with respect to fire safety. For example, are car drivers expected to carry a fire extinguisher?

14. Can running an underinflated tire cause the tire to catch fire and burn?

K. Chapter 10: Fire and Explosion Case Study

1. How far would the firemen have to have been from either explosion to have had a reasonable chance in surviving the blast?

2. If glass windows broke out from the blast in a nearby building, would there likely also have been damages due to ground vibrations?

3. If a building did not sustain any damages from ground vibrations, could the air blast have broken out its windows?

4. How much air pressure does it take to cause a medium-sized car to be turned over?

5. What is the chemical formula for ANFO? What is the chemical formula for nitroglycerin? Can the latter be created from the former through thermal decomposition? If so, how much could theoretically be made?

6. In the analysis, it was assumed that the trailer structures themselves offered no significant containment of the explosions. Explain why this assumption is reasonable. Why was this assumption important?

7. What is the speed of sound in combustion gases at elevated temperatures? What would have been the speed of sound inside a trailer before the explosions occurred?

8. Explain the use of scaling factors in both air blast calculations and ground vibration propagation calculations. Can you give the theoretical underpinnings?

9. If the recommended scaling factor for ground vibrations is 50 ft/lb$^{1/2}$, then what was the margin of safety for the area where blasting was being done in Kansas City? Using the "safe blasting formula" and the recommended scaling factor, what would the actual ground PPV values be when the formula indicates 2.0 in/sec?

10. As populations increase and urban areas become more dense, where are blasting materials to be kept and stored? What about the "not in my backyard" feelings of neighbors?

J. Chapter 11: Study Problems

1. Explain thermodynamic entropy.

2. What is Gibbs Free Energy? What is the equation that relates entropy, enthalpy, and Gibbs Free Energy? How can this quantity be used to predict the direction of a chemical reaction?

3. If the entropy of water actually decreases when ice melts, how can this happen spontaneously?

> *One man's word is no man's word;*
> *we should quietly hear both sides.*
>
> Johann Wolfgang von Goethe

BIBLIOGRAPHY

A. General

The following bibliography lists reference materials that the reader will find useful in augmenting his or her knowledge about fire and explosion reconstruction. I have relied on the information contained in some of these references in writing this text; some references have been included because they corroborate or further amplify ideas and information presented in the text, and a few items are listed simply because I think they relate to the over-all topic of fire and explosion analysis and are interesting. Where appropriate, I have added comments to let the reader know something about what the reference contains.

There is no particular significance to the order of the list, and it is certainly not to be considered exhaustive. However, I do believe that the list constitutes a core upon which an undergraduate educational program could be developed. A person knowledgeable about the material in these references would have a sound understanding of fire and accident reconstruction principles. I have listed more books and bound collections of papers than single papers because the former are easier to obtain by inter-library loan, and provide more "good stuff" for less effort. Of course, a serious student will find many more references listed within the various items.

B. Books

Fire Investigation Handbook, U.S. Department of Commerce, National Bureau of Standards, NBS Handbook 134, Edited by Francis Brannigan, August 1980.

This is a very readable text on fire analysis. The text is a practical amalgam of theory and experience and contains a number of instructive photographs. It is often used as a basic text in fire academies and training schools. Persons in the business should have a copy on hand since it is often referenced as an authoritative source in court proceedings.

Investigation of Fire and Explosion Accidents in the Chemical, Mining, and Fuel Related Industries - A Manual, by Joseph Kuchta, United States Department of the Interior, Bureau of Mines, Bulletin 680, 1985.

Despite the formidable title, this is an excellent engineering reference source for fires and deflagration type explosions. It is not a primer. To properly understand it, the reader should have previous knowledge in chemistry and basic thermodynamics. The text is to the point, is written well, and is a cornucopia of reference information.

Introduction to Forensic Engineering, by Randall Noon, P.E., CRC Press, ISBN 0-8493-8102-9, 1992.

This introductory text contains a number of chapters about fire and explosions which are useful to the novice in fire and explosion reconstruction. Chapter 3 is noteworthy because it provides an excellent discussion of the scientific method as it applies to forensic engineering in general. Chapter 20 is useful because it describes the process of being an expert witness, and Chapter 21 gives some practical tips for preparing an investigative report.

The Condensed Chemical Dictionary, revised by Gessner Hawley, Ninth Edition, Van Nostrand Reinhold Company, 1977.

Newer editions of this standard reference text are also available. This is a very useful reference concerning chemical terms, chemicals and trade name items. Thumbnail descriptions of each chemical's properties and hazards are listed.

Handbook of Chemistry and Physics, edited by Robert Weast, Ph.D., CRC Press, 71st Edition.

This is the mother lode of information concerning chemical compounds, heats of reaction, solubility, etc. It is hard to imagine a practical reference shelf without this volume. I have listed a specific edition, but new ones come out annually.

Standard Handbook for Mechanical Engineers, by Baumeister and Marks, Seventh Edition, McGraw-Hill, 1967.

A standard reference book for mechanical engineers, this handbook contains information on fuels, explosives, machinery, gases, materials, circuitry, switch gear, and many types of equipment that may be involved in fires and explosions. This is very useful when a person is trying to understand what used to be there before the fire or explosion and how it worked. Newer editions than the one listed are also available.

A Pocket Guide to Arson and Fire Investigation, Factory Mutual Engineering Corporation, Third Edition, 1992.

A small booklet that can provide handy information in the field. It fits in a shirt pocket or briefcase.

General Chemistry, by Linus Pauling, Dover Publications, Inc, 1988.

I believe this is the best reference text on general chemistry available, and at a very modest price. Dr. Pauling, of course, received the chemistry Nobel prize in 1954. With respect to fires and explosions, I recommend the following: chapter 10, chemical thermodynamics; chapter 11, chemical equilibrium; chapter 15, oxidation-reduction reactions; and chapter 16, the rate of chemical reactions. I also recommend the various discussions about entropy in the text.

Rego LP-Gas Serviceman's Manual, Rego Company, 4201 West Peterson Avenue, Chicago, IL, 60646.

This handy reference will fit in a shirt pocket or briefcase. It contains most of the basic information about LPG installations for residences. The section on leak testing an LPG installation is the same technique used after a fire or explosion to check out the remaining pipework.

Explosive Shocks in Air, Kinney and Graham, Springer Verlag, Second Edition, 1985. ISBN 3-540-15147-8 and 0-387-15147-8.

This is probably the best text on air blasts written for engineers and physicists. For those already familiar with basic thermodynamics, I recommend chapters 6–8, and 10–11. These chapters deal specifically with topics of concern to engineers involved in diagnosing the hows and whys of blast damage. However, I think the whole book deserves a reading by those serious students of fires and explosions.

NFPA 495: Explosive Materials Code, National Fire Protection Association, 1990 Edition.

These are the basic regulations that deal with the handling of explosive materials. It contains things like minimum distances from storage facilities to inhabited areas, etc. It is the "building code" of storage facilities for explosive materials.

NFPA Life Safety Code (NFPA 101), National Fire Protection Association, February 8, 1991. Also listed as ANSI 101.

This is the general fire code adopted by many units of government around the US and in other countries. It covers fire exit requirements, safety equipment, fire detection systems, etc.

Gas Transmission and Distribution Piping Systems (ANSI/ASME B31.8-1982), American Society of Mechanical Engineers, 1983.

These are general regulations that cover the construction and maintenance of pipeline systems that carry natural gas, and similar. The book includes design standards, testing procedures, maintenance procedures, and sections dealing with off-shore facilities and arctic facilities.

Manual for the Investigation of Automobile Fires, National Automobile Theft Bureau.

This booklet was not easy to find; I finally obtained a copy through an inter-library loan that took nearly two weeks. Apparently it was self-published by the NATB and only a handful of copies were printed. My copy had no publication or copyright date. At any rate, I found that the booklet has some useful tips concerning the examination of a fire damaged vehicle and the collection of evidence, especially with respect to what to look for in an arson case. It was presumably prepared for insurance adjusters and private investigators.

Code of Federal Regulations 29, Parts 1900 to 1910, and Part 1926 (two volumes).

These are the basic OSHA regulations that govern LPG, gas fuels, welding, storage of explosives, fire protection and prevention, etc. This is usually the first set of regulations checked when it is suspected that a compliance problem led to a fire or explosion.

ATF Arson Investigation Guide, published by the Department of the Treasury (no date).

Mostly this is a compendium of investigative check lists and Federal resources used in the investigation of arson by the ATF. The book has a nice glossary of terms in the back, and there are a number of excerpts from the federal laws concerning arson and explosions.

Manual for the Determination of Electrical Fire Causes - 1988 Edition, NFPA 907M.

This is a useful check-list type document for the investigation of electrically caused fires. It is not an engineering technical text, but it does contain very useful qualitative information and investigative procedures concerning electrically caused fires. The document is sometimes cited in courtroom proceedings as the standard for electrical fire investigations. This is an exaggeration of the document's technical importance, and certainly short shrifts other authoritative texts on the subject. However, because of this attitude, it is recommended that people involved in fire investigation work be familiar with it.

Fire and Explosion Investigations - 1992 Edition, NFPA 921.

Like its sister publication NFPA 907M, NFPA 921 is sometimes cited in courtroom proceedings as "the standard" for fire investigation work. As its scope indicates, the purpose of the publication "...is to establish guidelines and a recommended practice for the systematic investigation or analysis of fire and explosion incidents." It is not an engineering text, but it does contain very useful qualitative information, explanations, and investigative procedures concerning fire C&O investigations. Like NFPA 907M, it is recommended that people involved in fire investigation work be familiar with NFPA 921.

To Engineer is Human, by Henry Petroski, Vintage Books, 1992, 251 pages.

This is not strictly a fire and explosion related book. It is, however, about failure with respect to engineering design and has an excellent chapter about forensic engineering (chapter 14). I highly recommend it for its insights into the workings of engineering failure. The principles are easily applied to fire and explosion type failure assessments. It is very readable.

Thermodynamics, by Ernst Schmidt, Dover Publications, Inc., 1966, 532 pages.

This is a classic engineering text on thermodynamics, which also contains excellent chapters on thermochemistry. Chapter XII, Combustion, is particularly relevant to the topic of the chemistry of fire. For the money, this is a first-rate text.

Treatise on Thermodynamics, by Max Planck, Dover Publications, Inc., Third English Edition, 1990, 297 pages.

Dr. Planck won the Nobel Prize in Physics in 1918 for his contribution to the study of quantum physics and black body radiation. This text is especially good for those with only a small amount of previous knowledge about thermodynamics but who have basic college level mathematical skills. Parts I and II are especially useful with regard to the study of fire chemistry and physics.

Handbook for Chemical Technicians, authored by Strauss and edited by Kaufman, McGraw-Hill, 1976.

This is a handy compendium of laboratory procedures, chemical data and chemical principles. Most of the data necessary to work and solve thermochemical equations are contained in this handbook. Section 10 is particularly useful as it discusses chemical fire hazards and hazardous materials.

Forensic Engineering, edited by Kenneth Carper, Elsevier, 1989, 353 pages.

This is an introductory text which explains and defines forensic engineering. There are fourteen chapters, each written by a different author, which describe some facet of forensic engineering. Chapter 3, authored by Paul E. Pritzker, P.E., is about forensic engineering with respect to fires, and discusses briefly the "investigative team" concept. I also recommend chapter 10 (photodocumentation), chapter 11 (reports), and chapter 12 (expert witness).

Principles of Combustion, by Kenneth Kuo, John Wiley and Sons, 1986, 810 pages.

This is a first-rate upper-level undergraduate or graduate level engineering text about combustion. While the notation is sometimes overdone, there is a rich range of topics and the technical depth is excellent. I recommend this to engineers who have already had basic thermodynamics and heat transfer, and are ready for the next level.

Similitude in Engineering, by Glenn Murphy, C.E., Ph.D., The Ronald Press Company, 1950, 302 pages.

While the publishing date on this text may make the reader believe this is more about history than engineering, I still highly recommend it as being the best and most complete text on the subject of model studies. The art and science of model studies has almost been forgotten in undergraduate study in favor of the more "hi-tech" computer simulation programs. Unfortunately, the computer simulations are only as good as the assumptions made when the program was set up; if an important assumption is left out, the simulation results may be only so much garbage. In model studies, no such assumptions are made; the engineer gets to "play" with the real phenomenon but on a small scale. To this end, modeling studies of fires, especially in large buildings and facilities, can be a valuable tool for safe design. Also, when the size of the fire warrants it, fire modeling studies can be a useful diagnostic tool.

Investigation of Motor Vehicle Fires, by Lee Cole, Lee Books, 1992, 183 pages.

This book is useful in that it has a lot of qualitative information useful to the novice in this field. In many respects, it is simply a collection of the author's anecdotal experiences in the investigation of vehicle fires. Technical particulars are not fully explained, and there is a lot of information in the text which appears to have dubious association with car fires (e.g., trends in the use of various metals used in car production). Despite its shortcomings, the book is worth a reconnoiter with regard to on-site investigative tips and is similar to the manual published by the National Automobile Theft Bureau (listed above).

C. Papers

"Influence of Containers on Sour Gas Samples," by Price and Cromer, Petroleum Engineer International, March 1980.

Excellent paper which describes how the concentration of sulfonated type odorant compounds drops over time in various types of gas sampling containers. The study found that the best containers for sampling sour gas were silanized glass sample containers.

"Hydrogen Sulfide and Mercaptan Sulfur in Natural Gas (Cadmium Sulfate-Iodometric Titration Method)," ANSI/ASTM D 2385–66 (reapproved 1976).

While not strictly a research paper, this standard describes the laboratory method to test natural gas for odorant.

"Aging Impairs the Ability to Detect Gas Odor," Fire Technology, August 1987.

This article discusses the results of two studies showing that smelling ability diminishes with age, and that the ability to detect odorant also diminishes with age.

"Characterization of LP Gas Odorant Fade," study prepared for the Consumer Product Safety Commission by Arthur D. Little, Inc., CPSC-C–86–1281, June 1987.

This study, commissioned by the CPSC, discusses LPG odorant fade in steel gas cylinders, and due to contact with masonry. The study found that under certain conditions, LPG gas could lose some of its odorant due to adsorption/absorption effects and surface oxidation/reduction reactions.

"Duty to Warn," LP/GAS, August 1983, Volume 43, Number 8, pages 19–27.

This is an excellent article which summarizes the legal responsibilities of the LPG distributor with respect to the "duty to warn" obligation. Aspects of warning labels, odorants, and obligations of service persons making hookups are discussed in easy to understand language.

"When is Seeing Believing?" by William Mitchell, Scientific American, Feb. 1994, Volume 270, Number 2, pages 68–75.

This is recommended reading for all persons involved in the presentation and examination of evidence. The article describes some of the ways in which computer graphics can be used to provide fake photographic evidence. A very brief discussion of this same topic was given in chapter 6 of the text, *Engineering Analysis of Vehicular*

Accidents, by this author, CRC Press, 1994. Unfortunately, one of the darker sides of the computer revolution is that photographic evidence, once considered quite reliable, is becoming increasingly easier to fake. It will not be long before unscrupulous forensic engineers use computerized faking techniques to persuade juries as to the "scientific" evidence in a case, especially when the monetary stakes are sufficiently high.

"Roots of Reason," by Bruce Bower, Science News, January 29, 1994, Volume 145, Number 5, pages 72–75.

This is an interesting piece about how and why people reason the way they do. The lessons noted in this short article should be heeded by anyone who hopes to write a convincing report or convince a jury. Importantly, it points out that classic deductive logic alone is not necessarily convincing; culture and environment influence personal perceptions of what is logical.

"Fire Storms," by Mark Wheeler, Discover, May 1994, pages 52–56.

This article is short, and does not contain much technical information. However, there are some excellent color photographs of fire-created vortices. The article does introduce the topic of fire-induced localized weather conditions.

"Air Blast Phenomena, Characteristics of the Blast Wave in Air," reprint of Chapter II from The Effects of Nuclear Weapons, Samuel Glasstone, Editor, April 1962, U.S. Atomic Energy Commission, pages 102–148.

Don't let the title fool you into thinking this is only about nuclear weapons. The article is excellent in its explanation of how blast waves from detonations propagate.

"Sensitivity of Explosives," by Andrej Macek, U.S. Naval Ordnance Laboratory, Chemical Reviews, 1962, Volume 41, pages 41–62.

The section on pages 44–50, the thermal decomposition of explosives, is pertinent to the Kansas City Firemen explosion discussed in Chapter 10. In that case, fires caused the detonation of stacked ANFO stores, which ordinarily are considered a "fire safe" type explosive glass sample containers.

Index